ASPEN PUBLISHERS

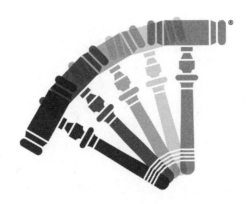

Casenote™ *Legal Briefs*

PATENT LAW

Keyed to Courses Using

Adelman, Rader, and Thomas's
Cases and Materials on Patent Law

Third Edition

D1261818

Wolters Kluwer

Law & Business

AUSTIN   BOSTON   CHICAGO   NEW YORK   THE NETHERLANDS

© 2010 Aspen Publishers, Inc. All Rights Reserved.
a Wolters Kluwer business
http://lawschool.aspenpublishers.com

No part of this publication may be reproduced or transmitted in any form or by any means, electronic or mechanical, including photocopy, recording, or any information storage and retrieval system, without permission in writing from the publisher. Requests for permission to make copies of any part of this publication should be mailed to:

> Aspen Publishers
> Attn: Permissions Dept.
> 76 Ninth Avenue, 7th Floor
> New York, NY 10011-5201

To contact Customer Care, e-mail customer.care@aspenpublishers.com, call 1-800-234-1660, fax 1-800-901-9075, or mail correspondence to:

> Aspen Publishers
> Attn: Order Department
> P.O. Box 990
> Frederick, MD 21705

Printed in the United States of America.

1 2 3 4 5 6 7 8 9 0

ISBN 978-0-7355-8605-5

About Wolters Kluwer Law & Business

Wolters Kluwer Law & Business is a leading provider of research information and workflow solutions in key specialty areas. The strengths of the individual brands of Aspen Publishers, CCH, Kluwer Law International and Loislaw are aligned within Wolters Kluwer Law & Business to provide comprehensive, in-depth solutions and expert-authored content for the legal, professional and education markets.

CCH was founded in 1913 and has served more than four generations of business professionals and their clients. The CCH products in the Wolters Kluwer Law & Business group are highly regarded electronic and print resources for legal, securities, antitrust and trade regulation, government contracting, banking, pension, payroll, employment and labor, and health-care reimbursement and compliance professionals.

Aspen Publishers is a leading information provider for attorneys, business professionals and law students. Written by preeminent authorities, Aspen products offer analytical and practical information in a range of specialty practice areas from securities law and intellectual property to mergers and acquisitions and pension/benefits. Aspen's trusted legal education resources provide professors and students with high-quality, up-to-date and effective resources for successful instruction and study in all areas of the law.

Kluwer Law International supplies the global business community with comprehensive English-language international legal information. Legal practitioners, corporate counsel and business executives around the world rely on the Kluwer Law International journals, loose-leafs, books and electronic products for authoritative information in many areas of international legal practice.

Loislaw is a premier provider of digitized legal content to small law firm practitioners of various specializations. Loislaw provides attorneys with the ability to quickly and efficiently find the necessary legal information they need, when and where they need it, by facilitating access to primary law as well as state-specific law, records, forms and treatises.

Wolters Kluwer Law & Business, a unit of Wolters Kluwer, is headquartered in New York and Riverwoods, Illinois. Wolters Kluwer is a leading multinational publisher and information services company.

Format for the Casenote Legal Brief

Nature of Case: This section identifies the form of action (e.g., breach of contract, negligence, battery), the type of proceeding (e.g., demurrer, appeal from trial court's jury instructions) or the relief sought (e.g., damages, injunction, criminal sanctions).

Fact Summary: This is included to refresh your memory and can be used as a quick reminder of the facts.

Rule of Law: Summarizes the general principle of law that the case illustrates. It may be used for instant recall of the court's holding and for classroom discussion or home review.

Facts: This section contains all relevant facts of the case, including the contentions of the parties and the lower court holdings. It is written in a logical order to give the student a clear understanding of the case. The plaintiff and defendant are identified by their proper names throughout and are always labeled with a (P) or (D).

Palsgraf v. Long Island R.R. Co.

Injured bystander (P) v. Railroad company (D)

N.Y. Ct. App., 248 N.Y. 339, 162 N.E. 99 (1928).

NATURE OF CASE: Appeal from judgment affirming verdict for plaintiff seeking damages for personal injury.

FACT SUMMARY: Helen Palsgraf (P) was injured on R.R.'s (D) train platform when R.R.'s (D) guard helped a passenger aboard a moving train, causing his package to fall on the tracks. The package contained fireworks which exploded, creating a shock that tipped a scale onto Palsgraf (P).

🏛 **RULE OF LAW**
The risk reasonably to be perceived defines the duty to be obeyed.

FACTS: Helen Palsgraf (P) purchased a ticket to Rockaway Beach from R.R. (D) and was waiting on the train platform. As she waited, two men ran to catch a train that was pulling out from the platform. The first man jumped aboard, but the second man, who appeared as if he might fall, was helped aboard by the guard on the train who had kept the door open so they could jump aboard. A guard on the platform also helped by pushing him onto the train. The man was carrying a package wrapped in newspaper. In the process, the man dropped his package, which fell on the tracks. The package contained fireworks and exploded. The shock of the explosion was apparently of great enough strength to tip over some scales at the other end of the platform, which fell on Palsgraf (P) and injured her. A jury awarded her damages, and R.R. (D) appealed.

ISSUE: Does the risk reasonably to be perceived define the duty to be obeyed?

HOLDING AND DECISION: (Cardozo, C.J.) Yes. The risk reasonably to be perceived defines the duty to be obeyed. If there is no foreseeable hazard to the injured party as the result of a seemingly innocent act, the act does not become a tort because it happened to be a wrong as to another. If the wrong was not willful, the plaintiff must show that the act as to her had such great and apparent possibilities of danger as to entitle her to protection. Negligence in the abstract is not enough upon which to base liability. Negligence is a relative concept, evolving out of the common law doctrine of trespass on the case. To establish liability, the defendant must owe a legal duty of reasonable care to the injured party. A cause of action in tort will lie where harm, though unintended, could have been averted or avoided by observance of such a duty. The scope of the duty is limited by the range of danger that a reasonable person could foresee. In this case, there was nothing to suggest from the appearance of the parcel or otherwise that the parcel contained fireworks. The guard could not reasonably have had any warning of a threat to Palsgraf (P), and R.R. (D) therefore cannot be held liable. Judgment is reversed in favor of R.R. (D).

DISSENT: (Andrews, J.) The concept that there is no negligence unless R.R. (D) owes a legal duty to take care as to Palsgraf (P) herself is too narrow. Everyone owes to the world at large the duty of refraining from those acts that may unreasonably threaten the safety of others. If the guard's action was negligent as to those nearby, it was also negligent as to those outside what might be termed the "danger zone." For Palsgraf (P) to recover, R.R.'s (D) negligence must have been the proximate cause of her injury, a question of fact for the jury.

▶ **ANALYSIS**

The majority defined the limit of the defendant's liability in terms of the danger that a reasonable person in defendant's situation would have perceived. The dissent argued that the limitation should not be placed on liability, but rather on damages. Judge Andrews suggested that only injuries that would not have happened but for R.R.'s (D) negligence should be compensable. Both the majority and dissent recognized the policy-driven need to limit liability for negligent acts, seeking, in the words of Judge Andrews, to define a framework "that will be practical and in keeping with the general understanding of mankind." The Restatement (Second) of Torts has accepted Judge Cardozo's view.

━

Quicknotes

FORESEEABILITY A reasonable expectation that change is the probable result of certain acts or omissions.

NEGLIGENCE Conduct falling below the standard of care that a reasonable person would demonstrate under similar conditions.

PROXIMATE CAUSE The natural sequence of events without which an injury would not have been sustained.

━

Party ID: Quick identification of the relationship between the parties.

Concurrence/Dissent: All concurrences and dissents are briefed whenever they are included by the casebook editor.

Analysis: This last paragraph gives you a broad understanding of where the case "fits in" with other cases in the section of the book and with the entire course. It is a hornbook-style discussion indicating whether the case is a majority or minority opinion and comparing the principal case with other cases in the casebook. It may also provide analysis from restatements, uniform codes, and law review articles. The analysis will prove to be invaluable to classroom discussion.

Issue: The issue is a concise question that brings out the essence of the opinion as it relates to the section of the casebook in which the case appears. Both substantive and procedural issues are included if relevant to the decision.

Holding and Decision: This section offers a clear and in-depth discussion of the rule of the case and the court's rationale. It is written in easy-to-understand language and answers the issue presented by applying the law to the facts of the case. When relevant, it includes a thorough discussion of the exceptions to the case as listed by the court, any major cites to the other cases on point, and the names of the judges who wrote the decisions.

Quicknotes: Conveniently defines legal terms found in the case and summarizes the nature of any statutes, codes, or rules referred to in the text.

Aspen Publishers is proud to offer *Casenote Legal Briefs*—continuing thirty years of publishing America's best-selling legal briefs.

Casenote Legal Briefs are designed to help you save time when briefing assigned cases. Organized under convenient headings, they show you how to abstract the basic facts and holdings from the text of the actual opinions handed down by the courts. Used as part of a rigorous study regimen, they can help you spend more time analyzing and critiquing points of law than on copying bits and pieces of judicial opinions into your notebook or outline.

Casenote Legal Briefs should never be used as a substitute for assigned casebook readings. They work best when read as a follow-up to reviewing the underlying opinions themselves. Students who try to avoid reading and digesting the judicial opinions in their casebooks or online sources will end up shortchanging themselves in the long run. The ability to absorb, critique, and restate the dynamic and complex elements of case law decisions is crucial to your success in law school and beyond. It cannot be developed vicariously.

Casenote Legal Briefs represents but one of the many offerings in Aspen's Study Aid Timeline, which includes:

- *Casenote Legal Briefs*
- *Emanuel Law Outlines*
- *Examples & Explanations* Series
- *Introduction to Law* Series
- Emanuel *Law in a Flash* Flashcards
- Emanuel *CrunchTime* Series

Each of these series is designed to provide you with easy-to-understand explanations of complex points of law. Each volume offers guidance on the principles of legal analysis and, consulted regularly, will hone your ability to spot relevant issues. We have titles that will help you prepare for class, prepare for your exams, and enhance your general comprehension of the law along the way.

To find out more about Aspen Study Aid publications, visit us online at *http://lawschool.aspenpublishers.com* or email us at *legaledu@wolterskluwer.com*. We'll be happy to assist you.

Get this Casenote Legal Brief as an AspenLaw Studydesk eBook today!

By returning this form to Aspen Publishers, you will receive a complimentary eBook download of this Casenote Legal Brief in the AspenLaw Studydesk digital format.* Learn more about AspenLaw Studydesk today at *www.AspenLaw.com*.

Name	Phone ( )

Address	Apt. No.

City	State	ZIP Code

Law School	Year (check one) ☐ 1st ☐ 2nd ☐ 3rd

Cut out the UPC found on the lower left corner of the back cover of this book. Staple the UPC inside this box. Only the original UPC from the book cover will be accepted. (No photocopies or store stickers are allowed.)

Attach UPC inside this box.

Email (Print legibly or you may not get access!)

Title of this book (course subject)

ISBN of this book (10- or 13-digit number on the UPC)

Used with which casebook (provide author's name)

Mail the completed form to:

Aspen Publishers, Inc.
Legal Education Division
130 Turner Street, Bldg 3, 4th Floor
Waltham, MA 02453-8901

* Upon receipt of this completed form, you will be emailed a code for the digital download of this book in AspenLaw Studydesk format. The AspenLaw Studydesk application is available as a 60-day free trial at *www.AspenLaw.com*.

For a full list of print titles by Aspen Publishers, visit *lawschool.aspenpublishers.com*.
For a full list of digital eBook titles by Aspen Publishers, visit *www.AspenLaw.com*.

Make a photocopy of this form and your UPC for your records.

For detailed information on the use of the information you provide on this form, please see the PRIVACY POLICY at www.aspenpublishers.com.

How to Brief a Case

A. Decide on a Format and Stick to It

Structure is essential to a good brief. It enables you to arrange systematically the related parts that are scattered throughout most cases, thus making manageable and understandable what might otherwise seem to be an endless and unfathomable sea of information. There are, of course, an unlimited number of formats that can be utilized. However, it is best to find one that suits your needs and stick to it. Consistency breeds both efficiency and the security that when called upon you will know where to look in your brief for the information you are asked to give.

Any format, as long as it presents the essential elements of a case in an organized fashion, can be used. Experience, however, has led *Casenotes* to develop and utilize the following format because of its logical flow and universal applicability.

NATURE OF CASE: This is a brief statement of the legal character and procedural status of the case (e.g., "Appeal of a burglary conviction").

There are many different alternatives open to a litigant dissatisfied with a court ruling. The key to determining which one has been used is to discover *who is asking this court for what.*

This first entry in the brief should be kept as *short as possible.* Use the court's terminology if you understand it. But since jurisdictions vary as to the titles of pleadings, the best entry is the one that addresses who wants what in this proceeding, not the one that sounds most like the court's language.

RULE OF LAW: A statement of the general principle of law that the case illustrates (e.g., "An acceptance that varies any term of the offer is considered a rejection and counteroffer").

Determining the rule of law of a case is a procedure similar to determining the issue of the case. Avoid being fooled by red herrings; there may be a few rules of law mentioned in the case excerpt, but usually only one is *the* rule with which the casebook editor is concerned. The techniques used to locate the issue, described below, may also be utilized to find the rule of law. Generally, your best guide is simply the chapter heading. It is a clue to the point the casebook editor seeks to make and should be kept in mind when reading every case in the respective section.

FACTS: A synopsis of only the essential facts of the case, i.e., those bearing upon or leading up to the issue.

The facts entry should be a short statement of the events and transactions that led one party to initiate legal proceedings against another in the first place. While some cases conveniently state the salient facts at the beginning of the decision, in other instances they will have to be culled from hiding places throughout the text, even from concurring and dissenting opinions. Some of the "facts" will often be in dispute and should be so noted. Conflicting evidence may be briefly pointed up. "Hard" facts must be included. Both must be *relevant* in order to be listed in the facts entry. It is impossible to tell what is relevant until the entire case is read, as the ultimate determination of the rights and liabilities of the parties may turn on something buried deep in the opinion.

Generally, the facts entry should not be longer than three to five *short* sentences.

It is often helpful to identify the role played by a party in a given context. For example, in a construction contract case the identification of a party as the "contractor" or "builder" alleviates the need to tell that that party was the one who was supposed to have built the house.

It is always helpful, and a good general practice, to identify the "plaintiff" and the "defendant." This may seem elementary and uncomplicated, but, especially in view of the creative editing practiced by some casebook editors, it is sometimes a difficult or even impossible task. Bear in mind that the *party presently* seeking something from this court may not be the plaintiff, and that sometimes only the cross-claim of a defendant is treated in the excerpt. Confusing or misaligning the parties can ruin your analysis and understanding of the case.

ISSUE: A statement of the general legal question answered by or illustrated in the case. For clarity, the issue is best put in the form of a question capable of a "yes" or "no" answer. In reality, the issue is simply the Rule of Law put in the form of a question (e.g., "May an offer be accepted by performance?").

The major problem presented in discerning what is *the* issue in the case is that an opinion usually purports to raise and answer several questions. However, except for rare cases, only one such question is really the issue in the case. Collateral issues not necessary to the resolution of the matter in controversy are handled by the court by language known as *"obiter dictum"* or merely *"dictum."* While dicta may be included later in the brief, they have no place under the issue heading.

To find the issue, ask *who wants what* and then go on to ask *why did that party succeed or fail in getting it.* Once this is determined, the "why" should be turned into a question.

The complexity of the issues in the cases will vary, but in all cases a single-sentence question should sum up the issue. *In a few cases,* there will be two, or even more rarely, three issues of equal importance to the resolution of the case. Each should be expressed in a single-sentence question.

Since many issues are resolved by a court in coming to a final disposition of a case, the casebook editor will reproduce the portion of the opinion containing the issue or issues most relevant to the area of law under scrutiny. A noted law professor gave this advice: "Close the book; look at the title on the cover." Chances are, if it is Property, you need not concern yourself with whether, for example, the federal government's treatment of the plaintiff's land really raises a federal question sufficient to support jurisdiction on this ground in federal court.

The same rule applies to chapter headings designating sub-areas within the subjects. They tip you off as to what the text is designed to teach. The cases are arranged in a casebook to show a progression or development of the law, so that the preceding cases may also help.

It is also most important to remember to *read the notes and questions* at the end of a case to determine what the editors wanted you to have gleaned from it.

HOLDING AND DECISION: This section should succinctly explain the rationale of the court in arriving at its decision. In capsulizing the "reasoning" of the court, it should always include an application of the general rule or rules of law to the specific facts of the case. Hidden justifications come to light in this entry; the reasons for the state of the law, the public policies, the biases and prejudices, those considerations that influence the justices' thinking and, ultimately, the outcome of the case. At the end, there should be a short indication of the disposition or procedural resolution of the case (e.g., "Decision of the trial court for Mr. Smith (P) reversed").

The foregoing format is designed to help you "digest" the reams of case material with which you will be faced in your law school career. Once mastered by practice, it will place at your fingertips the information the authors of your casebooks have sought to impart to you in case-by-case illustration and analysis.

B. Be as Economical as Possible in Briefing Cases

Once armed with a format that encourages succinctness, it is as important to be economical with regard to the time spent on the actual reading of the case as it is to be economical in the writing of the brief itself. This does not mean "skimming" a case. Rather, it means reading the case with an "eye" trained to recognize into which "section" of your brief a particular passage or line fits and having a system for quickly and precisely marking the case so that the passages fitting any one particular part of

the brief can be easily identified and brought together in a concise and accurate manner when the brief is actually written.

It is of no use to simply repeat everything in the opinion of the court; record only enough information to trigger your recollection of what the court said. Nevertheless, an accurate statement of the "law of the case," i.e., the legal principle applied to the facts, is absolutely essential to class preparation and to learning the law under the case method.

To that end, it is important to develop a "shorthand" that you can use to make margin notations. These notations will tell you at a glance in which section of the brief you will be placing that particular passage or portion of the opinion.

Some students prefer to underline all the salient portions of the opinion (with a pencil or colored underliner marker), making marginal notations as they go along. Others prefer the color-coded method of underlining, utilizing different colors of markers to underline the salient portions of the case, each separate color being used to represent a different section of the brief. For example, blue underlining could be used for passages relating to the rule of law, yellow for those relating to the issue, and green for those relating to the holding and decision, etc. While it has its advocates, the color-coded method can be confusing and time-consuming (all that time spent on changing colored markers). Furthermore, it can interfere with the continuity and concentration many students deem essential to the reading of a case for maximum comprehension. In the end, however, it is a matter of personal preference and style. Just remember, whatever method you use, underlining must be used sparingly or its value is lost.

If you take the marginal notation route, an efficient and easy method is to go along underlining the key portions of the case and placing in the margin alongside them the following "markers" to indicate where a particular passage or line "belongs" in the brief you will write:

N (NATURE OF CASE)
RL (RULE OF LAW)
I (ISSUE)
HL (HOLDING AND DECISION, relates to the RULE OF LAW behind the decision)
HR (HOLDING AND DECISION, gives the RATIONALE or reasoning behind the decision)
HA (HOLDING AND DECISION, APPLIES the general principle(s) of law to the facts of the case to arrive at the decision)

Remember that a particular passage may well contain information necessary to more than one part of your brief, in which case you simply note that in the margin. If you are using the color-coded underlining method instead of margin notation, simply make asterisks or checks in the margin next to the passage in question in the colors that indicate the additional sections of the brief where it might be utilized.

The economy of utilizing "shorthand" in marking cases for briefing can be maintained in the actual brief writing process itself by utilizing "law student shorthand" within the brief. There are many commonly used words and phrases for which abbreviations can be substituted in your briefs (and in your class notes also). You can develop abbreviations that are personal to you and which will save you a lot of time. A reference list of briefing abbreviations can be found on page xii of this book.

C. Use Both the Briefing Process and the Brief as a Learning Tool

Now that you have a format and the tools for briefing cases efficiently, the most important thing is to make the time spent in briefing profitable to you and to make the most advantageous use of the briefs you create. Of course, the briefs are invaluable for classroom reference when you are called upon to explain or analyze a particular case. However, they are also useful in reviewing for exams. A quick glance at the fact summary should bring the case to mind, and a rereading of the rule of law should enable you to go over the underlying legal concept in your mind, how it was applied in that particular case, and how it might apply in other factual settings.

As to the value to be derived from engaging in the briefing process itself, there is an immediate benefit that arises from being forced to sift through the essential facts and reasoning from the court's opinion and to succinctly express them in your own words in your brief. The process ensures that you understand the case and the point that it illustrates, and that means you will be ready to absorb further analysis and information brought forth in class. It also ensures you will have something to say when called upon in class. The briefing process helps develop a mental agility for getting to the *gist* of a case and for identifying, expounding on, and applying the legal concepts and issues found there. The briefing process is the mental process on which you must rely in taking law school examinations; it is also the mental process upon which a lawyer relies in serving his clients and in making his living.

Abbreviations for Briefs

acceptance	acp		offer	O
affirmed	aff		offeree	OE
answer	ans		offeror	OR
assumption of risk	a/r		ordinance	ord
attorney	atty		pain and suffering	p/s
beyond a reasonable doubt	b/r/d		parol evidence	p/e
bona fide purchaser	BFP		plaintiff	P
breach of contract	br/k		prima facie	p/f
cause of action	c/a		probable cause	p/c
common law	c/l		proximate cause	px/c
Constitution	Con		real property	r/p
constitutional	con		reasonable doubt	r/d
contract	K		reasonable man	r/m
contributory negligence	c/n		rebuttable presumption	rb/p
cross	x		remanded	rem
cross-complaint	x/c		res ipsa loquitur	RIL
cross-examination	x/ex		respondeat superior	r/s
cruel and unusual punishment	c/u/p		Restatement	RS
defendant	D		reversed	rev
dismissed	dis		Rule Against Perpetuities	RAP
double jeopardy	d/j		search and seizure	s/s
due process	d/p		search warrant	s/w
equal protection	e/p		self-defense	s/d
equity	eq		specific performance	s/p
evidence	ev		statute of limitations	S/L
exclude	exc		statute of frauds	S/F
exclusionary rule	exc/r		statute	S
felony	f/n		summary judgment	s/j
freedom of speech	f/s		tenancy in common	t/c
good faith	g/f		tenancy at will	t/w
habeas corpus	h/c		tenant	t
hearsay	hr		third party	TP
husband	H		third party beneficiary	TPB
in loco parentis	ILP		transferred intent	TI
injunction	inj		unconscionable	uncon
inter vivos	I/v		unconstitutional	unconst
joint tenancy	j/t		undue influence	u/e
judgment	judgt		Uniform Commercial Code	UCC
jurisdiction	jur		unilateral	uni
last clear chance	LCC		vendee	VE
long-arm statute	LAS		vendor	VR
majority view	maj		versus	v
meeting of minds	MOM		void for vagueness	VFV
minority view	min		weight of the evidence	w/e
Miranda warnings	Mir/w		weight of authority	w/a
Miranda rule	Mir/r		wife	W
negligence	neg		with	w/
notice	ntc		within	w/i
nuisance	nus		without prejudice	w/o/p
obligation	ob		without	w/o
obscene	obs		wrongful death	wr/d

Table of Cases

A aaiPharma Inc. v. Thompson 128
Abbott Laboratories v. Geneva
    Pharmaceuticals, Inc. 29
A.C. Aukerman Co. v. R.L. Chaides
    Construction Co. 113
Agawam Woolen Co. v. Jordan 40
Alexander Milburn Co. v.
    Davies-Bournonville Co. 39
Al-Site Corp. v. VSI International, Inc. 71
Amsted Industries Inc. v. Buckeye Steel
    Castings Co. 124
Apotex USA, Inc. v. Merck & Co., Inc. 38
Aristocrat Technologies Australia Pty Ltd. v.
    International Game Technology 72
Atlantic Thermoplastics Co., Inc. v.
    Faytex Corp. 70
Atlas Powder Co. v. E.I. du Pont
    De Nemours & Co. 59
Autogiro Co. of America v. United States 91
Aventis Pharma S.A. v. Amphastar
    Pharmaceuticals, Inc. 82

B Bergy, In re 3
BIC Leisure Products, Inc. v. Windsurfing
    International, Inc. 120
Bilski, In re 10
Bonito Boats, Inc. v. Thunder
    Craft Boats, Inc. 2
Brenner, Commissioner of Patents v.
    Manson 16

C Catalina Marketing International, Inc. v.
    Coolsavings.com, Inc. 69
Chemcast Corp. v. Arco Industries Corp. 66
Clay, In re 55
Computer Docking Station Corp. v. Dell, Inc. 96
Corning Glass Works v. Sumitomo
    Electric USA, Inc. 99
Cybor Corp. v. FAS Technologies, Inc. 93

D Datamize, LLC v. Plumtree Software, Inc. 75
Deuel, In re 53
Diamond, Commissioner of Patents and
    Trademarks v. Chakrabarty 6
Diamond v. Diehr 9
Dillon, In re 52
DSU Medical Corporation v. JMS
    Company, Ltd. 104

E eBay Inc. v. MercExchange, L.L.C. 116
Egbert v. Lippman 24
E.I. duPont deNemours & Co. v.
    Christopher 4
Electric Storage Battery Co. v.
    Shimadzu 28

Elizabeth, City of v. American
    Nicholson Pavement Co. 26
Enzo Biochem, Inc. v. Gen-Probe Inc. 65
Ethicon, Inc. v. United States Surgical Corp. 79

F Festo Corp. v. Shoketsu Kinzoku Kogyo
    Kabushiki Co., Ltd. 100
Fisher, In re 17
Foster, In re 54
Fressola, Ex parte 68

G The Gentry Gallery, Inc. v. The Berkline Corp. 63
Georgia-Pacific Corp. v. United States
    Plywood Corp. 121
Gillman v. Stern 33
Gosteli, In re 87
Gottschalk v. Benson 8
Gould v. Hellwarth 58
Gould v. Schawlow 36
Graham v. John Deere Co. 44
Graver Tank Co. v. Linde Air Products Co. 97
Great A. & P. Tea Co. v. Supermarket
    Equipment Corp. 43

H Hewlett-Packard Co. v. Bausch & Lomb, Inc. 86
Hilmer, In re 88
Hotchkiss v. Greenwood 42

J Jazz Photo Corp. v. International
    Trade Comm. 106
Johnson & Johnston Associates, Inc. v.
    R.E. Service Co., Inc. 102
Juicy Whip, Inc. v. Orange Bang, Inc. 15

K Kingsdown Medical Consultants, Ltd. v.
    Hollister Inc. 81
Kirin-Amgen Inc. and Others v. Hoechst
    Marion Roussel Limited and Others 107
KSR International Co. v. Teleflex, Inc. 45

L Laboratory Corporation of America
    Holdings v. Metabolite Laboratories, Inc. 7
Lowell v. Lewis 14

M Madey v. Duke University 111
Markman v. Westview Instruments, Inc. 92
McElmurry v. Arkansas Power & Light Co. 114
MedImmune, Inc. v. Genentech, Inc. 130
Merck KGaA v. Integra
    Lifesciences I, Ltd. 126
Metallizing Engineering Co. v. Kenyon
    Bearing & Auto Parts 25
Metroprolol Succinate Patent Litigation, In re 85
Mylan Pharmaceuticals, Inc. v. Thompson 127
Mylan Pharmaceuticals, Inc. v. U.S.
    Food and Drug Administration 133

O   Oka v. Youssefyeh 34
Ormco Corp. v. Align Technology, Inc. 49
Orthokinetics, Inc. v. Safety
       Travel Chairs, Inc. 74

P   Panduit Corp. v. Stahlin Bros.
       Fibre Works, Inc. 118
Papesch, In re 51
Pfaff v. Wells Electronics, Inc. 27
Pharmaceutical Resources, Inc. v.
       Roxane Laboratories, Inc. 61
Phillips v. AWH Corporation 94

R   Regents of the University of California v.
       Eli Lilly & Co. 64
Rite-Hite Corp. v. Kelley Co. 119
Roche Products, Inc. v. Bolar
       Pharmaceutical Co., Inc. 110

S   Sanofi-Synthelabo v. Apotex, Inc. 117
Schering Corp. v. Geneva
       Pharmaceuticals, Inc. 21
Scott v. Finney 35
Seagate Technology, LLC, In re 122

T   Teva Pharmaceuticals USA, Inc. v.
       Novartis Pharmaceuticals Corp. 131
Titanium Metals Corp. of America v.
       Banner 20
Transco Products Inc. v. Performance
       Contracting, Inc. 78
Translogic Technology, Inc., In re 47
Tsubakimoto Seiko Co. Ltd. v.
       Thk K.K. 108

U   USM Corp. v. SPS Technologies, Inc. 112

V   Vas-Cath Inc. v. Mahurkar 62
Vogel, In re 84

W   Warner-Jenkinson Company v.
       Hilton Davis Chemical Co. 98
Wilson Sporting Goods Co. v.
       David Geoffrey & Associates 103
W.L. Gore & Associates v. Garlock, Inc. 30
Woodcock v. Parker 32
Woodland Trust v. Flowertree
       Nursery, Inc. 37
Wright, In re 60

Introduction

Quick Reference Rules of Law

PAGE

1. **Foundations of the United States Patent System.** States may not offer patent-like   2
   protections to intellectual creations that would otherwise remain unprotected as a matter of
   federal law. (Bonito Boats, Inc. v. Thunder Craft Boats, Inc.)

2. **Origins of the patent system.** The purpose of granting patent rights to inventors for their   3
   discoveries is to promote progress in the useful arts or technological arts, rather than in
   science or knowledge in general. (In re Bergy)

3. **Other Forms of Intellectual Property Protection: Misappropriation.** To obtain   4
   knowledge of a trade secret without spending the time and money to discover it
   independently is improper and gives rise to a cause of action unless the holder voluntarily
   discloses it or fails to take reasonable precautions to ensure its secrecy.
   (E.I. duPont deNemours & Co. v. Christopher)

Bonito Boats, Inc. v. Thunder Craft Boats, Inc.

Boat designer (P) v. Competitor (D)

489 U.S. 141 (1989).

NATURE OF CASE: Appeal from judgment striking down a statute prohibiting "direct molding process" in reproducing unpatented designs.

FACT SUMMARY: Bonito Boats, Inc.'s (P) fiberglass recreational hull was molded and reproduced by Thunder Craft (D), whereupon Bonito (P) sued in state court under a Florida statute prohibiting direct molding of unpatented designs.

> 🏛 **RULE OF LAW**
> States may not offer patent-like protections to intellectual creations that would otherwise remain unprotected as a matter of federal law.

FACTS: In 1976, Bonito Boats (P) produced a popular recreational fiberglass boat design and sold it under the trade name 5VBR. There was no record of a patent application for the design. In 1983, a Florida statute was passed making it unlawful for anyone to duplicate a manufactured vessel hull using the direct molding process without permission. Bonito (P) sued Thunder Craft (D) under this statute, which granted damages, injunctive relief and attorney fees. The Florida Supreme Court struck down the law, finding that it conflicted with the balance struck by Congress in the federal patent statute between the encouragement of invention and free access to unpatented ideas. A few years earlier, a California appeals court had upheld a similar law. The Supreme Court granted certiorari to resolve the conflict.

ISSUE: May states offer patent-like protections to intellectual creations that would otherwise remain unprotected as a matter of federal law?

HOLDING AND DECISION: (O'Connor, J.) No. Article I, § 8, cl. 8 of the Constitution (The Patent and Copyright Clause) reflects a balance between the need to encourage innovation and the avoidance of monopolies that stifle competition. Imitation and refinement through imitation lead to innovation, yet there must be an incentive to disclose the innovation to the public, hence the grant of a time-constrained monopoly. The inventor could keep his invention a secret and reap its fruits indefinitely, but federal law rewards its disclosure and the benefit to the community this way. For those inventors with a nonobvious, novel, useful product or idea who opt for federal patent protection, the protection offers exclusive rights to the inventor for a period of twenty (20) years. The attractiveness of the bargain depends on a backdrop of free competition in unpatented designs and innovations. These are fostered by the nonobvious, novelty, and utility requirements of patent registry. Patent protection also requires affirmative action because a patent is not available to a person who places the new product in public commerce prior to seeking patent protection. That person clearly did not seek exclusivity and does not deserve the protection of a federal patent. Inventors may submit the new product or idea into the public market or choose federal patent protection. The federal patent system is a careful balance between protection and disclosure.

▶ ANALYSIS

The federal patent protection grants powers but also limits that grant so that ideas and products are not monopolized. Much of the patent system involves choices on the part of the inventor. The inventor may choose to submit the idea or product to the marketplace without the protection of a patent, keep the idea or product secret indefinitely, share the idea or product with the community at large, or seek federal patent protection to receive exclusivity for a number of years while still sharing the information with the public.

■=■

Quicknotes

U.S. CONSTITUTION, ART. 1, § 8 Gives Congress the authority to promote science by securing limited exclusive rights to inventors.

PATENT A limited monopoly conferred on the invention or discovery of any new or useful machine or process that is novel and non-obvious.

■=■

In re Bergy

N/A

596 F.2d 952 (C.C.P.A. 1979).

NATURE OF CASE: [Nature of case not stated in case-book excerpt.]

FACT SUMMARY: Article I, § 8, clauses 8 and 18, of the Constitution are analyzed.

🏛 RULE OF LAW
The purpose of granting patent rights to inventors for their discoveries is to promote progress in the useful arts or technological arts, rather than in science or knowledge in general.

FACTS: Article I, § 8, clauses 8 and 18, of the Constitution grants to Congress the power to establish both a copyright system and a patent system. It states that: (The Congress shall have Power) . . . (8) To promote the Progress of Science and useful Arts, by securing for limited Times to Authors and Inventors the exclusive Right to their respective Writings and Discoveries; . . . (And) (18) To make all Laws which shall be necessary and proper for carrying into Execution the foregoing Powers . . .

ISSUE: What is the purpose of granting patent rights?

HOLDING AND DECISION: (Rich, J.) The purpose of granting patent rights to inventors for their discoveries is the promotion of progress in the useful arts or technological arts rather than in science or knowledge in general. When Congress enacted the Patent Act in 1952, it adopted this construction of the Constitution. In its report it stated that science, or knowledge in general, is to be promoted by giving authors the exclusive right to their writings, and the progress of the useful arts is to be promoted by giving inventors the exclusive right to their discoveries. The first patent law and many more that followed were thus entitled "Acts to promote the progress of useful arts." Furthermore, the Constitution did not give inventors any right to the patentability of any individual invention, but rather empowered Congress to secure to inventors an exclusive right for a limited time for the stated purpose of promoting the useful arts.

▌ANALYSIS

The inclination against national involvement in economic matters by the delegates to the Constitutional Convention is probably why the clause is limited to exclusive rights alone.

■▬■

E.I. duPont deNemours & Co. v. Christopher

Chemical producer (P) v. Photographer (D)

431 F.2d 1012 (5th Cir. 1970).

NATURE OF CASE: Action for damages for and to enjoin use of appropriated trade secrets.

FACT SUMMARY: A third party hired photographer Christopher (D) to take aerial photographs of a Du Pont (P) plant under construction to uncover trade secrets.

🏛 RULE OF LAW
To obtain knowledge of a trade secret without spending the time and money to discover it independently is improper and gives rise to a cause of action unless the holder voluntarily discloses it or fails to take reasonable precautions to ensure its secrecy.

FACTS: Christopher (D), a photographer, was hired by a party whose identity he refused to disclose. His job was to take aerial pictures from a plane flying over a plant which Du Pont (P) was in the process of building. The object was to use such pictures to uncover trade secrets regarding Du Pont's (P) secret process for producing methanol. When Du Pont (P) brought an action for damages and an injunction against further use of the pictures, Christopher (D) argued that his activities were conducted in public airspace and that for an appropriation of trade secrets to be wrongful there must be a trespass, other illegal conduct, or breach of a confidential relationship, none of which existed. He appealed an adverse decision.

ISSUE: Unless the secret's holder voluntarily disclosed it or failed to take reasonable precautions to ensure its secrecy, does one act wrongfully by obtaining knowledge of a trade secret without spending the time and money to discover it independently?

HOLDING AND DECISION: (Goldberg, J.) Yes. It is improper to obtain knowledge of a trade secret without spending the time and money to discover it independently unless the holder voluntarily discloses it or fails to take reasonable precautions to ensure its secrecy. Thus, a cause of action for wrongful appropriation of trade secrets does not require that there have been a breach of confidence or some illegal conduct like trespass. In this case, Du Pont (P) took reasonable precautions (fencing the construction site, etc.) to ensure secrecy. It is not required to go so far as to put a roof over its unfinished plant to guard its secrets. Thus, a cause of action was stated in this case. Affirmed and remanded.

▶ ANALYSIS

Although the decision represents an expansion of the concept of wrongful appropriation of trade secrets to deal with

sophisticated methods of industrial espionage not contemplated when the concept arose, the protection is not total. The court itself said it did "not mean to imply . . . that everything not in plain view is within the protected value, nor that all information obtained through every extra optical extension is forbidden."

Quicknotes

TRADE SECRET Consists of any formula, pattern, plan, process, or device known only to its owner and business which gives an advantage over competitors.

RESTATEMENT OF TORTS § 757 One who discloses or uses a trade secret is liable if the discovery of the secret was by improper means or disclosure breaches a confidence.

CHAPTER 2

Patent Eligibility

Quick Reference Rules of Law

PAGE

1. **Biotechnology and Products of Nature.**   Living organisms are patentable. (Diamond, Commissioner of Patents and Trademarks v. Chakrabarty)   *6*

2. **Biotechnology and Products of Nature.**   [Rule of Law not included in casebook excerpt.] (Laboratory Corporation of America Holdings v. Metabolite Laboratories, Inc.)   *7*

3. **Computer-Related Inventions and Methods of Doing Business.**   A mathematical formula, having no substantial practical application except in connection with a digital computer, cannot be patented. (Gottschalk v. Benson)   *8*

4. **Computer-Related Inventions and Methods of Doing Business.**   Patentable claims do not become invalid because they include mathematical formulas. (Diamond v. Diehr)   *9*

5. **Computer-Related Inventions and Methods of Doing Business.**   The machine-or-transformation test is the applicable test to determine whether a claim is drawn to a patent-eligible process pursuant to § 101. (In re Bilski)   *10*

Diamond, Commissioner of Patents and Trademarks v. Chakrabarty

Patent office (D) v. Doctor (P)

447 U.S. 303 (1980).

NATURE OF CASE: Review of reversal of Examiner's rejection of patent claim.

FACT SUMMARY: Dr. Chakrabarty (P) sought a patent for an artificially created oil-eating bacterium.

RULE OF LAW
Living organisms are patentable.

FACTS: Dr. Chakrabarty (P) artificially created an oil-eating bacterium and filed a patent application with three claims. The first two were method claims regarding the method of making the bacterium and the application of the bacteria to oil. Both of these were approved. The third claim was for the bacterium itself, and the Patent and Trademarks Office (PTO) (D) rejected this on the grounds it was living matter, and, thus, outside the scope of Title 35. The appellate court reversed. The Supreme Court granted certiorari.

ISSUE: Are living organisms patentable?

HOLDING AND DECISION: (Burger, C.J.) Yes. Living organisms are patentable. The judiciary must proceed cautiously when asked to extend patent law to areas that Congress had not foreseen. However, the judiciary shall apply the statute if it is clear, and Title 35 contains no ambiguity in the present case. Title 35 contains broad language as to its subject matter requirements. Such broad language is not ambiguous when it is needed to serve a congressional objective. Here, the objective is the promotion of "Progress of Science and Useful Arts," and limiting it by the PTO's (D) proposed interpretation fails this purpose. The PTO's (D) second argument is that the Court should reject the patenting of living organisms as against public policy. This is not the province of the judiciary. It is a matter of high policy to be resolved by the legislative process after the kind of investigation, examination, and study that legislative bodies cannot. Reversed.

▌ ANALYSIS

Chakrabarty may not have been as problematical as the PTO (D) feared in terms of creating a slippery slope. No matter the decision reached, it was still accepted that the products created by a genetically engineered object and the processes of genetic engineering were patentable. *Chakrabarty* expanded the scope to the organism itself. The larger effect was felt on Wall Street as opposed to the PTOs (D) and the courts, for biotechnology stocks received a big boost. The PTO (D) has since approved patents for several animals, including mammals. The opinions issued on the subject

gave little weight to proposed ethical or moral arguments. In fact, one decision requiring such a discussion was brought by several animal rights groups, but it was dismissed for lack of standing. See *Animal Legal Defense Fund v. Quigg*, 932 F.2d 920, 18 U.S.P.Q.2d 1677 (Fed. Cir. 1991).

■=■

Quicknotes

35 U.S.C. § 101 Whoever invents a new and useful process, machine, or composition of matter may obtain a patent.

■=■

Laboratory Corporation of America Holdings v. Metabolite Laboratories, Inc.

Alleged infringer (D) v. Patent licensee (P)

548 U.S. 124 (2006).

NATURE OF CASE: Writ of certiorari from liability for infringement of process patent.

FACT SUMMARY: Metabolite Laboratories, Inc. (P) licensed a patent for testing and correlating homocysteine and vitamin deficiency. Laboratory Corporation of America Holdings ("Lab Corp") (D) used the tests and paid royalties for each use. Abbott Labs then developed a test which Lab Corp (D) alternately used and did not pay Metabolite (P) royalties. Metabolite (P) sued Lab Corp (D) for infringement. Lab Corp (D) was found liable and assessed damages. Lab Corp (D) appealed and then filed for a writ of certiorari.

RULE OF LAW
[Rule of Law not stated in casebook excerpt.]

FACTS: University doctors developed a method to test for levels of homocysteine and use the results to determine vitamin deficiencies of folate and cobalamin. The doctors obtained a patent, which Metabolite (P) licensed. Lab Corp (D) then licensed the patented tests from Metabolite (P) and paid Metabolite (P) royalties for each use of the test. Lab Corp (D) then began using a similar but superior test developed by Abbott Labs. Lab Corp (D) did not pay Metabolite (P) royalties when it used the Abbott Labs test although Lab Corp (D) did continue to occasionally use, and pay royalties for, the Metabolite (P) test. Metabolite (P) sued Lab Corp (D) for patent infringement and breach of the license agreement. Metabolite (P) claimed that Lab Corp's (D) use of the Abbott Labs test violated claim 13 of its licensed patent, which prohibited the correlation of test results and potential vitamin deficiencies. Metabolite (P) claimed Lab Corp (D) induced physicians to infringe upon the patent each time a physician reviewed any homocysteine test result and determined a vitamin deficiency. The jury found Lab Corp (D) liable and assessed damages. Lab Corp (D) appealed on the basis the lower court had interpreted claim 13 too broadly. The Federal Circuit affirmed the finding of liability and Lab Corp (D) filed its writ of certiorari, which the Supreme Court granted.

ISSUE: [Issue not stated in casebook excerpt.]

HOLDING AND DECISION: [Holding not stated in casebook excerpt.] Writ dismissed as improvidently granted.

DISSENT: (Breyer, J.) A method patent on correlating test results cannot prohibit physicians from applying knowledge after looking at test results. Lab Corp (D) argues that claim 13 is an attempt to patent "phenomena of nature" which are not patent-eligible. The scope of the "phenomena of nature" doctrine is difficult to discern, but unnecessary to analyze here because claim 13 simply is invalid. Metabolite (P) attempts to argue that claim 13 is a process patent because of the process taken to correlate the test results, but the "process" is just a natural correlation of applying medical knowledge to numbers on a test result. The Court should decide this case because the lower court's decision places doctors in jeopardy when they cannot use their best medical judgment out of fear of breaching licensing agreements or infringing upon patents.

ANALYSIS

Five justices of the Supreme Court determined to dismiss the writ on a procedural basis because Lab Corp (D) had not referenced § 101 in the lower courts, which is the section of the Patent Act that addresses the "phenomena of nature" doctrine. Two other justices joined Justice Breyer in his dissent and Chief Justice Roberts was not involved in the case. The Supreme Court's refusal to provide clear direction on the subject of patentable subject matter in the area of natural correlation has left patent attorneys tiptoeing around the clear disapproval expressed in the dissent and the long-standing approval of the Federal Circuit cases.

Gottschalk v. Benson

Patent office (D) v. Inventor (P)

409 U.S. 63 (1972).

NATURE OF CASE: Appeal from decision reversing rejection of patent claims.

FACT SUMMARY: Gottschalk (D), the Acting Commissioner of Patents, appealed the reversal of his rejection of patent claims relating to the programmed conversion of numerical information.

🏛 **RULE OF LAW**
A mathematical formula, having no substantial practical application except in connection with a digital computer, cannot be patented.

FACTS: Benson (P) submitted patent claims for a method for converting binary-coded-decimal (BCD) numerals into pure binary numerals. The claims were not limited to any particular art or technology, to any particular apparatus or machinery, or to any particular end use. They purported to cover any use of the claimed method in a general purpose digital computer of any type. Gottschalk (D), the Acting Commissioner of Patents, appealed the reversal of his rejection of the patent claims.

ISSUE: Can a mathematical formula, having no substantial practical application except in connection with a digital computer, be patented?

HOLDING AND DECISION: (Douglas, J.) No. A mathematical formula, having no substantial practical application except in connection with a digital computer, cannot be patented. One may not patent an idea. But in practical effect that would be the result if the formula for converting binary code into pure binary were patented in this case. A procedure for solving a given type of mathematical problem is known as an "algorithm." The procedures set forth in the present claims are of formulation for programs to solve that kind, i.e., a generalized formulation for programs to solve mathematical problems of converting one form of numerical representation to another. A patent on the formula would in practical effect be a patent on the algorithm itself. If programs such as this are to be patentable, considerable problems are raised which only committees of Congress can manage. Reversed.

▶ *ANALYSIS*

The *Benson* decision is the leading one on the question of whether or not computer programs are patentable. The history of the case reveals the typical positions which have been taken by the Patent Office and the Court of Customs and Patent Appeals. The patent claims were rejected by the Patent Office, reflecting its usual opposition to patenting computer programs. The Court of Customs and Patent Appeals, typically defiant of the Patent Office, reversed. In subsequent decisions, the Court of Customs and Patent Appeals seemed to even defy the Supreme Court in attempting to gain patents for computer programs.

■═■

Diamond v. Diehr

Patent office (D) v. Rubber manufacturer (P)

450 U.S. 175 (1981).

NATURE OF CASE: Appeal from patent rejection.

FACT SUMMARY: In Diehr's (P) suit against the patent examiner, Diamond (D), for rejection of Diehr's (P) patent on a process for curing synthetic rubber, Diamond (D) contended that the steps in Diehr's (P) claims that were carried out by a computer under control of a stored program constituted nonstatutory subject matter under 35 U.S.C. § 101.

> 🏛 **RULE OF LAW**
> Patentable claims do not become invalid because they include mathematical formulas.

FACTS: Diehr (P) developed a process for curing synthetic rubber which included in several of its steps the use of a mathematical formula and a programmed digital computer. Diamond (D), the patent examiner, rejected Diehr's (P) claims, contending that the steps in Diehr's (P) claims that were carried out by computer under control of a stored program, constituted nonstatutory subject matter under 35 U.S.C. § 101. Diamond (D) concluded that Diehr's (P) claims defined and sought protection of a computer program for operating a rubber-molding press and thus could not be patented. At trial, the Court of Customs and Patent Appeals ruled in Diehr's (P) favor, stating that Diehr's (P) claims used a mathematical formula in a process which, when considered as a whole, performed a function which the patent laws were designed to protect. Diamond (D) appealed.

ISSUE: Do patentable claims become invalid because they include mathematical formulas?

HOLDING AND DECISION: (Rehnquist, J.) No. Patentable claims do not become invalid because they include mathematical formulas. It is now commonplace that an application of a law of nature or mathematical formula to a known structure or process may well be deserving of patent protection. In deciding the eligibility of Diehr's (P) claimed process for patent protection under § 101, the claims must be considered as a whole. Diehr's (P) claims are nothing more than a process for molding rubber products and not an attempt to patent a mathematical formula, when considered as a whole. Diehr's (P) claims, which contain a mathematical formula, implement that formula in a process which is performing a function which the patent laws were designed to protect—that is, transforming an article to a different state or thing. Affirmed.

▶ *ANALYSIS*

In determining the eligibility of a claimed process for patent protection under § 101, their claims must be considered as a whole. It is inappropriate to dissect claims into old and new elements and then to ignore the presence of the old elements in the analysis. This is especially true in a process claim because a new combination of steps in a process may be patentable even though all the constituents of the combination were well known and in common use before the combination was made.

■■■

Quicknotes

35 U.S.C. § 101 Whoever invents a new and useful process, machine, or composition of matter may obtain a patent.

■■■

In re Bilski

Patent applicants (P)

545 F.3d 943 (2008).

NATURE OF CASE: Appeal from Board of Patent Appeals and Interferences sustaining rejection of eleven claims of Bilski's (P) patent application.

FACT SUMMARY: Bernard L. Bilski (P) and Rand A. Warsaw (P) submitted a patent application containing eleven claims related to hedging risk in consumer commodities trading. The examiner rejected all eleven claims as not directed to § 101 patent-eligible subject matter. Bilski (P) and Warsaw (P) appealed to the Board of Patent Appeals and Interferences ("Board") on the basis of examiner error; the Board sustained the rejection. Bilski (P) and Warsaw (P) appealed the Board's final determination.

RULE OF LAW
The machine-or-transformation test is the applicable test to determine whether a claim is drawn to a patent-eligible process pursuant to § 101.

FACTS: Bilski (P) and Warsaw (P) submitted a patent application containing eleven claims related to a method for managing consumption risk of a consumer commodity. The Applicants (P) admitted that the commodity may not be a physical commodity but could be options for future purchases. The examiner determined the method was manipulating an abstract idea, did not involve a specific apparatus, and was therefore not directed to the "technological arts." The examiner rejected all eleven claims of the application. Bilski (P) and Warsaw (P) appealed to the Board, which held the examiner applied the wrong test when using the "technological arts" test and should not have required a specific apparatus because "transformation" of physical subject matter was patent-eligible and may not require a specific apparatus. The Board sustained the rejection, however, on the grounds the claims did not involve a transformation, attempted to patent an abstract idea, and did not produce a "useful, concrete and tangible result." Bilski (P) and Warsaw (P) appealed the Board's final determination.

ISSUE: Is the machine-or-transformation test the applicable test to determine whether a claim is drawn to a patent-eligible process pursuant to § 101?

HOLDING AND DECISION: (Michel, C.J.) Yes. The machine-or-transformation test is the applicable test to determine whether a claim is drawn to a patent-eligible process pursuant to § 101. A claim's threshold inquiry is whether the claim is drawn to a patent-eligible subject matter under § 101. The statute includes four categories of eligible patent subject matter, i.e., processes, machines, manufactures, and compositions of matter. Applicants' (P) claims admittedly fail to meet three of the four, so the Court must consider whether the claims fall under "processes." The

Supreme Court has defined "process" in § 101 to exclude fundamental principles that should remain free knowledge to all persons. The Supreme Court in *Diamond v. Diehr*, 450 U.S. 175 (1981), distinguished between fundamental principles and a particular application of a fundamental principle. *Diehr* essentially requires an inquiry into whether the claim forecloses substantially all applications of the fundamental principle or whether the claim applies the fundamental principle in a specific fashion. *Diehr* involved the application of a particular algorithm to a process for curing rubber. The algorithm still could be used in any application other than the specific steps outlined in the claim to cure rubber, so it was a patent-eligible process. A contrasting Supreme Court case arose in *Gottschalk v. Benson*, 409 U.S. 63 (1972), where the claim was for a mathematical formula to convert BCD numerals to pure binary numerals using a digital computer. If approved, no one else could use the conversion algorithm because it had no other practical application. The claim was therefore rejected. The issue before the Court then is whether Applicants' (P) claim involves a fundamental principle, and if so, whether patenting the claim substantially precludes use of that fundamental principle for any other application. The Supreme Court provides the definitive test to determine if the claim preempts other applications of the fundamental principle. The claim is patent-eligible under § 101 if the claim is tied to a particular machine or apparatus or transforms a particular article into a different state or thing. The case law supports the machine-or-transformation test and the Supreme Court reaffirmed it in *Diehr*. A claim does not become patent-eligible just by limiting it to a particular field or including an "insignificant post-solution activity." Further, although § 101 refers to "new and useful" processes, that phrase is not a requirement independent of § 102 (novelty) and § 103 (non-obviousness). Novelty and non-obviousness do not come under consideration in a § 101 analysis. Similarly, a non-patent-eligible step in the claim does not render the entire claim ineligible. Other case law articulations of § 101 tests are overruled. The *Freeman-Walter-Abele* test, which includes determining whether the claim uses an algorithm and then evaluating the application of that algorithm, is inadequate because it evaluates individual steps rather than the claim as a whole. The "useful, concrete, and tangible result" test is invalid as insufficient and not intended to supplant the machine-or-transformation test. Finally, the "technological arts" test fails because the terms "technological arts" and "technology" are ever-evolving. The correct test determines whether a transformation occurs or whether a machine or apparatus is involved in more than

Continued on next page.

an insignificant extrasolution manner. The transformation should be the transformation of an article into a different state or thing, even if the transformation involves raw data. The data gathering step inherent in an algorithm does not, however, transform a non-patent-eligible claim into a patent-eligible claim. Here, the Applicants' (P) process does not transform an article into a different state or thing. The "article" might even be a mere option to buy in the future. The claim admittedly fails the machine test also, so is thus not drawn to patent-eligible subject matter. The examiner did err in applying the "technological arts" test, but the application does not meet the machine-or-transformation test either. The process encompasses a purely mental process of mathematics, which would preempt all applications of any mental process to hedge risk. Applicants' (P) claims are not drawn to patent-eligible subject matter. Affirmed.

DISSENT: (Newman, J.) The Court today errs in redefining "process" to exclude electronic and photonic technologies. The Court ignores its prior decisions and strikes down the "useful, concrete, and tangible result" as well as failing to recognize that the patent application must meet all elements of the statute including novelty, non-obviousness, and utility. The public has relied on the prior Court holdings, particularly in the area of "intangibles." The Court applies new standards, such as transformation as "central to the purpose" but does not specify what types of transformations qualify. The property rights of the inventors who received patents under the prior tests and definitions are now at risk. The Court has ignored the actual text of the statute, its legislative history, application, and Court interpretation.

DISSENT: (Mayer, J.) The Court should overrule its prior decisions that provide patent protection to business methods. Congress did not intend to permit patents of business methods; patenting has occurred through a misapprehension of the statute's legislative history, and patents are meant to protect technological innovations rather than methods for running a business. Business method patents do not promote the useful arts and are typically of poor quality. Business methods belong in the public domain. Bilski's (P) claims include methods of running a business to hedge risk, are broadly drafted, and prohibit the free-flow of ideas to hedge risk. The machine-or-transformation test will do little to limit the patents on business methods. Bilski's (P) claims arguably involve a physical transformation as market participants go from a state of not being involved in a transaction to a state of being involved. The transformation should be directed to an advance in science or technology.

DISSENT: (Rader, J.) The Court could simply have stated Bilski's (P) claim involves an abstract idea and is therefore not patent-eligible. In its unending opinion, however, it disrupts well-settled principles of law. The Court ignores the broad "process" definition in favor of defining "process" in a limited fashion and thus undermining Congressional intention. Even if the claim slips in under a broader reading of § 101, it still must meet the requirements of the remainder of the chapter. The Court has no authority to impose "transformation" when the statute does not use that term.

▶ ANALYSIS

Multiple corporations filed amicus briefs in the *Bilski* case to discourage the continued granting of business method patents, which appeared to be the focus of the claims set out in the Bilski (P) application. The concern is that continued mental/business method patent-granting could lead to the patenting of truly mental processes, including jury selection. The other side argued that patents should be freely granted as the digital age progresses because inventors have an incentive then to develop new ways to apply digital information. *Bilski* has been appealed to the U.S. Supreme Court.

■▬■

Utility

Quick Reference Rules of Law

PAGE

1. **General Principles.**   The usefulness requirement of the Patent Act is satisfied so long as the invention is not frivolous or injurious to the well-being, good policy, or sound morals of society. (Lowell v. Lewis) ... 14

2. **General Principles.**   The statutory requirement of utility is satisfied if one product can be altered to make it look like another because that in and of itself is a benefit. An invention does not lack utility for patent purposes simply because it can fool the public, through imitation, in a manner that is designed to increase product sales. (Juicy Whip, Inc. v. Orange Bang, Inc.) ... 15

3. **The Utility Requirement in Chemistry and Biotechnology.**   A process or a product which has no known use or is useful only in the sense that it may be the object of scientific research is not patentable because it is not "useful." (Brenner, Commissioner of Patents v. Manson) ... 16

4. **The Utility Requirement at the Federal Circuit.**   A patent application that discloses general generic uses of a claimed invention, the claimed inventions of which are mere research intermediaries, lacks utility and lacks enablement. (In re Fisher) ... 17

Lowell v. Lewis

[Parties not identified.]

15 Fed. Cas. 1018 (D. Mass. 1817).

NATURE OF CASE: Patent claim brought in Massachusetts circuit court.

FACT SUMMARY: Lowell (P) must prove his pump invention is useful.

RULE OF LAW
The usefulness requirement of the Patent Act is satisfied so long as the invention is not frivolous or injurious to the well-being, good policy, or sound morals of society.

FACTS: Lowell (P) argued that his pump satisfies the "useful" requirement of The Patent Act of 1793 and thereby deserved patent protection.

ISSUE: Is the usefulness requirement of the Patent Act satisfied so long as the invention is not frivolous or injurious to the well-being, good policy, or sound morals of society?

HOLDING AND DECISION: (Story, J.) Yes. The usefulness requirement of the Patent Act is satisfied so long as the invention is not frivolous or injurious to the well being, good policy, or sound morals of society. Lewis (D) contends that Lowell's (P) pump must supersede the pumps in common use in order to receive patent protection. This is incorrect. The Patent Act of 1793 uses the term "useful invention" incidentally. It occurs only in the first section and is merely descriptive of the application's subject matter or the applicant's conviction. If the invention is mischievous or immoral, such as a method to poison or assassinate, then it would be unpatentable. However, if the invention steers clear of this limited category, it would be patentable. This is true even if the invention serves no purpose. In that case, the invention may sink into contempt and disregard, but it will remain patentable.

ANALYSIS

While on the circuit in New England, Justice Story provided several influential decisions concerning U.S. patent law. In 1818, he expounded upon the definition of utility by defining it as an invention that may be applied to a beneficial use in society. *See Bedford v. Hunt*, 3 Fed. Cas. 37 (D. Mass. 1817). Given this liberal standard, it is hardly surprising that utility is rarely litigated. Courts are not necessarily looking for something better, just different.

Quicknotes

PATENT ACT OF 1793 Allows for patents on "useful inventions."

Juicy Whip, Inc. v. Orange Bang, Inc.

Beverage dispenser manufacturer (P) v. Infringer (D)

185 F.3d 1364 (Fed. Cir. 1999).

NATURE OF CASE: Appeal of grant of summary judgment.

FACT SUMMARY: Juicy (P) sued Orange (D), alleging it was infringing on its beverage-dispensing patent. Orange (D) alleged the dispenser was unpatentable because it lacked utility.

🏛 RULE OF LAW
The statutory requirement of utility is satisfied if one product can be altered to make it look like another because that in and of itself is a benefit. An invention does not lack utility for patent purposes simply because it can fool the public, through imitation, in a manner that is designed to increase product sales.

FACTS: Juicy (P) has a patent for a post-mix beverage dispenser that is designed to look like a pre-mix beverage dispenser. A post-mix dispenser stores beverage syrup concentrate and water in separate locations until the beverage is ready to be dispensed. A pre-mix beverage dispenser, on the other hand, pre-mixes the syrup concentrate and water and the beverage is stored in a display reservoir bowl until it is ready to be dispensed. A pre-mix dispenser's display bowl stimulates impulse buying. However, it creates the need to clean the bowl frequently because of bacterial build-up. The patented dispenser thus has the appearance of a pre-mix dispenser but functions as a post-mix dispenser, thereby alleviating the required maintenance. Juicy (P) sued Orange (D), alleging it was infringing on the patent. The district court granted Orange's (D) motion for summary judgment and held the patent invalid for lack of utility.

ISSUE: Does the post-mix dispenser that looks like a pre-mix dispenser lack utility?

HOLDING AND DECISION: (Bryson, J.) No. The post-mix dispenser does not lack utility. The Patent Act provides that whoever invents any useful machine may obtain a patent for it. An invention is useful if it is capable of providing some identifiable benefit. Although inventions that are injurious to the well-being of society are considered unpatentable, the principle that inventions are invalid if they are principally designed to serve immoral purposes has not recently been applied broadly. The district court's reliance on the cases of *Rickard v. Du Bon*, 103 F. 868 (2d Cir. 1900), and *Scott & Williams v. Aristo Hosiery Co.*, 7 F.2d 1003 (2d Cir. 1925), is thus misplaced because they do not represent the correct view of the doctrine of utility under the Patent Act of 1952. The statutory requirement of utility is satisfied if one product can be altered to make it look like another, because that in and of itself is a benefit. It is common for a product to be designed to appear to viewers to be something that it is not and there are many patents directed at making one product imitate another. The value of such products is that they appear to be something that they are not. In this case, the post-mix dispenser has utility because it embodies the features of a post-mix dispenser while imitating the visual appearance of a pre-mix dispenser. Just because customers may believe that they are receiving fluid directly from the display tank does not mean the invention has no utility. Even if it was considered deceptive, that does not mean it is unpatentable. Other agencies, and not the Patent and Trademark Office, are delegated the task of protecting customers from fraud and deception in the sale of food products. Furthermore, it is up to Congress to declare particular types of inventions unpatentable. Reversed and remanded.

▌ *ANALYSIS*

This case centered on the reasoning that the invention was useful in and of itself because it was able to create more sales by fooling the public into believing that it was getting a certain product when it was really getting a different product. The real utility of the product was that it was increasing sales by providing customers with the appearance of the product but eliminating the work of cleaning and maintenance which would have been involved in creating the actual product.

■═■

Brenner, Commissioner of Patents v. Manson

Patent office (D) v. Chemist (P)

383 U.S. 519 (1966).

NATURE OF CASE: Appeal from affirmation of a denial of an application for an "interference."

FACT SUMMARY: The Patent Office found Manson's (P) process for making certain steroids unpatentable due to a failure to disclose any utility for the steroids.

🏛 RULE OF LAW
A process or a product which has no known use or is useful only in the sense that it may be the object of scientific research is not patentable because it is not "useful."

FACTS: Manson (P) wanted to patent a process to produce certain known steroids and requested "interference" be declared to establish that his patent application had priority over one filed earlier by Ringold and Rosenkranz and allegedly covering the process. An "interference" proceeding is used to settle the priority of patent applications filed close in time on substantially the same invention. Manson's (P) patent application was rejected for "failure to disclose any utility for" the chemical compound produced by the process. In appealing the decision, Manson (P) noted that steroids of a class which included the compound his process produced were undergoing screening for possible tumor-inhibiting effects in mice, and that a homologue adjacent to his steroid had proven effective in that role. He also argued that his process would be useful as a step in further research which might develop other useful processes and compounds. The Court of Customs and Patent Appeals held for Manson (P).

ISSUE: Is a process or product patentable if it has no known uses or is useful only in the sense that it may be the subject of scientific research?

HOLDING AND DECISION: (Fortas, J.) No. A process or a product which has no known use or is useful only in the sense that it may be the object of scientific research is not patentable because it is not "useful." Even if a showing that the steroid produced by this process would be likely to have a tumor-inhibiting effect in mice would be sufficient to establish "utility," the Patent Office determined that no such showing was made. Thus, this process is not patentable. Reversed.

DISSENT IN PART: (Harlan, J.) In chemistry, one discovery builds upon the next and new processes and products without "utility," as the majority too narrowly defines it, may permit someone else to take a further step leading to a commercially useful item. To encourage such activity is one job of the patent laws.

▶ ANALYSIS

Before 1950, the question of whether the chemical compound produced by a process which was the subject of a patent application was "useful" was not addressed. Prior to that time, the Patent Office seemed to assume that chemical compounds were necessarily useful. Thus, it failed to conduct any specific inquiries other than ascertaining that the process did indeed produce the designated chemical compound.

■■■

Quicknotes

35 U.S.C. § 101 Whoever invents a new and useful process, machine, or composition of matter may obtain a patent.

■■■

In re Fisher

N/A

421 F.3d 1365 (Fed. Cir. 2005).

NATURE OF CASE: Appeal from affirmance of a decision denying patentability for lack of utility and lack of enablement.

FACT SUMMARY: Fisher (P) contended that his claimed invention, relating to five purified nucleic acid sequences (genes), commonly referred to as expressed sequence tags (ESTs), that encoded proteins and protein fragments in maize plants, had a specific and substantial utility and that his patent application enabled one of ordinary skill in the art to use the invention.

🏛 RULE OF LAW
A patent application that discloses general generic uses of a claimed invention, the claimed inventions of which are mere research intermediaries, lacks utility and lacks enablement.

FACTS: Fisher (P) submitted a patent application (the '643 application) that related to five purified nucleic acid sequences (genes), commonly referred to as expressed sequence tags (ESTs), that encoded proteins and protein fragments in maize plants. When Fisher (P) filed the '643 application, he did not know the precise structure or function of either the genes or the proteins encoded for by those genes. The '643 application disclosed that the five claimed ESTs could be used in a variety of ways. These included: (1) serving as a molecular marker for mapping the entire maize genome, which consists of ten chromosomes that collectively encompass roughly 50,000 genes; (2) measuring the level of mRNA in a tissue sample via microarray technology to provide information about gene expression; (3) providing a source for primers for use in the polymerase chain reaction (PCR) process to enable rapid and inexpensive duplication of specific genes; (4) identifying the presence or absence of a polymorphism; (5) isolating promoters via chromosome walking; (6) controlling protein expression; and (7) locating genetic molecules of other plants and organisms. The patent examiner found that none of the recited uses for the ESTs satisfied the "substantial utility" standard and "enablement" standard required for patentability. The board of appeals and interferences affirmed, and the court of appeals granted review.

ISSUE: Does a patent application that discloses general generic uses of a claimed invention, the claimed inventions of which are mere research intermediaries, lack utility and lack enablement?

HOLDING AND DECISION: (Michel, C.J.) Yes. A patent application that discloses general generic uses of a claimed invention, the claimed inventions of which are mere research intermediaries, lacks utility and lacks enablement.

Fisher's (P) argument that the claimed ESTs provide seven specific and substantial uses, regardless whether the functions of the genes corresponding to the claimed ESTs are known is not convincing. Essentially, the claimed ESTs act as no more than research intermediates that may help scientists to isolate the particular underlying protein-encoding genes and conduct further experimentation on those genes. The overall goal of such experimentation is presumably to understand the maize genome. Therefore, the claimed ESTs are mere "objects of use-testing," i.e., objects upon which scientific research could be performed with no assurance that anything useful will be discovered in the end. Fisher's (P) comparison of the ESTs to a patentable microscope is also unconvincing. A microscope can immediately reveal an object's structure, whereas the claimed ESTs can only be used to detect the presence of genetic material having the same structure as the EST itself. It is unable to provide any information about the overall structure let alone the function of the underlying gene. Accordingly, while a microscope can offer an immediate, real-world benefit in a variety of applications, the same cannot be said for the claimed ESTs. The claimed ESTs themselves are not an end of Fisher's (P) research effort, but only tools to be used along the way in the search for a practical utility. Thus, while Fisher's (P) claimed ESTs may add a noteworthy contribution to biotechnology research, they are not of sufficient utility to merit patentability because Fisher (P) does not identify the function for the underlying protein-encoding genes. Absent such identification, the claimed ESTs have not been researched and understood to the point of providing an immediate, well-defined, real world benefit to the public meriting the grant of a patent. Therefore, Fisher's (P) asserted uses are insufficient to meet the standard for a "substantial" utility under § 101. The claimed inventions also lack enablement under § 112. Affirmed.

DISSENT: (Rader, J.) The invention here, ESTs, has a utility as a research tool to isolate and study other molecules. Granted, the ESTs are only useful in a research context but they are still useful and patentable. The Court determines the utility would not produce enough valuable information, but the existence of any information shows a utility. The ESTs are similar to a microscope in that they are a tool to enable a researcher to move one step closer to a discovery. The Patent Office is in an unenviable position because they have to distinguish between an appropriately protectable incremental tool and a tool that fails to provide sufficient advancement to justify patent protection. The Patent Office must do this without the benefit of an obviousness requirement for

Continued on next page.

genomic inventions. The current law, however, includes research tools providing a cognizable benefit and the ESTs have "utility" under § 101.

▶ *ANALYSIS*

A research tool may not immediately benefit the public at large, but Judge Rader points out, and other scholars agree, that the incremental benefit offered to researchers should count as utility deserving of patent protection. The utility requirement as it stands is narrowly applied.

■▬■

Quicknotes

PATENT   A limited monopoly conferred on the invention or discovery of any new or useful machine or process that is novel and nonobvious.

■▬■

CHAPTER 4

Anticipation

Quick Reference Rules of Law

PAGE

1. **Anticipation.** Patents may not be issued on anticipated claims pursuant to § 102, which are claims that can be found within the scope of a prior art reference. (Titanium Metals Corp. of America v. Banner) — 20

2. **Anticipation.** A patent claim is anticipated if a single prior art reference expressly or inherently discloses or enables the later claim. (Schering Corp. v. Geneva Pharmaceuticals, Inc.) — 21

Titanium Metals Corp. of America v. Banner

Corporate patent application licensee (P) v. Comm'r of Patents and Trademarks (D)

778 F.2d 775 (1985).

NATURE OF CASE: Appeal from order authorizing Banner (D) to issue a patent to Titanium Metals Corp. of America (P).

FACT SUMMARY: Inventor-employees licensed their patent application to the employer, Titanium Metals Corp. of America (P). The application contained three claims related to titanium alloy. The examiner rejected the claims on the bases of obviousness and anticipation. Titanium (P) appealed and Banner (D) sustained the rejection. Titanium (P) filed a civil action in the U.S. District Court for the District of Columbia against Banner (D) and the District Court ordered Banner (D) to issue the patent based on claims 1 and 2. Banner (P) appealed.

> ## RULE OF LAW
> Patents may not be issued on anticipated claims pursuant to § 102, which are claims that can be found within the scope of a prior art reference.

FACTS: Loren C. Covington and Howard R. Palmer filed an application to patent an alloy they developed. They then licensed their patent application and the invention to their employer, Titanium Metals Corp. of America (P). The alloy consists primarily of titanium with small amounts of other metals and a preferred absence of iron. The application consisted of three claims related to the alloy and its preferred compositions. The examiner rejected the claims, finding claims 1 and 2 were anticipated by a Russian article related to alloys such as the claims at issue, and claim 3 would have been obvious after reading the article. Titanium (P) appealed the examiner's decision to the Patent and Trademark Office Board of Appeals ("Board"), which affirmed the rejection but on the mistaken assumption that all three claims were anticipated by the Russian article. The Board determined the technical Russian article disclosed and described the alloys falling within the claims at issue, thus the claims were not new. The article did not discuss the corrosion resistance of the alloy, which is one of the claims submitted, but the Board determined that was of no consequence and the claim was anticipated. Titanium (P) brought a civil action against Brenner (D) in the District Court. The Court considered Titanium's (P) expert witness's testimony, the pre-trial and post-trial briefs, and ordered Brenner (D) to issue the patent based on claims 1 and 2. Brenner (D) appealed.

ISSUE: May patents be issued on anticipated claims pursuant to § 102, which are claims that can be found within the scope of a prior art reference?

HOLDING AND DECISION: (Rich, J.) No. Patents may not be issued on anticipated claims pursuant

to § 102, which are claims that can be found within the scope of a prior art reference. Patent law, specifically § 101 and § 102, requires that the subject matter of the patent application be new. No one in the lower court considered whether the alloy at issue was new. The issue should have been whether claims 1 and 2 related to, or read on, an alloy already disclosed by the Russian article. Section 102 requires the claim to not be described in a domestic or foreign publication printed before the invention date or more than one year before the allowable application date. Here, the Russian article was printed five years prior to application and its "prior art" status is unquestionable. An expert witness affidavit in the instant case demonstrates without question that claims 1 and 2 read on the alloys disclosed in the Russian article and therefore are fully anticipated. The Court seems to have misinterpreted the law to permit a patent because the applicants disclosed many things that cannot be learned from reading the Russian article, such as the alloys' good corrosion resistance. The Court did not consider, however, the primary issue of whether the patent could issue on an alloy that is not new even when persons discover that old alloy's corrosion resistance. Here, the claim covered several compositions of the alloy, but the alloy itself is covered in prior art, and thus each claim fails. The claims are anticipated and not allowed under § 102. Reversed.

ANALYSIS

An anticipated claim relates to a product already disclosed in a prior art even if that claim involves a new process to develop the product. Frustrating to many patent applicants, even a missing material element in the prior art can be considered inherent in the prior art and thus still be anticipated. The courts must heavily rely on expert testimony in the particular technological area to determine if the prior art fully discloses all material elements included in the claim.

Quicknotes

PRIOR ART Any prior knowledge or activity regarding a particular invention that may be considered by the Patent and Trademark Office in granting or denying a patent application or by the court in determining a patent infringement action.

Schering Corp. v. Geneva Pharmaceuticals, Inc.

Patent applicant (P) v. Alleged infringer (D)

339 F.3d 1373 (Fed. Cir. 2003).

NATURE OF CASE: Appeal from summary judgment invalidating patent claims.

FACT SUMMARY: Schering Corp. (P) owns two patents on antihistamines. The first patent's claims expired and the second patent's claims were about to expire. Geneva Pharmaceuticals, Inc. (D) began marketing generic antihistamine, which Schering (P) claimed infringed upon its second patent's claims. The District Court determined that two of the second patent's claims were anticipated by the first patent and thus invalidated those two claims by summary judgment.

🏛 RULE OF LAW
A patent claim is anticipated if a single prior art reference expressly or inherently discloses or enables the later claim.

FACTS: Schering (P) owned the '233 patent and the '716 patent on antihistamines. Schering marketed the '233 patented non-drowsy antihistamine loratadine as Claritin. When a patient ingests Claritin, that patient forms the metabolite DCL, which is the subject matter of Claims 1 and 3 of the '716 patent. The '233 patent issued on August 4, 1981, while the earliest priority date of the '716 patent was February 15, 1984, which makes the '233 patent prior art to the '716 patent. The '233 patent does not expressly disclose DCL or metabolites of loratadine. The '233 patent expired and Geneva (D) and other manufacturers began to market generic loratadine. Schering (P) filed a lawsuit claiming patent infringement based on the alleged infringement of the '716 patent which would not expire until 2004. The District Court determined patent '233 anticipated claims 1 and 3 of the '716 patent and thus granted summary judgment to Geneva (D). Schering (P) appealed.

ISSUE: Is a patent claim anticipated if a single prior art reference expressly or inherently discloses or enables the later claim?

HOLDING AND DECISION: (Rader, J.) Yes. A patent claim is anticipated if a single prior art reference expressly or inherently discloses or enables the later claim. Anticipation invalidates a patent if each limitation of the claimed invention is disclosed in a single prior art reference. Even if a feature is not expressly disclosed, the claim is anticipated if the feature is inherent in the reference. This Court holds that a person of ordinary skill in the art at the time would not have had to recognize or reproduce the inherent feature for the claim to be anticipated. Schering's (P) reliance on *Continental Can Co. v. Monsanto Co.*, 948 F.2d 1264 (Fed. Cir. 1991) is misplaced because that case did not consider whether the inherent feature was recognized

before or after the patent at issue. The other cited cases also do not stand for the proposition that inherency requires recognition. The instant case does not even involve accidental anticipation because DCL inevitably forms when loratadine is ingested. This may be a case of first impression as the '233 patent does not disclose DCL. The prior art reference can be either express or inherent. If the public could not practice the prior art without infringing upon the new claim, then the new claim is wholly anticipated. Here, Geneva's (D) use of loratadine (i.e. the prior art) infringes upon claims 1 and 3 of the '716 patent (i.e. the new claim) because all loratadine metabolizes into DCL. Thus, the prior art of loratadine, patent '233, anticipates claims 1 and 3 of patent '716. Schering (P) next argues that the tests of loratadine were secret and thus DCL was not in public domain prior to the critical date of February 15, 1983. Anticipation, however, does not require actual disclosure or creation; only that one skilled in the prior art is enabled to create based on the express or inherent reference. Metabolites are capable of patent protection. For example, a more pure version of a naturally occurring metabolite can receive protection. Compound claims, such as the one here, are not patent-eligible. Affirmed.

DISSENT from denial of rehearing en banc: (Newman, J.) The Court today holds that DCL was anticipated although it did not previously exist and was not known to the prior art. The issue in the suit was infringement, not validity. The Court correctly held no liability for infringement but unnecessarily strained to find the patent claims invalid. A previously existing but unknown product is not unpatentable. Here, the panel sought to overturn precedent that analyzes inherency as applied to subject matter not taught in the single prior art reference. The panel held that no one knew of the existence of DCL, so no person of ordinary skill in the prior art could have known that loratadine ingestion resulted in DCL. The Court en banc should have heard the case to determine the inherency issue.

▶ ANALYSIS

Schering (P) appealed to the Court en banc to hear the case, but the Court declined, which led to Judge Newman's dissent. The case originally arose because Geneva (D) sought to market a generic Claritin while claiming its generic form did not infringe upon Schering's (P) Clarinex—the brand name for DCL—because the Clarinex patent was invalid. The parent drug, loratadine, necessarily formed DCL, so the knowledge required for the patent on DCL

Continued on next page.

predated the patent by more than one year and was thus anticipated. This case drastically altered metabolite patent practices because the pharmaceutical companies could no longer stagger the introduction and marketing of the parent drug with the later introduction and marketing of the metabolite drug without fear that a competitor would patent a nonobvious metabolite from the parent drug first.

■═■

Quicknotes

PRIOR ART Any prior knowledge or activity regarding a particular invention that may be considered by the Patent and Trademark Office in granting or denying a patent application or by the court in determining a patent infringement action.

■═■

CHAPTER 5

Statutory Bars

Quick Reference Rules of Law

PAGE

1. **Applicant Activities § 102(b): "Public Use."** If an inventor gives or sells a device to another without limitation or restriction, or injunction or secrecy, and it is used, such use is public and places the invention "in public use." (Egbert v. Lippmann) — 24

2. **Applicant Activities § 102(b): "Public Use."** Commercial exploitation of an invention, even if done in secret, constitutes a "public use" under § 102(b) of the Patent Act. (Metallizing Engineering Co. v. Kenyon Bearing & Auto Parts) — 25

3. **Applicant Activities § 102(b): Experimental Use.** Public experimentation does not put an invention in "public use." (City of Elizabeth v. American Nicholson Pavement Co.) — 26

4. **Applicant Activities § 102(b): "On Sale."** An invention may not be patented a year after it was ready for patenting and was the subject of a commercial offer for sale. (Pfaff v. Wells Electronics, Inc.) — 27

5. **Third-Party Activities § 102(b): Informing Uses.** A third party's innocent use of an invention in its factory to create a commercial product is a "public use" under § 102(b). (Electric Storage Battery Co. v. Shimadzu) — 28

6. **Third-Party Activities § 102(b): Non-informing Uses.** The on-sale bar doctrine applies, when before one year prior to the date of application for the patent, the invention is both the subject of a commercial sale or offer for sale and is ready for patenting. (Abbott Laboratories v. Geneva Pharmaceuticals, Inc.) — 29

7. **Third-Party Activities § 102(b): Secret Uses.** A third party's secret commercial use of a process is not a "public use" under § 102(b). (W.L. Gore & Associates v. Garlock, Inc.) — 30

Egbert v. Lippmann

Executor of original patentee's estate (P) v. Alleged patent infringer (D)

104 U.S. (14 Otto) 333 (1881).

NATURE OF CASE: Action alleging patent infringement.

FACT SUMMARY: Lippmann (D) fought a patent infringement charge by asserting that Barnes, the original patentee, had permitted the corset steels he had invented to be "in public use" long before he patented them.

🏛 RULE OF LAW
If an inventor gives or sells a device to another without limitation or restriction, or injunction or secrecy, and it is used, such use is public and places the invention "in public use."

FACTS: Barnes invented improved corset steels between January and May of 1855, according to the testimony given by the executrix of his estate, Egbert (P), in an action she brought against Lippmann (D) for patent infringement. Egbert (P) contended that she and a friend, Mrs. Cugier, had complained in Barnes's presence about how their corset steels would break, and that he had said he could make a pair that would not break. When they next met, he presented a pair of corset steels he had made to Egbert (P), and she wore them for quite some time. She further testified that Barnes presented another pair to her in 1858 and that when the corsets in which they were placed wore out, she ripped them out and put them in new corsets several times. Sturgis testified that Barnes spoke of the invention to him in 1863, that he went to Barnes's home to see the invention, and that Barnes had his wife remove her corset and take a pair of scissors to it to remove the steels so that he could explain to Sturgis how they were made and used. This evidence, contended Lippmann (D), established that the steels were "in public use" long before a patent application was made, thus making the patent ultimately issued void. From a circuit court decision in favor of Lippmann (D), Egbert (P) appealed.

ISSUE: Does an inventor put his invention "in public use" by giving it or selling it to another to be used without limitation or restriction or injunction of secrecy?

HOLDING AND DECISION: (Woods, J.) Yes. If an inventor gives or sells a device without limitation or restriction or injunction of secrecy, and it is used, the invention has been placed in "public use." Whether the use of an invention is public or private does not depend upon the number of persons to whom its use is known. Furthermore, to constitute the public use of an invention, it is not necessary that more than one of the patented articles be publicly used. Some inventions, like the one at issue here, are by their very character capable of being used only where they cannot be seen or observed by the public eye. Nevertheless, if the inventor allows it to be used without any restriction of any kind, the use is a public one. Tested by these principles, the evidence in this case showed there was a public use of the invention. Affirmed.

DISSENT: (Miller, J.) With an article of this nature it may well be imagined that an inventor's warning not to expose one's use of the steel spring to public observation would have been a piece of irony. Thus, failure to issue it should not defeat a patent that is otherwise meritorious.

▶ *ANALYSIS*

Exposure to public view is not and never has been the test of a public-use bar. The idea that a public use can be found even if the invention is not observable by the public is an important rationale whose present-day consequences could not be fathomed when this case was decided. It is now frequently applied to technological advancements in sophisticated machinery, etc., the insides of which are seldom seen by anyone.

■■■

Quicknotes

35 U.S.C. § 102 A person is entitled to a patent unless the invention was already known or used, has been abandoned or was previously invented.

■■■

Metallizing Engineering Co. v. Kenyon Bearing & Auto Parts

Metals manufacturer (P) v. Competitor (D)

153 F.2d 516 (2d Cir. 1946).

NATURE OF CASE: Appeal from judgment holding patent valid and infringed.

FACT SUMMARY: Metallizing (P) had commercially utilized their patented process over a year prior to filing.

RULE OF LAW
Commercial exploitation of an invention, even if done in secret, constitutes a "public use" under § 102(b) of the Patent Act.

FACTS: Metallizing Engineering (P) assigned a patent to Meduna concerning a new metallizing process. Metallizing is a process by which worn metal parts of a machine are replenished by adding "spray metal" to the parts. The application for the patent was filed on August 6, 1942, but the Patent Law required that the invention not be in "public use" prior to a year before this date. Before August 6, 1941, Meduna had used the process for commercial gain, but had kept it a closely guarded secret. When Kenyon (D) later used the process, Metallizing (P) sued for infringement. Kenyon (D) claimed that Metallizing (P) lost all patent rights with its earlier public use. The lower court found for Metallizing (P), and Kenyon (D) appealed.

ISSUE: Does commercial exploitation of an invention, even if done in secret, constitute a "public use under § 102(b) of the Patent Act"?

HOLDING AND DECISION: (Hand, J.) Yes. Commercial exploitation of an invention, even if done in secret, constitutes a "public use" under § 102(b) of the Patent Act. The lower court correctly followed precedent, but this precedent confused two separate doctrines: (1) the effect an inventor's commercial exploitation has upon patent rights for a machine or process; and (2) the effect that the prior use of others has upon patent rights. As to the first doctrine, an inventor cannot commercially exploit his invention longer than the statutorily required time to file for an application. Regardless of how little the public learned of the invention or process, an inventor loses his patent rights once it is commercially utilized. He must either choose secrecy or a legal monopoly. Judgment reversed, complaint dismissed.

▶ ANALYSIS

The *Metallizing* opinion is somewhat difficult, for Justice Hand was forced to distort his definitions of common words so that "public" meant "secret" when modifying "use." Had Hand reached the opposite conclusion, an inventor could commercially exploit his discovery while keeping it secret as long as possible. Once someone else "discovered" the invention, the original inventor could then apply for a patent and receive protection. Thus, he could maintain exclusivity for much longer than the limited number of years that Congress has decided accounts for the "Progress of Science and the Useful Arts."

■■■

Quicknotes

35 U.S.C. § 102 A person is entitled to a patent unless the invention was already known or used, has been abandoned, or was previously invented.

■■■

City of Elizabeth v. American Nicholson Pavement Co.

City (D) v. Inventor (P)

97 U.S. (7 Otto) 126 (1877).

NATURE OF CASE: Review of judgment finding patent infringement.

FACT SUMMARY: Nicholson (P) charged the City of Elizabeth (D) with patent infringement when it laid down a wooden pavement in conformity with his patented process.

🏛 RULE OF LAW
Public experimentation does not put an invention in "public use."

FACTS: Nicholson (P) patented a process in 1854 for laying down wooden pavement that was cheaper, more durable, and safer than the norm. While developing the process, Nicholson (P) experimented by laying down, at his own expense, pavement on a public road in Boston in 1848. It was assumed that people and horses would travel along it. The City of Elizabeth (D) laid down wooden pavements in substantial conformity with the patented process. Nicholson (P) successfully brought an action for patent infringement, and the Supreme Court granted review.

ISSUE: Does public experimentation place the invention within the statutory meaning of "public use?"

HOLDING AND DECISION: [Judge not stated in casebook excerpt.] No. Public experimentation does not put the invention in "public use." It is not enough that the public know of the invention; public use or sale must occur. The policy of abandonment requires that if the invention is in public use or sale prior to the statutory two years before filing, the inventor loses all rights. However, the nature of street pavement is that it cannot be experimented upon satisfactorily without public use. The public had incidental use of Nicholson's (P) pavement, but not "public use" within the meaning of the statute. It would have been different if Nicholson (P) had allowed Boston to lay down pavement elsewhere in the city or he had sold it, but Nicholson (P) never let the invention beyond his control. Public knowledge of the invention does not preclude the inventor from receiving a patent. It is the public use or sale of the object that will preclude the patent. Affirmed.

▶ ANALYSIS

Although *Elizabeth* seemingly undercuts Story's opinion in *Pennock v. Adam Dialogue*, 27 U.S. (1829), in that it does not necessarily encourage early filing, the policy reasons are obvious. Certain inventions require public experimentation, while others do not. What is less obvious is whether public experimentation is an exception to the "public use" rule or is it simply not a "public use." The Federal Circuit in *TP Laboratories, Inc. v. Professional Positioners, Inc.*, 724 F.2d

965, 220 U.S.P.Q. 577 (Fed. Cir. 1984), *cert. denied*, 469 U.S. 826 (1984), implies it is not an exception. Judge Nies wrote that it is incorrect to ask first whether it is a public use and, second, whether it is experimental. Rather, the correct question is whether it is a "public use" under § 102(b).

■=■

Quicknotes

35 U.S.C. § 102 A person is entitled to a patent unless the invention was already known or used, has been abandoned, or was previously invented.

■=■

Pfaff v. Wells Electronics, Inc.

Inventor (P) v. Alleged infringer (D)

525 U.S. 55 (1998).

NATURE OF CASE: Appeal from judgment in a patent infringement action.

FACT SUMMARY: Pfaff (P), the inventor of a computer chip socket, filed for a patent over a year after offering it for sale.

> ## 🏛 RULE OF LAW
> An invention may not be patented a year after it was ready for patenting and was the subject of a commercial offer for sale.

FACTS: Pfaff (P) began work on a computer chip socket in November 1980. He prepared detailed engineering drawings that described the design, dimensions, and materials in March 1981. The following month, Texas Instruments ordered 30,100 of the sockets from Pfaff (P) although there was no prototype yet. Pfaff (P) did not fill the order until July 1981. Subsequently, Pfaff (P) was issued a patent on January 1, 1985, and brought a patent infringement action against Wells (D), the maker of a competing socket. The court of appeals ruled that Pfaff's (P) claims were invalid because he had filed for the patent more than a year after the sale to Texas Instruments. Pfaff (P) argued that his invention was not "on sale" for this purpose until it had been actually reduced to practice.

ISSUE: May an invention be patented a year after it was ready for patenting and was the subject of a commercial offer for sale?

HOLDING AND DECISION: (Stevens, J.) No. An invention may not be patented a year after it was ready for patenting and was the subject of a commercial offer for sale. The Patent Act of 1952 does not require that an invention be reduced to practice before it can be patented. Assuming diligence on the part of the applicant, it is normally the first inventor to conceive, rather than the first to reduce to practice, who establishes the right to patent. In the present case, it is evident that Pfaff (P) could have obtained a patent on his socket when he accepted the Texas Instruments purchase order. Section 102 of the Patent Act limits patents on ideas that are in the public domain. Thus, an inventor loses patent rights when the inventor puts the invention into public use before filing an application, although private testing is permitted. For purposes of the one-year filing period, two conditions cause the period to commence. When the invention is the subject of a commercial offer for sale and is qualified for a patent, the inventor has one year in which to file an application. This standard is perfectly clear and allows the inventor control over the timing of an invention's public use. In the present case,

Pfaff's (P) invention was ready for patenting because he had detailed drawings of the socket prior to its actual manufacture. Thus, the one-year period began to run when it was offered for sale to Texas Instruments. Since Pfaff (P) did not file a patent application within a year, the patent is invalid. Affirmed.

▶ ANALYSIS

Courts often used a totality of the circumstances test for the on-sale and public use limitations prior to this decision. Following the Court's ruling in this case, this test seems to be completely outdated. However, it may still play a role in determining whether a use was experimental or commercial.

■≡■

Quicknotes

PATENT ACT § 102(b) Prohibits a patent for an invention that has been in public use more than a year prior to the application date.

■≡■

Electric Storage Battery Co. v. Shimadzu

Battery manufacturer (D) v. Japanese inventor (P)

307 U.S. 5 (1939).

NATURE OF CASE: Appeal from judgment holding patents valid and infringed.

FACT SUMMARY: American company Electric Storage (D) used a process to develop lead powder two years before Japanese citizen Shimadzu (P) sought a U.S. patent for it.

RULE OF LAW
A third party's innocent use of an invention in its factory to create a commercial product is a "public use" under § 102(b).

FACTS: On July 14, 1923, and April 27, 1926, Shimadzu (P), a Japanese citizen, applied for patents concerning an apparatus and process by which fine lead powder was developed. Electric Storage Battery Co. (D), without knowledge of Shimadzu's (P) inventions, began the use of a machine that involved the use of Shimadzu's (P) method and apparatus. Electric's (D) machine was set up in early 1921, and it attained commercial production in June 1921. Shimadzu (P) sued successfully for patent infringement, and the Supreme Court granted review.

ISSUE: Is a third party's innocent use of an invention in its factory to create a commercial product a "public use" under § 102(b).

HOLDING AND DECISION: (Roberts, J.) Yes. A third party's innocent use of an invention in its factory to create a commercial product is a "public use" under § 102(b). Prior public use two years prior to an application for a patent renders a patent invalid. Experimental use is not public use, but the unhidden use of a machine in a factory process to produce commercial products for profit is a public use. In this case, the machine, process, and product were not hidden from employees in Electric Storage's (D) plant and no efforts were made to conceal them from anyone who may have had a legitimate interest. The machine was in use two years prior to Shimadzu's (P) applications, so his patent claims were invalid, and, thus, they could not be infringed. Reversed.

ANALYSIS

As the opinion noted, predecessor statutes to 35 U.S.C. § 102(b) imposed a bar only when the applicant used or consented to the use of his invention before the statutory time. *Electric Storage* revealed that § 102(b) extended this bar to the use by third persons other than the patent applicant and/or inventor. The statutory time that limits the date of public use prior to a patent applicant has changed over the years. During *Electric Storage* it was two years, but in 1939, Congress shortened it to its present state of one year.

Quicknotes

PATENT ACT § 102(b) Prohibits a patent for an invention which has been in public use more than a year prior to the application date.

Abbott Laboratories v. Geneva Pharmaceuticals, Inc.

Pharmaceutical manufacturer (P) v. Competitor (D)

182 F.3d 1315 (Fed. Cir. 1999).

NATURE OF CASE: Appeal of summary judgment.

FACT SUMMARY: Geneva (D) sought to market a generic form of Hytrin. Hytrin was being sold at that time by Abbott (P), and Abbott (P) moved to prevent Geneva (D) from so selling. Geneva (D) claimed that Abbott's (P) patent for Hytrin was invalid based on the on-sale bar doctrine.

🏛 RULE OF LAW
The on-sale bar doctrine applies, when before one year prior to the date of application for the patent, the invention is both the subject of a commercial sale or offer for sale and is ready for patenting.

FACTS: Abbott (P) marketed terazosin hydrochloride, a treatment for hypertension, exclusively under the name Hytrin beginning in 1987. Terazosin hydrochloride exists in four anhydrous forms and Claim 4 of Abbott's (P) patent for the product claims the Form IV anhydrate. Geneva (D) sought to market a generic form of Hytrin using the Form IV anhydrate and Abbott (P) sued. Geneva (D) argued that Form IV was anticipated because it was sold in the United States more than one year before Abbott's (P) patent filing date of October 18, 1994. Byron Chemical Company, Inc. had made three sales of Form IV terazosin hydrochloride anhydrate in the United States more than one year before Abbott's (P) patent filing date. Byron itself had bought the substance at issue from two foreign manufacturers. At the time of the Byron sales in the United States, the parties did not know the identity of the particular form with which they were dealing. It was not until after the sales were made that samples were tested and it was determined that Form IV had been sold. The district court granted Geneva's (D) motion for summary judgment and held Claim 4 of the patent to be invalid under the on-sale provision. Abbott (P) appealed.

ISSUE: Is Claim 4 of Abbott's (P) patent invalid under the on-sale provision?

HOLDING AND DECISION: (Lourie, J.) Yes. Claim 4 of Abbott's (P) patent is invalid under the on-sale provision. A patent is invalid if the invention was on sale in the United States more than one year prior to the date of the application for the patent in the United States. Before October 18, 1993, the invention must both be the subject of a commercial sale or offer for sale and be ready for patenting. The invention may be shown to be ready for patenting by proof of reduction to practice before October 18, 1993. It is undisputed that Form IV was the subject matter of at least three commercial sales in the United States before October 18, 1993. The invention was also ready for patenting because

at least two foreign manufacturers had already reduced it to practice. Proof of conception of the invention is not required. The fact that the claimed material was sold under circumstances in which no question existed that it was useful means that it was reduced to practice. Since the material in this case was sold, it was useful and appreciated. The fact that the parties to the sales transactions did not know they were dealing with Form IV at the time of the sales is irrelevant to the question of whether it was on sale before October 18, 1993. Affirmed.

▶ ANALYSIS

The on-sale bar doctrine is meant to prevent the withdrawal of inventions that have been placed into the public domain through commercialization.

■■■■

Quicknotes

PATENT ACT § 102(b) Prohibits a patent for an invention that has been in public use more than a year prior to the application date.

■■■■

W.L. Gore & Associates v. Garlock, Inc.

Tape manufacturer (P) v. Alleged patent infringer (D)

721 F.2d 1540 (Fed. Cir. 1983).

NATURE OF CASE: Appeal from judgment holding patents invalid.

FACT SUMMARY: TEFLON tape, developed by a secret process, is sold prior to one year before Gore (P) applied for a patent on the process.

🏛 RULE OF LAW
A third party's secret commercial use of a process is not a "public use" under § 102(b).

FACTS: Dr. Gore, Vice President of W.L. Gore and Associates (Gore) (P), discovered that, contrary to traditional thinking, stretching TEFLON (a du Pont invention) tape very quickly and at high heat would not break the tape. Instead, it created a soft, flexible, but strong material. Gore (P) filed a patent application with twenty-four claims related to this process on May 21, 1970. In New Zealand in 1966, Cropper created a machine for producing stretched and unstretched TEFLON tape and offered to sell the machine to a company in Massachusetts. After being rebuffed, Cropper sold the machine to Budd with an attached secrecy agreement. A former Budd employee claimed that Budd made no effort to keep the machine secret. Budd offered and sold tape created by the process outlined in Gore's (P) claim. Gore (P) brought an action against Garlock (D) for infringement, but Garlock (D) argued "public use" was made over one year before Gore's (P) patent application. The lower court held for Garlock (D), and Gore (P) appealed.

ISSUE: Is a third party's secret commercial use of a process a "public use" under § 102(b)?

HOLDING AND DECISION: (Markey, C.J.) No. A third party's secret commercial use of a process is not a "public use" under § 102(b). Assuming that Cropper's machine used the patented process, there was no evidence that someone viewing Cropper's machine, even while in operation, could discern the process. There is no evidence that the public could learn of the claimed process by examining the tape product. Thus, the district court erred in holding that Budd's secret use of the machine and sale of tape made the patent invalid. Judgment reversed and remanded.

▶ ANALYSIS

Chief Judge Markey appears to have conflated § 102(a) and (b). Recall that § 102(a) requires that the invention not be "known or used by others," and § 102(b) uses the term "public use" in creating the public use bar. Most analysts discuss the "public use" clauses together and note that the difference is that § 102(a) applies only to the inventor, while § 102(b) applies to both the inventor and third parties.

■■■

Quicknotes

35 U.S.C. § 102(a) Disallows patents for inventions already known or used in the United States or patented in a foreign country.

PATENT ACT § 102(b) Prohibits a patent for an invention which has been in public use more than a year prior to the application date.

■■■

Novelty

Quick Reference Rules of Law

PAGE

1. **Prior Invention Under § 102(a).**   If the first inventor of a machine obtains a patent, a second inventor, regardless of his lack of awareness of the first invention, cannot then obtain a patent on the machine. (Woodcock v. Parker) — *32*

2. **Prior Invention Under § 102(a).**   An inventor who strictly conceals the operation and composition of his machine while operating it commercially is not the first inventor if another made the first public use. (Gillman v. Stern) — *33*

3. **The Elements of "Invention" Under § 102(g): Conception.**   Conception requires proof that the junior party knew of the means of carrying out the conception and proof of an exact date of conception. (Oka v. Youssefyeh) — *34*

4. **The Elements of "Invention" Under § 102(g): Reduction to Practice.**   The standard to determine whether sufficient testing has occurred to show reduction to practice is a commonsense assessment of whether the invention in fact solved the problem. (Scott v. Finney) — *35*

5. **The Elements of "Invention" Under § 102(g): Diligence.**   A party chargeable with diligence must account for the entire period during which diligence is required and prove reasonable diligence during that time. (Gould v. Schawlow) — *36*

6. **The Elements of "Invention" Under § 102(g): Corroboration.**   Uncorroborated oral testimony by interested parties concerning long-past events does not provide the clear and convincing evidence required to invalidate a patent on the grounds of prior knowledge and use. (Woodland Trust v. Flowertree Nursery, Inc.) — *37*

7. **Patent Award to the Second Inventor.**   A patent will be invalid if another entity invents the product at issue within the United States prior to the patent holder and if that entity does not abandon, suppress, or conceal the invention. (Apotex USA, Inc. v. Merck & Co., Inc.) — *38*

8. **Disclosure in United States Patent Applications—§ 102(e).**   A United States patent disclosing an invention dates from the date of filing of the application for the purpose of anticipating a subsequent invention. (Alexander Milburn Co. v. Davis-Bournonville Co.) — *39*

9. **Derivation—Theft from a Prior Inventor—§ 102(f).**   When an employer is engaged in experiments on a new invention, any suggestions by employees that do not themselves amount to a new invention are the property of the employer. (Agawam Woolen Co. v. Jordan) — *40*

Woodcock v. Parker

Inventor (P) v. Inventor (D)

30 Fed. Cas. 491 (D. Mass. 1813).

NATURE OF CASE: Action brought in circuit court.

FACT SUMMARY: Woodcock (P) sought to use a machine patented by Parker (D).

🏛 RULE OF LAW
If the first inventor of a machine obtains a patent, a second inventor, regardless of his lack of awareness of the first invention, cannot then obtain a patent on the machine.

FACTS: Parker (D) invented a machine and operated it to produce useful effects. Parker (D) then obtained a patent from the Department of State and passed title of the machine to others. Woodcock (P) sought to bar the use of the machine, claiming he had invented the same machine and obtained a patent on it.

ISSUE: Does the first to invent retain the patent right?

HOLDING AND DECISION: (Story, J.) Yes. If the first inventor of a machine obtains a patent, a second inventor, regardless of his lack of awareness of the first invention, cannot then obtain a patent on the machine. If the members of the jury are satisfied that Parker (D) was the first inventor, then Woodcock cannot bring an action. If Parker (D) had abandoned the invention, the issue may be different, but there is no evidence of abandonment.

▶ ANALYSIS

Woodcock stood for the first-to-invent principle, a principle favored by the United States over a first-to-file concept. The first-to-invent system is entirely unique to the United States. The Statute of Monopolies never clearly spoke to which principle was correct, merely stating patents issue "to the first and true inventor." Whether this implied the first to invent or the first to file is unclear, and Justice Story's opinion is among the earliest to favor the first-to-invent concept. This concept was then explicitly written down in the Patent Act of 1836.

■■■

Gillman v. Stern

Inventor (P) v. Inventor (D)

114 F.2d 28 (2d Cir. 1940).

NATURE OF CASE: Appeal from judgment of invalid patent.

FACT SUMMARY: Stern (D) claimed that Gillman's (P) patent was invalid since Haas had secretly invented a similar "puffing machine" years earlier.

🏛 RULE OF LAW
An inventor who strictly conceals the operation and composition of his machine while operating it commercially is not the first inventor if another made the first public use.

FACTS: Gillman (P) sought an injunction for a patent infringement on a "puffing machine." The machine operated pneumatically to blow thread or yarn into packets formed in fabric to create a design. Stern (D) raised several defenses, one of which being that there had been a prior use of the machine by Haas. Haas had invented a puffing machine similar to the patented one in the autumn of 1929. Haas kept it a strict secret and carefully kept people out of the shop where his four machines were kept. He enjoined his wife and four employees to the strictest secrecy. Haas did reveal how the machine performed to two investors who attempted to, but never did, raise the money for a patent. The lower court held Gillman's (P) patent invalid. Both sides appealed.

ISSUE: Is an inventor who strictly conceals the operation and composition of his machine while operating it commercially always the "first inventor?"

HOLDING AND DECISION: (Hand, J.) No. An inventor who strictly conceals the operation and composition of his machine while operating it commercially is not the first inventor if another made the first public use. A patentee must be a "first and original inventor." In *Gayler v. Wilder*, 10 How. 477, it was held that the first inventor must make his results public to satisfy this part of the statute. Just as a secret use is not a "public use," a secret inventor is not a "first inventor." In this case, Haas's use was clearly not public, and he was clearly not a "first inventor." Reversed and remanded.

▶ ANALYSIS

Judge Learned Hand points out that it is arguable that the statute should confine prior "public uses" to the patentee only and that "first inventor" should apply to the first who conceives the invention in tangible form. However, the law did not develop in that way and the results are as seen in *Gillman*. Canada originally utilized a pure first-to-invent system so that if anyone in the world were to invent something, a second inventor would be barred from obtaining a patent on the item. This system was created in a judicial decision, but the Canadian Parliament found it too much and modified it in 1935 to a more realistic system. Canada abandoned the first-to-invent system in 1989.

■=■

Oka v. Youssefyeh

Inventor (P) v. Inventor (D)

849 F.2d 581 (Fed. Cir. 1988).

NATURE OF CASE: Appeal from Board award of priority.

FACT SUMMARY: Two parties invented the same compound; Oka (P) was the first to file, but Youssefyeh (D) filed interference and claimed he invented it prior to Oka's (P) filing.

RULE OF LAW
Conception requires proof that the junior party knew of the means of carrying out the conception and proof of an exact date of conception.

FACTS: The patent concerned a class of compounds with a complex composition. However, two of the more typical subspecies of the class contained either a 2-indanyl group or a 5-indanyl group. Youssefyeh (D) had the idea for a 2-indanyl class of compounds on February 27, 1980, and he was in possession of a method of making other compounds on October 10, 1980. During the last week of October 1980, Youssefyeh's (D) partner, co-applicant Suh, directed an assistant to use the October 10 method to prepare a species of 5-indanyl class of compounds. The assistant did so in December 1980, and Youssefyeh (D) reduced the invention to practice on January 9, 1981. Oka (P) filed his application for the compounds on October 31, 1980.

ISSUE: Does proof of conception require that the junior party knew of the means of carrying out the conception and the exact date of conception?

HOLDING AND DECISION: (Markey, C.J.) Yes. Conception requires proof that the junior party knew of the means of carrying out the conception and proof of an exact date of conception. Youssefyeh (D), as the junior filing party, bears the burden of showing he had conception and reduced it to practice prior to Oka's (P) filing date. Conception requires both the idea of the structure of the chemical compound and possession of an operative method of making it. Therefore, Youssefyeh (D) lacked conception when he had the 2-indanyl idea on February 27, 1980, for he must show he had the means. Youssefyeh (D) had the ultimate means at his disposal on October 10, but he had not recognized that it could be used to create this class of compounds. Instructions to use this method were not given until the last week of October 1980. In addition, Youssefyeh (D) lacked the idea of a 5-indanyl compound at that time, so he had conception of neither species until the last week of October. When setting a date of conception, if a party merely states a period of time, he has not set a date for his activities earlier than the last day of the period. Therefore, Youssfyeh (D) established a conception date at October 31,

1980. Oka's (P) filing date was October 31, 1980, and, as senior party, Oka (P) earns priority in a tie. Judgment reversed.

▶ *ANALYSIS*

The decision of which of several parties with identical priority patent dates should receive the patent is not unique to first-to-invent systems. Although it appears unlikely, a first-to-file regime could face the same problem when multiple inventors file for the same invention on the same day. The Japanese Patent Act addresses this issue and requires the parties to resolve the dispute or else none of the applicants will obtain a patent.

Quicknotes

CONCEPTION An inventor's devising of an invention of sufficient comprehensiveness so that it is capable of being reduced to practice.

Scott v. Finney

Doctor (P) v. Doctor (D)

34 F.3d 1058 (Fed. Cir. 1994).

NATURE OF CASE: Appeal from Board award of priority.

FACT SUMMARY: Dr. Scott (P) contended that his testing of a penile implant was adequate to show reduction to practice.

🏛 RULE OF LAW
The standard to determine whether sufficient testing has occurred to show reduction to practice is a commonsense assessment of whether the invention in fact solved the problem.

FACTS: Dr. Finney (D) and Dr. Scott (P) filed for patents concerning a penile implant for impotent patients. This implant was to consist of a rod that would rigidize upon being filled with liquid that would enter the rod through a pump-and-valve mechanism. Dr. Finney (D) was the senior party, and his filing date was May 15, 1980. Dr. Scott's (P) evidence of reduction to practice before this date consisted of a videotape of implantation of a prototype device in an anesthetized patient. Dr. Scott (P) operated the device in the patient several times to simulate an erection before removing it. Dr. Scott's (P) test consisted only of one valve-and-rod mechanism although the invention in practice would require one on each side of the penis. In addition to the video, Dr. Scott (P) supplied evidence of testing for leakage. The Board found that Dr. Scott (P) had failed to show the device would successfully operate under actual use conditions for a reasonable length of time, so he had failed to show reduction to practice. Dr. Scott (P) appealed.

ISSUE: Is the standard to determine whether sufficient testing has occurred to show reduction to practice a commonsense assessment of whether the invention in fact solved the problem?

HOLDING AND DECISION: (Rader, J.) Yes. The standard to determine whether sufficient testing has occurred to show reduction to practice is a commonsense assessment of whether the invention in fact solved the problem. In proving reduction to practice, the junior party must show utility, i.e., that the device would successfully operate under actual use for a reasonable length of time. This is often done with testing, and the court should apply a reasonableness standard. Testing need not show utility beyond a possibility of failure, but only beyond a probability of failure. There is much case law concerning the adequate amount of testing to meet this requirement, but one theme throughout is that the court should apply a commonsense approach. The character of the testing required varies with the character of the invention and the problem it solves. Here, the Board

erred in requiring human testing in actual use circumstances for a period of time. Dr. Scott's (P) testing showed a reasonable expectation that his invention would work under normal conditions for its intended purpose beyond a probability of failure. Reversed and remanded.

▶ ANALYSIS

If an applicant files for a patent but fails to pursue his invention, it may be ruled that he has not satisfied the reduction to practice element. In that case, the abandoned application's filing date is instead the date of conception. It should be noted that testing is not always required. Some inventions are so simple and their purpose and efficacy so obvious that construction alone is sufficient to demonstrate workability. See *King Instr. Corp. v. Otari Corp.*, 767 F.2d 853, 226 U.S.P.Q. 402 (Fed. Cir. 1985).

■=■

Quicknotes

REDUCTION TO PRACTICE The method of determining priority of patentability by assessing when the inventor's conception is rendered capable of use.

■=■

Gould v. Schawlow

Inventor (P) v. Inventor (D)

363 F.2d 908 (C.C.P.A. 1966).

NATURE OF CASE: Appeal from Board award of priority.

FACT SUMMARY: Gould (P) conceived of a laser, but lacked the resources to reduce it to practice before Schawlow (D).

🏛 RULE OF LAW
A party chargeable with diligence must account for the entire period during which diligence is required and prove reasonable diligence during that time.

FACTS: On July 30, 1958, Schawlow (D) applied for a patent on a "laser." Gould (P) applied for a patent on the same invention on April 6, 1959. Gould (P) challenged Schawlow's (D) patent, and both parties claimed their filing dates as reduction-to-practice dates. Gould (P) bore the burden of proving reasonable diligence from prior to July 30, 1958, to April 6, 1959. Gould (P) was able to prove conception of the laser as early as November 1957, but he did not begin construction since he wanted to find variations that were easier to build. The Board of Patent Interferences found that Gould's evidence was insufficient in that there was no corroboration for the work done in the critical period.

ISSUE: Must a party chargeable with diligence account for the entire period during which diligence is required and prove reasonable diligence during that time?

HOLDING AND DECISION: (Worley, C.J.) Yes. A party chargeable with diligence must account for the entire period during which diligence is required and prove reasonable diligence during that time. Gould (P) made little attempt to identify particular activity at particular times during the critical period of July to December 1958. Nor did he establish how such activity related to a reduction to practice. Gould (P) must show facts proving what exactly he did and when exactly he did it. Gould (P) also argued that the Board used a "formalistic approach" creating a higher standard. "Reasonable diligence" is the correct standard. An inventor will not be penalized if he has limited resources as long as he devotes those resources with reasonable and continuous diligence. Gould (P) failed to show evidence meeting this standard. Affirmed.

▌ ANALYSIS

One policy underlying the diligence requirement is to create a form of equality. A person may have a good idea but lack the resources to reduce it to practice. Thus, if she works diligently in either trying to marshal resources or engage a patent attorney, she will not lose her privileged status. It may have appeared that this policy goal was not met in Gould, but Chief Justice Worley's lengthy factual discussion, coupled with his emphasis on protecting inventors with limited resources, indicate Gould lost due to evidentiary matters.

■=■

Quicknotes

DILIGENCE The exercise of care or attentiveness; the law sets forth three degrees of diligence: ordinary, slight, and extraordinary.

■=■

Woodland Trust v. Flowertree Nursery, Inc.

Inventor (P) v. Infringer (D)

148 F.3d 1368 (Fed. Cir. 1998).

NATURE OF CASE: Appeal of invalid patent determination in infringement action.

FACT SUMMARY: Woodland (P) sued Flowertree (D) alleging patent infringement of its foliage protection system. Flowertree (D) argued the patent was invalid because the system had been known and in use for more than a year prior to the patent application being filed.

🏛 RULE OF LAW
Uncorroborated oral testimony by interested parties concerning long-past events does not provide the clear and convincing evidence required to invalidate a patent on the grounds of prior knowledge and use.

FACTS: Woodland (P) holds a patent, whose application was filed in 1983, for an invention that protects foliage plants from freezing by establishing an insulating covering of ice over ground level watering. Woodland (P) sued Flowertree (D) alleging patent infringement. Flowertree (D) defended arguing patent invalidity in that the patented method had been known and used by an owner of Flowertree (D) and the owner of a different nursery in the 1960s and 1970s. It was discontinued in 1978 and reconstructed in 1988. Four witnesses testified in support of the defense of prior knowledge and use. Each of the witnesses either used the method himself or was related to, employed by, or the friend of someone who used the method. The district court found the patent to be invalid based on prior knowledge and use by others. Woodland (P) appealed.

ISSUE: Was the claimed invention anticipated by the Flowertree (D) system in that it constituted prior art that was known publicly and used?

HOLDING AND DECISION: (Newman, J.) No. The apparatus claimed in the patent was not anticipated by the Flowertree (D) systems. The uncorroborated oral testimony by interested parties of long-past events does not provide the clear and convincing evidence required to invalidate a patent. Oral testimony in this context is regarded with skepticism and must be supported with corroboration. In assessing corroboration, the following criteria are considered: the relationship between the witness and the prior user; the time period between the event and trial; the interest of the corroborating witness in the subject matter in suit; contradiction or impeachment of the witness's testimony; how detailed the testimony is; witness's familiarity with the patented subject matter and the prior use; probability that a prior use could occur; and impact of the invention on the industry. In this case, there is no physical record to support the oral evidence. The relationship of the witnesses and the fact that the prior use ended twenty years before the trial (and was abandoned until Flowertree (D) learned of Woodland's (P) practices) highlight the failure of this oral evidence to provide clear and convincing evidence of prior knowledge and use. Reversed and remanded.

▶ ANALYSIS

Federal Rules of Evidence 803(6) has been held not to apply to prove dates of inventive activity.

■■■

Apotex USA, Inc. v. Merck & Co., Inc.

Drug manufacturer (P) v. Competitor (D)

254 F.3d 1031 (Fed. Cir. 2001).

NATURE OF CASE: Appeal of allowed motion for summary judgment.

FACT SUMMARY: Apotex (P) sued Merck (D) alleging infringement of its patent. Merck (D) argued that Apotex's (P) patent was invalid because Merck (D) invented the product at issue before Apotex (P) did.

RULE OF LAW
A patent will be invalid if another entity invents the product at issue within the United States prior to the patent holder and if that entity does not abandon, suppress, or conceal the invention.

FACTS: Apotex (P) has two patents that relate to a process for making enalapril sodium, which is used for the treatment of high blood pressure. Merck (D) has manufactured and sold enalapril sodium under the trademark Vasotec since 1983. Merck (D) owns patents covering the enalapril sodium compound but does not own a patent covering its process of manufacturing Vasotec. In 1992, Merck (D) disclosed the ingredients it used in its Vasotec manufacturing in a Canadian product monograph of which 30,000 copies were distributed. Merck (D) also disclosed in a French dictionary the ingredients used in manufacturing its enalapril sodium product, which was sold in various foreign countries. In 1991, Merck (D) sued Apotex (P) in Canada for infringement of Merck's (D) patent covering the enalapril sodium compound. During the trial, a demonstration of Merck's (D) process of manufacturing Vasotec was performed. Within days, an Apotex (P) employee conceived of the patented product at issue. Apotex (P) subsequently sued Merck (D) alleging that Merck (D) infringed on its patents for enalapril sodium. Merck (D) alleged that the patents were invalid. Cross-motions for summary judgment were filed. The district court granted Apotex's (P) motion for summary judgment on infringement but also granted Merck's (D) motion for summary judgment that the patent was invalid. Apotex (P) appealed.

ISSUE: Are the patents invalid because Merck (D) (1) invented the enalapril sodium process within the United States before Apotex (P) and (2) did not abandon, suppress, or conceal that invention?

HOLDING AND DECISION: (Lourie, J.) Yes. The patents are invalid because Merck (D) invented the enalapril sodium process within the United States before Apotex (P) and did not abandon, suppress, or conceal that invention. It is conceded that Merck (D) invented the process before Apotex (P) and that Merck (D) did not abandon its process of manufacturing Vasotec. Nor did Merck (D) conceal or suppress the process. The type of alleged concealment involved in this case is a legal inference of suppression or

concealment whereby there was allegedly an unreasonable delay in filing a patent application. Absent a satisfactory explanation for the delay, a prior invention will be deemed suppressed or concealed if within a reasonable time after completion, no steps are taken to make the invention publicly known. Although Congress made it clear that the product had to be made in the United States, the statutory language and legislative history does not require suppression or concealment to occur in this country. Furthermore, since Merck (D) has established priority of invention, Apotex (P) has the burden of producing evidence indicating that Merck (D) suppressed or concealed that invention. Merck (D) then bears the ultimate burden of persuasion and must rebut any alleged suppression or concealment with clear and convincing evidence to the contrary. In the present case, Apotex (P) has produced evidence sufficient to create a genuine issue of material fact as to whether Merck (D) suppressed or concealed its process of manufacturing enalapril sodium tablets. Merck (D) failed to make its invention publicly known. Merck (D) perfected its process and began commercially using the process to manufacture Vasotec no later than 1983 but didn't make the invention publicly known until 1988 when it published the ingredients in the French dictionary. A delay of five years suggests that Merck (D) suppressed or concealed its invention. Merck (D), however, has rebutted the inference by showing by clear and convincing evidence that it resumed activity, making the benefits of the invention known to the public, before Apotex's (P) entry into the field, and therefore it did not suppress or conceal the invention. Merck's (D) disclosures in the French dictionary, monographs, and trial testimony following its period of suppression or concealment made the invention publicly known before Apotex's (P) entry into the field in 1994. Moreover, the statements of Apotex's (P) own employee in his deposition for this case and the employee's statement of facts in the Canadian trial regarding the composition of the Vasotec tablets and the starting ingredients, in conjunction with Merck's various disclosures, prove that Merck (D) made the knowledge of its invention available to the public. Affirmed.

ANALYSIS

Diligence plays no role in determining suppression or concealment.

∎▬∎

Quicknotes

35 U.S.C. § 102(g) Denies patent if the invention has already been made by someone else who has not abandoned, suppressed, or concealed it.

∎▬∎

Alexander Milburn Co. v. Davis-Bournonville Co.

[Parties not identified.]

270 U.S. 390 (1926).

NATURE OF CASE: Action charging patent infringement.

FACT SUMMARY: Davis (D) defended a patent infringement charge by asserting that the application for patent filed by Milburn's (P) assignor was subsequent to Clifford's patent application that disclosed the invention but did not result in a patent until after Milburn's (P) assignor applied.

> 🏛 **RULE OF LAW**
> A United States patent disclosing an invention dates from the date of filing of the application for the purpose of anticipating a subsequent invention.

FACTS: Milburn (P) claimed that Davis (D) was infringing the Whitford patent it had been assigned. As a defense, Davis (D) contended that Clifford had filed a patent application disclosing the invention prior to the date when Whitford filed his patent application, although the Clifford patent was not issued until after the Whitford application had been filed. It thus argued that Whitford was not the first inventor of the thing patented. The district court found the Whitford patent valid and returned a decision for Milburn (P). The court of appeals affirmed. Both considered the effective date of the Clifford patent to be the date it was granted, which was after the Whitford application was filed. Thus, it would not be available as a reference to bar issuance of a patent to Whitford. Davis (D) appealed.

ISSUE: For the purposes of anticipating a subsequent invention, does a United States patent disclosing an invention date from the date of the filing of the patent application?

HOLDING AND DECISION: (Holmes, J.) Yes. The effective date of a United States patent for purposes of anticipating a subsequent invention is considered to be the date on which the patent application was filed. If an invention is disclosed by a patent where the application and patent grant both took place before a subsequent patent application covering the same invention was filed, it is clear that the second patent would be barred. The delays of the Patent Office ought not to cause a different result to obtain when the first patent is not actually granted until after the second patent application is filed. In both cases, the second patent should be barred because the second one to apply was not the first inventor and the first applicant has done all he can do to make the description public. All that remains is for the Patent Office to do its work. Under the aforementioned rule, the Clifford application served as a bar to issuance of a patent on the same invention to Whitford. Reversed.

▶ **ANALYSIS**

The *Milburn* rule has been criticized for using as prior knowledge information which was secret at the time it was used, i.e., patent applications whose contents are secret. Nonetheless, it has been codified in § 102(e) of the 1952 Patent Act.

∎━∎

Quicknotes

35 U.S.C. § 102(e) Denies patent if the invention is the subject of another patent or application.

∎━∎

Agawam Woolen Co. v. Jordan

Alleged infringer (D) v. Inventor (P)

74 U.S. (7 Wall.) 583 (1868).

NATURE OF CASE: Appeal from award of patent.

FACT SUMMARY: Jordan (P) argued that Agawam (D) had infringed on his patent on a weaving apparatus.

🏛 RULE OF LAW
When an employer is engaged in experiments on a new invention, any suggestions by employees that do not themselves amount to a new invention are the property of the employer.

FACTS: Jordan (P) had spent his entire life working with machinery and weaving machines. Jordan (P) developed a weaving apparatus utilizing a key device he termed a "traverser." The traverser allowed endless "roving," i.e., weaving. While experimenting, an employee of Jordan's (P), Winslow, suggested that spools be used rather than cans. According to Winslow, he made the spools and attached it to the apparatus. Jordan (P) sued Agawam Woolen Co. (D) for patent infringement, but Agawam argued that Winslow held the rights to the apparatus. Jordan (P) won, and Agawam (D) appealed.

ISSUE: Does an employee's suggestions to an employer engaged in experiments on a new invention that do not themselves amount to a new invention, belong to the employer?

HOLDING AND DECISION: (Clifford, J.) Yes. When an employer is engaged in experiments on a new invention, any suggestions by employees that do not themselves amount to a new invention are the property of the employer. This principle derives from the fact that when an inventor enlists aid in carrying out his experiments, and such aid makes ancillary discoveries or suggested improvements, these improvements are deemed to be embodied in the inventor's patent. Even granting the credibility of Agawam's (D) witness, Jordan (P) as the original patentee should retain the rights to the apparatus. The apparatus would be incomplete without the traverser. The spool and drum, while perhaps better than cans, are mere improvements upon the apparatus, while the traverser is the key device. Reversed.

▶ ANALYSIS

The *Agawam* decision is the precursor to the modern § 102(f) that bars an applicant "who did not himself invent the subject matter sought to be patented." Agawam also provided a standard addressing communications of invention. For instance, must the entire conception be communicated to invoke the § 102(f) bar? *Agawam*'s standard still exists: it is enough of a communication if it "enabled an ordinary mechanic, without the exercise of any ingenuity and special skill on his part, to construct and put the improvement in successful operation." Theft from an inventor, either through communications or the more outright kind found in *Agawam*, is termed derivation in patent law.

■■■

CHAPTER 7

Nonobviousness

Quick Reference Rules of Law

PAGE

1. **The Historical Standard of Invention.**   A patent will not be held valid if it merely improves an old device by the substitution of materials better suited to the purpose of the device. (Hotchkiss v. Greenwood) — 42

2. **The Historical Standard of Invention.**   A patent will not be sustained if the patentee merely brings together segments of prior art, with no change in their respective functions. (Great A. & P. Tea Co. v. Supermarket Equipment Corp.) — 43

3. **The Modern Standard of Nonobviousness.**   Determination of the non-obviousness of a claimed invention as to a prior art requires a case-by-case analysis of the scope and content of the prior art, the differences between the prior art and claims at issue, and the level of ordinary skill in the pertinent art. (Graham v. John Deere Co.) — 44

4. **The Modern Standard of Nonobviousness.**   In determining the obviousness of a patent claim, the courts must consider the prior art, the differences between the prior art and the subject matter of the claim, and the level of ordinary skill a person must have in the subject matter of the claim before considering secondary factors and the test for teaching, suggestion, or motivation of the patentee. (KSR International Co. v. Teleflex, Inc.) — 45

5. **The Modern Standard of Nonobviousness.**   If the differences in the patented subject matter and the subject matter of the prior art would have been obvious to a person of ordinary skill in the art at the time of invention, then the subject matter is not patent-eligible under § 103(a). (In re Translogic Technology, Inc.) — 47

6. **The Objective Tests.**   Sections 102(a) and 103(a) prohibit patents on claims that would be obvious or anticipated from prior art references unless the patent applicant demonstrates a suggestion or motivation to modify the teachings of the prior art, or secondary considerations, such as commercial success, rebut the finding of obviousness. (Ormco Corp. v. Align Technology, Inc.) — 49

7. **Obviousness in Chemistry and Biotechnology: Composite Claims.**   A prima facie case of obviousness due to structural similarity of compounds can be overcome by showing a difference in the compound's properties. (In re Papesch) — 51

8. **Obviousness in Chemistry and Biotechnology: Composite Claims.**   A prima facie case of obviousness does not require both structural similarity and a suggestion in or expectation from the prior art that the claimed compound will have the same or a similar utility as the one newly discovered by the applicant. (In re Dillon) — 52

9. **Obviousness for Biotechnology.**   When a chemical entity is structurally new, a prima facie case of obviousness requires that the teachings of the prior art suggest the claimed compounds to a person of ordinary skill in the art. (In re Deuel) — 53

10. **Prior Art for Obviousness: Prior Art Under Section 102.**   A patent must be denied where an applicant undertakes, under Rule 131, to swear back of a reference having an effective date more than a year before his filing date if the reference contains enough disclosure to make his invention obvious. (In re Foster) — 54

11. **Prior Art for Obviousness: Analogous Arts.**   Prior art is analogous if it is in the same field of endeavor or if it is still reasonably pertinent to the particular problem with which the inventor is involved. (In re Clay) — 55

Hotchkiss v. Greenwood

[Parties not identified.]

52 U.S. (11 How.) 248 (1850).

NATURE OF CASE: On writ of error to the Circuit Court for the District of Ohio, to review an allegedly erroneous jury instruction in an infringement case.

FACT SUMMARY: Hotchkiss (P) contended that Greenwood (D) had infringed upon his patented design for knobs made of clay or porcelain.

🏛 RULE OF LAW
A patent will not be held valid if it merely improves an old device by the substitution of materials better suited to the purpose of the device.

FACTS: Hotchkiss (P) claimed as his invention an improvement in the manufacture of clay or porcelain knobs, such as doorknobs. He dovetailed the cavity where the screw was to be inserted making it largest at the bottom, then formed the screw by pouring metal into the cavity. Greenwood (D) defended the infringement suit, arguing that the improvement was obvious and therefore not patentable in the first place. The court charged the jury that if it found such knobs had been similarly manufactured using metal, wood, or some other material rather than clay or porcelain, the patent was invalid. After the jury found for Greenwood (D), Hotchkiss (P) claimed the instruction was erroneous, and moved for a new trial.

ISSUE: Will a patent be held valid if it merely improves an old device by the substitution of different materials?

HOLDING AND DECISION: (Nelson, J.) No. A patent is not valid if it merely improves an old device by the substitution of materials better suited to the purpose of the device. The clay or porcelain knob so manufactured by Hotchkiss (P) may have been made more durable by the mode of fastening the shank to the knob, but the effect would be the same in the case of knobs made of wood, and the method was already known and commonly used with wooden knobs. The improvement here is the work of the skillful mechanic, not that of the inventor. The judgment for Greenwood (D) is affirmed.

▶ ANALYSIS

The inventiveness standard articulated in *Hotchkiss* was not new. However, it was the first meaningful attempt by the court to define the vague requirement that an invention be more than a novelty to be patentable. Judge Learned Hand stated over a century later that invention is "as fugitive, impalpable, wayward and vague a phantom as exists in the whole paraphernalia of legal concepts." *Harries v. King Prods.*, 183 F.2d 158 (2d Cir. 1950).

Great A. & P. Tea Co. v. Supermarket Equipment Corp.

[Parties not identified.]

340 U.S. 147, 87 U.S.P.Q. 303 (1950).

NATURE OF CASE: Review of appellate court decision upholding judgment of infringement.

FACT SUMMARY: Great A. & P. (P) sued Supermarket (D) for infringement of its patent on a rack to move groceries along a supermarket counter to the checking clerk.

🏛 RULE OF LAW
A patent will not be sustained if the patentee merely brings together segments of prior art, with no change in their respective functions.

FACTS: Great A. & P.'s (P) patented device equipped cashiers' counters with a three-sided frame, which, when pushed or pulled, would move groceries deposited within it by a customer to the checking clerk. The district court denied Supermarket's (D) claim that the device was obvious and therefore could not be the subject of a patent, much less an infringement suit. The court found that the conception of a counter with an extension to receive the contents of a bottomless self-unloading tray was a decidedly novel feature and constituted a new and useful combination. The court of appeals upheld the judgment, regarding the finding of the district court as to obviousness as one of fact and not clearly erroneous.

ISSUE: Will a patent be sustained if the patentee merely brings together segments of prior art, with no change in their respective functions?

HOLDING AND DECISION: (Jackson, J.) No. A patent will not be sustained if the patentee merely brings together segments of prior art, with no change in their respective functions. The conjunction of known elements must contribute something; only when the whole in some way exceeds the sum of its parts is the accumulation of old devices patentable. Here the counter supports merchandise, as counters have always done; the rack draws or pushes goods, as racks have always done; and the guide rails keep the merchandise from falling off the surface, as guide rails have always done. Two and two have been added together, and still they make only four. Great A. & P. (P), the patentee, has added nothing to the total stock of knowledge, but has merely brought together segments of prior art and claims them in concert as a monopoly. The patents are invalid and the judgment is reversed.

CONCURRENCE: (Douglas, J.) A patent is a monopoly, and the Framers did not want such monopolies freely granted. It is not enough that an invention is new and useful. It must make a distinctive contribution to scientific knowledge, and demonstrate "inventive genius."

▶ ANALYSIS

It may be argued that nearly every invention can be reduced to the combination of old elements, and that the invention lies not in the elements functioning differently within the combination, but in cleverly seeing the utility of such combinations. Following *Great A. & P.*, Congress passed the 1952 Patent Act, codifying the prerequisites to patentability without any reference to "invention" as a legal requirement.

■■■

Quicknotes

PRIOR ART Any prior knowledge or activity regarding a particular invention that may be considered by the Patent and Trademark Office in granting or denying a patent application or by the court in determining a patent infringement action.

■■■

Graham v. John Deere Co.

Inventor (P) v. Farm equipment manufacturer (D)

383 U.S. 1 (1966).

NATURE OF CASE: Review of judgment invalidating a patent in one case and judgment sustaining a patent in consolidated case.

FACT SUMMARY: John Deere (D) defended an infringement action on obvious grounds.

🏛 RULE OF LAW
Determination of the non-obviousness of a claimed invention as to a prior art requires a case-by-case analysis of the scope and content of the prior art, the differences between the prior art and claims at issue, and the level of ordinary skill in the pertinent art.

FACTS: Graham (P) filed suit against John Deere Co. (D) claiming patent infringement on a device consisting of old mechanical elements that absorbed shock from plow shanks as they plowed through rocky soil. In a previous case, the Fifth Circuit had held the patent valid, ruling that a combination was patentable when it produced an "old result in a cheaper and otherwise more advantageous way." In the instant case, the Eighth Circuit said that since there was no new result or combination, the patent was invalid. Graham (P) petitioned for certiorari, which the Supreme Court granted to resolve the conflict.

ISSUE: Does the determination of the non-obviousness of a claimed invention as to a prior art require a case-by-case analysis of the scope and content of the prior art, the differences between the prior art and claims at issue, and the level of ordinary skill in the pertinent art?

HOLDING AND DECISION: (Clark, J.) Yes. Determination of the non-obviousness of a claimed invention as to a prior art requires a case-by-case analysis of the scope and content of the prior art, the differences between the prior art and claims at issue, and the level of ordinary skill in the pertinent art. The Patent Act of 1952 added the statutory non-obviousness requirement. However, this was merely a codification of judicial precedent first laid out in *Hotchkiss v. Greenwood*, 11 How. 248 (1851). Although § 103 of the Act uses the term "non-obviousness" instead of "invention," the general level of innovation needed to sustain a patent remains the same. The determination of whether an invention is patentable or merely an obvious improvement upon a prior art requires a case-by-case analysis of the criteria listed above. Secondary considerations such as commercial success, long-felt but unsolved needs, and the failure of others may also be relevant in considering the obviousness of an invention. With regard to the patent at issue in these cases, the differences between the patented invention and prior art would have been obvious to one reasonably skilled in the art. Therefore, the patent is invalid. Affirmed.

▶ ANALYSIS

The 1952 Patent Act was written in response to dissatisfaction with the Supreme Court's increasingly strict standard of "invention." There was also great criticism of the various judicial decisions applying this test in that they led to subjective and inconsistent determinations. Congress intentionally omitted any use of the word "invention" in the Act, so no past requirements would be referred to. Instead, Congress took the hundreds of different ways the case law doctrine had been read and codified them into a single statutory form. Judicial interpretation of this Act was still open to question, however, as the above decision demonstrated."

Quicknotes

U.S. CONSTITUTION, ART. 1 § 8 Gives Congress the authority to promote science by securing limited exclusive rights to inventors.

35 U.S.C. § 103 Denies patent if the invention of the subject matter would have been obvious to a person based on prior inventions.

PRIOR ART Any prior knowledge or activity regarding a particular invention that may be considered by the Patent and Trademark Office in granting or denying a patent application or by the court in determining a patent infringement action.

KSR International Co. v. Teleflex, Inc.

Alleged infringer (D) v. Patent license holder (P)

550 U.S. 398 (2007).

NATURE OF CASE: Writ of certiorari to resolve obviousness issue in patent infringement case.

FACT SUMMARY: Teleflex (P) sued KSR (D) for patent infringement based on an electronic sensor addition to an existing KSR (D) pedal design. KSR (D) argued the addition was obvious, so Teleflex's (P) patent claim was invalid.

> 🏛 **RULE OF LAW**
> In determining the obviousness of a patent claim, the courts must consider the prior art, the differences between the prior art and the subject matter of the claim, and the level of ordinary skill a person must have in the subject matter of the claim before considering secondary factors and the test for teaching, suggestion, or motivation of the patentee.

FACTS: Teleflex, Inc. (P) held the exclusive license to the patent entitled "Adjustable Pedal Assembly with Electronic Throttle Control." One claim of the patent involved the addition of an electronic sensor to the pedal which then transmitted information to the computer controlling the engine's throttle. KSR International Co. (D) added an electronic sensor to its existing pedal design. Teleflex (P) sued KSR (D) for patent infringement. KSR (D) argued the Teleflex (P) claim was invalid under 35 U.S.C. § 103 because the addition of the electronic sensor was obvious. The district court granted summary judgment to KSR (D) and Teleflex (P) appealed. The court of appeals applied the "teaching, suggestion, or motivation" [TSM] test and reversed. KSR (D) filed for a writ of certiorari, which the Supreme Court granted to address the obviousness analysis.

ISSUE: In determining the obviousness of a patent claim, must the courts consider the prior art, the differences between the prior art and the subject matter of the claim, and the level of ordinary skill a person must have in the subject matter of the claim before considering secondary factors and the test for teaching, suggestion, or motivation of the patentee?

HOLDING AND DECISION: (Kennedy, J.) Yes. In determining the obviousness of a patent claim, the courts must consider the prior art, the differences between the prior art and the subject matter of the claim, and the level of ordinary skill a person must have in the subject matter of the claim before considering secondary factors and the test for teaching, suggestion, or motivation of the patentee. 35 U.S.C. § 103 prohibits issuance of a patent when the subject matter as a whole is obvious to a person with ordinary skill in the art to which the subject matter pertains. [The Court reviewed the prior art of pedal and sensor technology.] The U.S. Patent and Trademark Office (PTO) rejected a prior

patent application for a pedal technology that, unlike the Teleflex (P) licensed patent at issue, did not involve a fixed pivot point because the technology was "obvious." The Teleflex (P) licensed patent was granted because of the limitation of the fixed pivot point. The district court considered the prior art, examined the differences between the patent claim and the prior art, and then found the skill level to be that of a mechanical engineer familiar with pedal designs. The district court found little difference between the prior art and the patent claim and no secondary factors sufficient to overcome the obviousness. The district court then had to apply the TSM test and found KSR (D) satisfied it because the industry inevitably led to the combination of electronic sensors and adjustable pedals plus the prior art suggested the combination. The court of appeals reversed on the ground that the district court was not strictly applying the TSM test. The appellate court looked at the purpose of the two pedal designs and found them to be different. The appellate court also held that "obvious to try" the pedal and sensor combination did not rise to the level of obviousness. This Court's precedents reflect a broader, more general inquiry into obviousness. The TSM test encourages the PTO to consider the reason a person of ordinary skill in the field combined two known elements in such a way to result in a potentially new patent subject matter. The general principle of the TSM test, however, cannot be applied rigidly. The appellate court cannot consider solely the motivation for the joining of two known elements because the joining may have been obvious to the patentee but that does not make the claim obvious under § 103. The appellate court also wrongly asserted that a person of ordinary skill might not put known elements together in a new fashion even when those elements were designed to individually accomplish a specific, alternate purpose. Finally, the appellate court erred in stating "obvious to try" was not "obvious" because sometimes it might rise to that level if a known problem has a finite number of solutions. In consideration of the facts here, the patent claim does rise to the level of obviousness. [The Court considered the prior art and differences between the claims]. The District court carefully and appropriately applied this Court's precedent and the statutory elements of § 103 when determining the patent claim was obvious and thus invalid. The court of appeals erred in applying too rigid a TSM test. Reversed and remanded.

▌ *ANALYSIS*

The Supreme Court ignored the Federal Circuit's well-established precedent applying the TSM test although it

Continued on next page.

retained the *Graham v. John Deere Co.*, 383 U.S. 1 (1966), elements for applying § 103 to a patent application. The impact of the decision, however, may be felt more by electrical and mechanical patent applicants than other applicants. The examiners can review the individual electrical/mechanical parts of the prior art to determine if the new claim would have been an obvious result even if it had not been accomplished previously.

■══■

Quicknotes

35 U.S.C. § 103   Denies patent if the invention of the subject matter would have been obvious to a person based on prior inventions.

PRIOR ART   Any prior knowledge or activity regarding a particular invention that may be considered by the Patent and Trademark Office in granting or denying a patent application or by the court in determining a patent infringement action.

■══■

In re Translogic Technology, Inc.

Patent applicant (P) v. Board (D)

504 F.3d 1249 (Fed. Cir. 2007).

NATURE OF CASE: Appeal from rejection of patent application for obviousness.

FACT SUMMARY: Translogic Technology, Inc. (Translogic) (P) applied for and received a patent, the '666 patent, related to multiplexers. On reexamination of patent '666, the United States Patent and Trademark Office's Board of Patent Appeals and Interferences (the Board) rejected certain of the claims of patent '666 as obvious due to prior art references. One reference was a technical article and the other was a textbook. The Board found a person of ordinary skill in the art would have used information from the textbook for the multiplexer stages in the article.

> ## 🏛 RULE OF LAW
> If the differences in the patented subject matter and the subject matter of the prior art would have been obvious to a person of ordinary skill in the art at the time of invention, then the subject matter is not patent-eligible under § 103(a).

FACTS: Translogic (P) applied for and received a patent, the '666 patent, related to multiplexers. The '666 patent claim specifically references a transmission gate multiplexer (TGM). One prior art reference, Gorai, is a technical article which discloses multiplexers but does not disclose use of a TGM. The other prior art reference, Weste, is a textbook which discloses and teaches a TGM. Translogic (P) filed a patent infringement suit against Hitachi, Ltd. claiming infringement of its '666 patent. Hitachi filed multiple requests for reexamination of patent '666, which the Board combined into one reexamination. The Board rejected several claims of the '666 patent based on obviousness in light of the prior art references. It determined a person of ordinary skill in the art would have applied the teaching in Weste to the technology disclosed in Gorai and thus the patent '666 claims were obvious. Translogic (P) appealed the rejection, which was affirmed. The Board then denied rehearing and Translogic (P) appealed to this court. In the infringement case, the district court imposed liability on Hitachi for inducing infringement. Hitachi filed an interlocutory appeal and the district court stayed its entry of permanent injunction. The district court then entered its final judgment and Hitachi appealed to this court. This court combined the infringement appeal with the reexamination appeal.

ISSUE: If the differences in the patented subject matter and the subject matter of the prior art would have been obvious to a person of ordinary skill in the art at the time of invention, is the subject matter patent-eligible under § 103(a)?

HOLDING AND DECISION: (Rader, J.) No. If the differences in the patented subject matter and the subject matter of the prior art would have been obvious to a person of ordinary skill in the art at the time of invention, then the subject matter is not patent-eligible under § 103(a). The Supreme Court affirmed this basic principle recently in *KSR Int'l Co. v. Teleflex, Inc.*, 550 U.S. 398 (2007). The Supreme Court in *KSR* also corrected this Court's "rigid" application of the "teaching, suggestion, and motivation" (TSM) test. The Court should use a broader approach to the TSM test. Here, the Gorai article predates the '666 patent and discloses multiplexer circuits. A person of ordinary skill in the art would have been well-versed in the TGM subject matter of the Weste textbook and would have applied that knowledge to the Gorai article disclosures. Translogic (P) argues that Gorai actually teaches away from multiplexers because it designs logic circuits. Translogic (P) is making the same error corrected in *KSR*. A variant does not need to address the same problem as the patent application so long as the variant is in the public domain and thus the common knowledge of a person of ordinary skill in the art. Translogic (P) also argues Weste provides not TSM on using TGMs in a series circuit as shown in Gorai. The Supreme Court in *KSR*, however, noted that the court can consider a person's creativity and inferences when determining a person of ordinary skill in the art would have found the patent subject matter obvious. Here, a person of ordinary skill in the art could have selected a TGM taught in Weste and applied it to the circuits shown in Gorai. The '666 is unpatentable under 35 U.S.C. § 103(a) for obviousness.

▶ ANALYSIS

This case highlights the tension between a parallel patent application review and infringement case. Here, the Board and the district court came to different conclusions (i.e., the Board rejected patent claims and the district court found Hitachi infringed upon those same claims). In the later analysis of the infringement claim, the Federal Circuit dismissed the infringement suit, overturned the district court imposition of damages, and lifted the injunction. In evaluating the patent claims, the Federal Circuit upheld its use of the TSM test but applied it in a flexible manner after *KSR*.

■=■

Continued on next page.

Quicknotes

35 U.S.C. § 103 Denies patent if the invention of the subject matter would have been obvious to a person based on prior inventions.

INTERLOCUTORY APPEAL The appeal of an issue that does not resolve the disposition of the case, but is essential to a determination of the parties' legal rights.

PRIOR ART Any prior knowledge or activity regarding a particular invention that may be considered by the Patent and Trademark Office in granting or denying a patent application or by the court in determining a patent infringement action.

■═■

Ormco Corp v. Align Technology, Inc.

Alleged infringer (D) v. Patent holder (P)

463 F.3d 1299 (Fed. Cir. 2006).

NATURE OF CASE: Appeal from summary judgment finding patent claims valid and liability for infringement.

FACT SUMMARY: Align Technology, Inc. (Align) (P) sued Ormco Corp. (D) for infringement of its patent '611 regarding orthodontic devices. Align (P) developed a series of retainer-like devices that straightened teeth. Ormco (D) argued the '611 claims would have been obvious and were thus invalid because of prior art references wherein another orthodontist developed a similar system but did not provide the devices in one package to the patient. The district court granted summary judgment to Align (P) that the patent claims were valid, and found Ormco (D) liable for infringing upon those claims.

🏛 **RULE OF LAW**

Sections 102(a) and 103(a) prohibit patents on claims that would be obvious or anticipated from prior art references unless the patent applicant demonstrates a suggestion or motivation to modify the teachings of the prior art, or secondary considerations, such as commercial success, rebut the finding of obviousness.

FACTS: Align (P) holds the '611 patent which includes claims related to orthodontic devices other than braces that straighten teeth. Claim 1 is an apparatus claim that describes a series of three retainer-like devices with different "geometries" that are provided to the patient in one package with instructions on use. The patient is to use the first device to move the teeth to an intermediate stage, the second device to the move the teeth to a successive stage, and the final device to move the teeth to the final stage. The patient does not have to, but can, see the orthodontist or dentist for various progress appointments. Ormco (D) developed the "Red, White & Blue" orthodontic product, which Align (P) claimed infringed upon its patent '611. Align (P) sued Ormco (D) for patent infringement and Ormco (D) argued the patent '611 claims were invalid for obviousness due to prior art references. The district court granted summary judgment to Align (P), holding the patent claims were valid. The district court also found Ormco (D) liable for infringement. Ormco (D) appealed.

ISSUE: Do §§ 102(a) and § 103(a) prohibit patents on claims that would be obvious or anticipated from prior art references unless the patent applicant demonstrates a suggestion or motivation to modify the teachings of the prior art, or secondary considerations, such as commercial success, rebut the finding of obviousness?

HOLDING AND DECISION: (Dyk, J.) Yes. Sections 102(a) and 103(a) prohibit patents on claims that would be obvious or anticipated from prior art references unless the patent applicant demonstrates a suggestion or motivation to modify the teachings of the prior art, or secondary considerations, such as commercial success, rebut the finding of obviousness. Ormco (D) argues the '611 patent claims were obvious pursuant to §§ 102(a) and 103(a) because of prior art references. The first reference is from Dr. Truax, an orthodontist, who developed a system of taking a mold of a patient's teeth, fashioning a device to move the teeth to a desired position, and then continuing to mold and move the teeth through a series of such appliances. The thinner appliance was applied before the thicker and Dr. Truax only provided one appliance at a time. The second reference is from Dr. Rains, another orthodontist, who practiced a similar technique using a series of three retainers to adjust a patient's teeth. The art must be accessible to the public to be recognized as prior art. Align (P) argued that Dr. Truax's materials were distributed only to orthodontists and thus not available to the general public. The promotion, however, was through seminars and clinics where his instruction sheet was distributed, so the prior art was sufficiently available to the general public. The district court concluded Dr. Truax's system used different thicknesses instead of different "geometries." The patent specification does not define the term "geometry," so the dictionary definition will be used, which defines "geometry" as "configuration" or "shape." Differing thicknesses fall within the dictionary definition, so the Truax devices fit the "geometries" limitation of Claim 1. The court also disagrees with the district court's finding that the devices are only capable of being provided in a single package. Claim 1 requires the devices are provided in a single package. Align (P) contends packaging the devices in such a manner would not have been obvious from Dr. Truax's reference. The suggestion, motivation, or teaching in the prior art does not have to be found explicitly within the prior art. The prior art, however, cannot "teach away" from the prior art modification. Align (P) argues Dr. Truax's reference teaches away from the single package because he requires the patient have an appointment to determine progress and the appropriate time to move to the next thickness. Here, the devices do not require a dentist or orthodontist to adjust and the patient can simply apply the next in the series. The claim, however, references periodic visits to the treating practitioner to ensure proper adjustment, which is just as Truax taught. Also, while the parties dispute whether Dr. Truax provided instructions to this patients, that limitation does not render Claim 1 nonobvious because the Food, Drug, and Cosmetic Act requires the provision of instructions with

Continued on next page.

medical devices. Finally, Align (P) argues the secondary considerations support a finding of nonobviousness. Secondary considerations may consist of commercial success, long felt but unsolved needs, or failure of others, among other indicia. It is true that Align's (P) product, Invisalign, has enjoyed tremendous commercial success, but even Align (P) concedes the success is due only partly to the claimed features of its patent. Truax had accomplished each of the claimed features prior to Invisalign's introduction. Similarly, the long-felt but unsolved needs and failure of others were not resolved or addressed by the claimed features. Claim 1 and its dependant claims are invalid as obvious. The court does not need to address the infringement finding. Reversed.

▌ ANALYSIS

The court is flexible in its application of the modification test, which differs from prior opinions. Align (P) did actually modify the prior teaching of Dr. Truax in that it provided the three devices in one package to the patient. Further, the court did not specifically find that the FDCA required instructions to be provided with these particular medical devices, so that was also a potential modification from the prior art.

■━■

Quicknotes

35 U.S.C. § 102(a) Denies patent for invention already known or used in the United States, or patented in a foreign country.

35 U.S.C. § 103 Denies patent if the invention of the subject matter would have been obvious to a person based on prior inventions.

PRIOR ART Any prior knowledge or activity regarding a particular invention, that may be considered by the Patent and Trademark Office, in granting or denying a patent application or by the court in determining a patent infringement action.

■━■

In re Papesch

N/A

315 F.2d 381 (C.C.P.A. 1963).

NATURE OF CASE: Appeal from patent rejection.

FACT SUMMARY: The applicant claimed that although his compound was structurally similar to a patented compound, its difference in properties rendered it patentable.

> ## 🏛 RULE OF LAW
> A prima facie case of obviousness due to structural similarity of compounds can be overcome by showing a difference in the compound's properties.

FACTS: Papesch sought a patent on a compound that was admittedly structurally obvious in light of an already patented compound. It differed only that Papesch had three ethyl groups while the prior art had three methyl groups. However, the triethyl compound had unexpected anti-inflammatory properties while the prior art had no usefulness in this area. The Board rejected the patent on the grounds of obviousness, and Papesch appealed.

ISSUE: Can a prima facie case of obviousness due to structural similarity of compounds be overcome by showing a difference in the compound's properties?

HOLDING AND DECISION: (Rich, J.) Yes. A prima facie case of obviousness due to structural similarity of compounds can be overcome by showing a difference in the compound's properties. In patent law, a compound and its properties are one and the same thing. The patentability of the thing does not depend on the similarity of its formula to a patented compound, but instead relies on the similarity of the two compounds. An assumed similarity based on a comparison of formulae must give way to evidence showing the assumption to be incorrect. Reversed.

▶ ANALYSIS

Two-dimensional representations, i.e., the structural formulas, are used to identify the structures to be patented in chemical and biotechnology fields. This map or label of the structure became of utmost importance to the Patent Office for several decades, so much so that the patent bar practically lost sight of the invention itself. Instead, one looked at the label, and if it was close to a prior label, then it was "structurally obvious." Consequently, if an inventor discovered an unexpected use for a structurally obvious compound, he would claim the method of use rather than the compound itself. *In re Papesch* marked a turning point where one could rebut a finding of structural obviousness and obtain a patent on the compound itself.

Quicknotes

35 U.S.C. § 103 Denies patent if the invention of the subject matter would have been obvious to a person based on prior inventions.

PRIMA FACIE CASE An action where the plaintiff introduces sufficient evidence to submit the issue to the judge or jury for determination.

In Re Dillon

N/A

919 F.2d 688 (Fed. Cir. 1990).

NATURE OF CASE: En banc hearing of appeal from finding of valid patent.

FACT SUMMARY: A structurally similar fuel additive disclosed in prior art acted as a dewatering agent, but the prior art did not suggest or disclose the fuel additive's use to reduce soot emissions. Dillon (P) sought to patent the additive to reduce soot emissions.

🏛 RULE OF LAW
A prima facie case of obviousness does not require both structural similarity and a suggestion in or expectation from the prior art that the claimed compound will have the same or a similar utility as the one newly discovered by the applicant.

FACTS: Dillon (P) sought a patent on tetra-orthoesters, useful as a fuel additive to reduce soot emissions. These compositions were structurally obvious from the already used tri-orthoesters, but the tri-orthoesters were used as a dewatering agent. The examiner and the PTO Board rejected Dillon's (P) application as obvious. A panel of the Federal Circuit reversed, then granted a petition for rehearing en banc.

ISSUE: Does a prima facie case of obviousness require both structural similarity and a suggestion in or expectation from the prior art that the claimed compound will have a similar utility as the one newly discovered by the applicant?

HOLDING AND DECISION: (Lourie, J.) No. A prima facie case of obviousness does not require both structural similarity and a suggestion in or expectation from the prior art that the claimed compound will have the same or a similar utility as the one newly discovered by the applicant. Exactly what constitutes a prima facie case varies from case to case. It is not the law, however, that if an applicant asserts a use not known to be possessed by the prior art, a prima facie case cannot then be established. Properties are relevant to establishing a prima facie case, but the prior art need not suggest or disclose the properties of the newly discovered compound to establish a prima facie case of obviousness. In this case, there are no references suggesting the fuel additive use that Dillon (P) has discovered, but there is a sufficient relationship between the two compounds in the fuel oil art to assume they would have similar properties, including water scavenging, and to provide motivation to make such new compounds. Dillon (P) failed to show her compound had different properties than the prior art or that hers performed to an unexpectedly higher degree. Reversed.

▶ ANALYSIS

There was a lengthy dissent in *Dillon* that the text does not print in its entirety. The dissent cited several cases, including *In re Papesch*, 315 F.2d 381 (C.C.P.A. 1963), to show that the court was going against precedent and reverting to a thirty year old "*Hass-Henze* Doctrine." *Papesch* did seem to state that if the new compound had different properties than its structurally similar brethren, it was patentable. *Dillon* distinguishes this in stating that *Papesch* did not deal with the requirements of establishing a prima facie case but, rather, with whether an examiner had to consider the properties of an invention at all. The majority strongly declared that it was not intending to "retreat from *Papesch* one inch."

Quicknotes

35 U.S.C. § 103 Denies patent if the invention of the subject matter would have been obvious to a person based on prior inventions.

EN BANC The hearing of a matter by all the judges of the court, rather than only the necessary quorum.

PRIOR ART Any prior knowledge or activity regarding a particular invention, that may be considered by the Patent and Trademark Office, in granting or denying a patent application or by the court in determining a patent infringement action.

In re Deuel

N/A

51 F.3d 1552 (Fed. Cir. 1995).

NATURE OF CASE: Appeal from Patent Board decision rejecting application for a patent.

FACT SUMMARY: The Patent Board declared Deuel's discovery of the sequences of similar tissue growing proteins in human and bovine cells obvious.

🏛 RULE OF LAW
When a chemical entity is structurally new, a prima facie case of obviousness requires that the teachings of the prior art suggest the claimed compounds to a person of ordinary skill in the art.

FACTS: Deuel's invention related to a protein, heparin-binding growth factor (HBGF), which facilitated the repair of damaged tissue. Deuel isolated and determined the DNA sequences and growth factor sequences of HBGF in both bovine uterine and human placental cells. His patent claims on these sequences were rejected as obvious. The patent examiner and the Board cited two prior references, Bohlen and Maniatis. Bohlen had ascertained that a similar protein, heparin-binding brain mitogen (HBBM), was identical in bovine and human brain tissues, but taught that this was brain-specific. Bohlen provided no teachings concerning DNA coding of HBBMs. Maniatis provided a method of gene cloning that Deuel utilized. Deuel appealed the rejection.

ISSUE: When a chemical entity is structurally new, does a prima facie case of obviousness require that the teachings of the prior art suggest the claimed compounds to a person of ordinary skill in the art?

HOLDING AND DECISION: (Lourie, J.) Yes. When a chemical entity is structurally new, a prima facie case of obviousness requires that the teachings of the prior art suggest the claimed compounds to a person of ordinary skill in the art. Here, the prior art did not disclose any relevant complementary DNA molecules, let alone any close relatives. The Board's theory that one might have been motivated to try to do what Deuel did amounts to speculation and impermissible hindsight. Bohlen actually taught against Deuel in that Bohlen claimed the proteins to be brain specific. As for Maniatis, the existence of a general method of isolating DNA is irrelevant to the question of whether the specific molecules would have been obvious. Reversed.

▶ ANALYSIS

Judge Lourie wrote the opinions for both *In re Dillon*, 919 F.2d 688 (Fed. Cir. 1990), and *In re Deuel*. The confusion in ascertaining the exact standards after both opinions reveals less about Lourie's judgment as much as it reveals the difficulty involved in patents in the field of biotechnology. The patenting of genes is very controversial in Europe, but Japan has proven more open to the idea. Some critics have contended that patenting complementary DNA sequence codes created from an obvious manipulation should not be patentable, but, rather, a "reasonable expectation of success" hurdle should be crossed. That is, if the prior art indicates it is reasonably likely that one could succeed in this manipulation, then it is prima facie obvious. See Varma and Abraham, "DNA is Different: Legal Obviousness and the Balance Between Biotech Inventors and the Market," 9 Harv. J.L. & Tech. 53 (1996).

Quicknotes

35 U.S.C. § 103 Denies patent if the invention of the subject matter would have been obvious to a person based on prior inventions.

PRIMA FACIE CASE An action where the plaintiff introduces sufficient evidence to submit the issue to the judge or jury for determination.

PRIOR ART Any prior knowledge or activity regarding a particular invention that may be considered by the Patent and Trademark Office in granting or denying a patent application or by the court in determining a patent infringement action.

In re Foster

N/A

343 F.2d 980 (C.C.P.A. 1965).

NATURE OF CASE: Appeal from a rejection of patent claims.

FACT SUMMARY: A prior art reference cited in rejecting Foster's patent claims had an effective date subsequent to the date of Foster's invention but more than one year prior to the date on which he finally filed his patent application.

🏛 RULE OF LAW
A patent must be denied where an applicant undertakes, under Rule 131, to swear back of a reference having an effective date more than a year before his filing date if the reference contains enough disclosure to make his invention obvious.

FACTS: Foster's patent application, filed August 21, 1956, was rejected on the basis of a magazine article in an August 1954 periodical that allegedly made the invention obvious (the Binder reference). He filed an affidavit under Rule 131 establishing that his invention date was prior to December 26, 1952. That meant the date of the Binder reference was subsequent to his date of invention but more than one year prior to the date he filed his patent application.

ISSUE: If an applicant swears back of a reference having an effective date more than a year before his filing date and the reference contains enough disclosure to make his invention obvious, must a patent be denied him?

HOLDING AND DECISION: (Almond, J.) Yes. In keeping with the principles underlying applicable statutes, a patent must be denied if an applicant undertakes to swear back of a reference having an effective date more than a year before his filing date if the reference contains enough disclosure to make his invention obvious. 35 U.S.C. § 102(b) provides that no patent should issue if the invention was patented or described in a printed publication in this or a foreign country or in public use or on sale in this country, more than one year prior to the date of the application for patent in the United States. The purpose of the statute is to require filing of the application within one year after the public comes into possession of the invention, whether by its being made obvious in a publication or combination of publications or otherwise.

▶ *ANALYSIS*

The one-year rule is designed to promote diligence in the filing of patent applications. Originally, a two-year period existed, but by 1939 Congress felt that improvements in communications were such that a one-year period was reasonable.

■■■

Quicknotes

PATENT ACT § 102(b) Prohibits a patent for an invention which has been in public use more than a year prior to the application date.

■■■

In re Clay

N/A

966 F.2d 656, 23 U.S.P.Q.2d 1058 (Fed. Cir. 1992).

NATURE OF CASE: Appeal from Board decision rejecting patent application.

FACT SUMMARY: Clay argued that his invention displacing the dead volume at the bottom of a tank with a gel was in a technical area too remote from a patented invention involving a similar gel so as to not be prior art.

🏛 RULE OF LAW
Prior art is analogous if it is in the same field of endeavor or if it is still reasonably pertinent to the particular problem with which the inventor is involved.

FACTS: Clay's invention, assigned to Marathon Oil Company, was a process for storing refined liquid hydrocarbon in a storage tank having a dead volume between the tank bottom and outlet port. The process involved preparing a gelatin solution that gelled after placement in the tank's dead volume, thereby raising the level of the liquid to a particular point, usually the outlet port. The Patent Board rejected the patent as obvious in light of two other inventions. The first, Hetherington, displaced the dead volume in the bottom of a tank with impervious bladders, or large bags. The second, Sydansk, reduced the permeability of hydrocarbon-bearing formations using a gel similar to Clay's invention. Clay argued that Sydansk's invention was not sufficiently germane to the technical area of the claimed invention and was thus too remote to be treated as prior art. Clay appealed.

ISSUE: Is prior art analogous if it is in the same field of endeavor or if it is still reasonably pertinent to the particular problem with which the inventor is involved?

HOLDING AND DECISION: (Lourie, J.) Yes. A prior art is analogous if it is in the same field of endeavor or if it is still reasonably pertinent to the particular problem with which the inventor is involved. This is the proper two-part test when determining the fact question of whether a reference in the prior art is analogous. Sydansk cannot be considered in Clay's field merely because they both relate to the petroleum industry. Sydansk's invention related to the extraction of crude petroleum, and Clay's to the storage of refined liquid hydrocarbons. Therefore, they were not in the same field of endeavor. Moreover, the problem addressed by Sydansk's invention, plugging of underground formation anomalies, does not relate to the problem faced by Clay, that is, preventing loss of a stored product. Thus, the reference was not reasonably pertinent. Since Sydansk came from a nonanalogous prior art, Clay's invention was not obvious. Reversed.

▶ ANALYSIS

It is interesting to note that only obviousness requires the prior art to be analogous. Novelty-defeating technology can come from a distantly related field. Some decisions in this area lead to seemingly strange results. In *Sage Products, Inc. v. Devon Industries Inc.*, 880 F. Supp. 718, 35 U.S.P.Q.2d 1321 (C.D. Cal. 1994), the court held a patent on a simple and secure street letter box was available as a prior art reference with regard to a disposal container for hazardous medical waste.

∎▬∎

Quicknotes

35 U.S.C. § 103 Denies patent if the invention of the subject matter would have been obvious to a person based on prior inventions.

PRIOR ART Any prior knowledge or activity regarding a particular invention that may be considered by the Patent and Trademark Office in granting or denying a patent application or by the court in determining a patent infringement action.

∎▬∎

The Patent Specification

Quick Reference Rules of Law

PAGE

1. **Enablement.** A patent application must have adequate disclosure sufficient for one skilled in the art to make an operable device. (Gould v. Hellwarth) — 58

2. **Enablement.** To be enabling under § 112, a patent must contain a description that enables one skilled in the art to make and use the claimed invention. (Atlas Powder Co. v. E.I. du Pont De Nemours & Co.) — 59

3. **Enablement.** An application containing a general description of processes, the subject matter, and methods of use, with only one working example, may be rejected as unsupported by an enabling disclosure. (In re Wright) — 60

4. **Enablement.** A patent application's specifications must enable a person skilled in the art to make the invention, so the claims cannot be so broad as to encompass unsuccessful examples in an unpredictable field. (Pharmaceutical Resources, Inc. v. Roxane Laboratories, Inc.) — 61

5. **"Written Description."** Drawings may be sufficient to provide the written description of the invention. (Vas-Cath Inc. v. Mahurkar) — 62

6. **"Written Description."** Patent claims may be no broader than the supporting disclosure and, thus, a narrow disclosure will limit claim breadth. (The Gentry Gallery, Inc. v. The Berkline Corp.) — 63

7. **"Written Description."** Claims for a DNA sequence will be considered invalid for failure to provide an adequate written description of the subject matter if a description of the DNA itself, which includes information pertaining to its relevant structure or physical characteristics, such as sequence information indicating which nucleotides constitute human cDNA, is not included. (Regents of the University of California v. Eli Lilly & Co.) — 64

8. **"Written Description."** [Rule of Law not stated in casebook excerpt.] (Enzo Biochem, Inc. v. Gen-Probe Inc.) — 65

9. **Best Mode.** Specifications must satisfy a dual-pronged best mode inquiry: subjectively, whether the inventor knew of a better method than the one disclosed, and objectively, whether the disclosure is adequate to direct those skilled in the art of practicing the best mode. (Chemcast Corp. v. Arco Industries Corp.) — 66

Gould v. Hellwarth

Laser inventor (P) v. Competitor (D)

472 F.2d 1383 (C.C.P.A. 1973).

NATURE OF CASE: Appeal from Board award of priority to the junior party.

FACT SUMMARY: Gould (P) applied for a patent on a Q-switch for a laser although lasers themselves were still theoretical.

⚖ RULE OF LAW
A patent application must have adequate disclosure sufficient for one skilled in the art to make an operable device.

FACTS: Both Gould (P) and Hellwarth (D) applied for patents on a Q-switch for a laser. Gould (P) filed on April 6, 1959, and Hellwarth (D) filed on August 1, 1961. However, Hellwarth (D) claimed Gould's (P) patent was invalid under 35 U.S.C. § 112, which requires the application to provide adequate instructions for a person skilled in the field to make an operable device. Gould's (P) application sufficiently described a Q-switch, but did not contain instructions on how to construct an operative laser. Masers, using microwaves instead of light waves, were well known, and it was understood that lasers were theoretically possible. However, a working laser was not developed until 1960 at the earliest. The Board ordered a priority hearing, and Hellwarth (D) won. Gould (P) appealed.

ISSUE: Must a patent application include adequate disclosure sufficient for one skilled in the art to make an operable device?

HOLDING AND DECISION: (Lane, J.) Yes. A patent application must have adequate disclosure sufficient for one skilled in the art to make an operable device. In this case, several expert witnesses testified that the application did not disclose a complete set of parameters for a laser and also failed to reveal the knowledge necessary to produce an operable laser. Gould (P) asserts that the necessary parameters were in a portion of the application suggesting use of a sodium and mercury gaseous atmosphere. Although the idea of a laser was understood, a working medium was not discovered until a scientist used pink ruby in April of 1960. As of 1968, no lasers using sodium-mercury were known to have been operated. The Gould (P) application fails to provide enabling disclosure on how to make the subject matter of the application. Affirmed.

▶ ANALYSIS

This decision may seem unfair to Gould (P). For instance, once workers in the field discovered how to make a laser, they could freely borrow his Q-switch idea, as it was not patented. However, creative patent attorneys were able to litigate successfully on Gould's (P) behalf with regard to his application in several other cases. In *Gould v. Control Laser Corp.*, 866 F.2d 1391 (Fed. Cir. 1989), a jury found laser devices infringed upon the "optical amplifier" outlined in Gould's (P) claim, and Gould (P) was awarded considerable royalties.

■■■

Quicknotes

35 U.S.C. § 112 Requires that patent applicants disclose how to make and use the invention and include a written description.

■■■

Atlas Powder Co. v. E.I. du Pont De Nemours & Company

Chemical company (P) v. Competitor (D)

750 F.2d 1569 (Fed Cir. 1984).

NATURE OF CASE: Appeal from judgment holding patent valid and infringed.

FACT SUMMARY: In Atlas's (P) suit against Du Pont (D) for patent infringement on a blasting agent, Du Pont (D) claimed that Atlas's (P) patent disclosure did not enable one of ordinary skill in the art to make and use the claimed invention and, thus, the invention was invalid under 35 U.S.C. § 112.

🏛 RULE OF LAW
To be enabling under § 112, a patent must contain a description that enables one skilled in the art to make and use the claimed invention.

FACTS: Atlas (P) developed the '978 patent for a blasting agent. When Du Pont (D) began to market a similar agent, Atlas (P) sued Du Pont (D) for infringement. At trial, Du Pont (D) contended that Atlas's (P) patent was invalid because the patent disclosure did not enable one of ordinary skill in the art to make and use the claimed invention pursuant to the dictates of 35 U.S.C. § 112. The court ruled for Atlas (P) on the grounds that Atlas's (P) '978 patent was different enough from the prior art and provided a solution to a detonation problem which others had not considered such that the patent was non-obvious. Du Pont (D) appealed.

ISSUE: To be enabling under § 112, must a patent contain a description that enables one skilled in the art to make and use the claimed invention?

HOLDING AND DECISION: (Baldwin, J.) Yes. To be enabling under § 112, a patent must contain a description that enables one skilled in the art to make and use the claimed invention. That some experimentation is necessary does not preclude ennoblement; the amount of experimentation, however, must not be unduly extensive. Determining ennoblement is a question of law. Here, Du Pont (D) argues that Atlas's (P) disclosure is nothing more than a list of "candidate ingredients" from which one skilled in the art would have to select and experiment unduly to find an operable emulsion. The district court held that it would have been impossible for Atlas (P) to list all operable emulsions and exclude the inoperable ones. Also, such a list would be unnecessary because one skilled in the art would know how to select a salt and fuel and then apply "Bancroft's Rule" to determine the proper emulsifier. The district court's holding was correct. Even if some of the claimed combinations were inoperative, the claims were not necessarily invalid. It is not a function of the claims to specifically exclude possible inoperative substances. Du Pont (D) has not persuaded this court that the district court was clearly erroneous in its findings. Affirmed.

▶ ANALYSIS

A specification will be sufficient even though a skilled person might have to make several trials or experiments before successfully making and using the invention. However, a skilled person is only required to use ordinary skill in making the invention. It is sufficient if the invention can be made operative by adjustments or corrections which would naturally occur to a worker skilled in the art.

Quicknotes

35 U.S.C. § 112 Requires that patent applicants disclose how to make and use the invention and include a written description.

In re Wright

N/A

999 F.2d 1557, 27 U.S.P.Q.2d 1510 (Fed. Cir. 1993).

NATURE OF CASE: Appeal from decision by the Board of Patent Appeals and Interferences of the United States Patent and Trademark Office (the Board) rejecting patent application.

FACT SUMMARY: Wright discovered a vaccine for a chicken RNA virus and sought a patent that extended to other vaccines.

> ## 🏛 RULE OF LAW
> An application containing a general description of processes, the subject matter, and methods of use, with only one working example, may be rejected as unsupported by an enabling disclosure.

FACTS: Wright applied for patents on the processes of producing live, non-pathogenic vaccines against pathogenic RNA viruses, the vaccines produced by these processes, and methods of using these vaccines. His application contained a general description of the processes, vaccines, and methods of use, but only a single working example. The example, fully described in the application, concerned a vaccine that confers immunity in chickens against the RNA tumor virus known as Prague Avian Sarcoma Virus (PrASV), a member of the Rous Associated Virus (RAV) family. Wright's application contained claims in many degrees, from the specific PrASV vaccine to a general non-pathogenic vaccine for an RNA virus. The examiner rejected the application as merely providing one working example that did not provide sufficient likelihood of creating other working examples without undue experimentation, or that these would be useful in the design of viral vaccines. Furthermore, the methods described in Wright's application were so undeveloped in 1983, the time of filing, as to not enable the design and production of vaccines against any and all RNA viruses. The Board affirmed the examiner's decision, and Wright appealed.

ISSUE: May an application containing a general description of processes, the subject matter, and methods of use, with only one working example, be rejected as unsupported by an enabling disclosure?

HOLDING AND DECISION: (Rich, J.) Yes. An application containing a general description of processes, the subject matter, and methods of use, with only one working example, may be rejected as unsupported by an enabling disclosure. The Board set forth a reasonable belief for its finding, so the burden shifts to Wright to provide persuasive arguments with sufficient evidence. The general description and single example in the application did nothing more in February of 1983 than invite experimentation to determine whether other vaccines having in vivo immunoprotective activity could be constructed for other RNA viruses. Wright's affidavits of support merely contain unsupported conclusory statements. Wright's argument that, at the least, his application should apply to vaccines against avian tumor viruses fails. There is no evidence that a skilled scientist could extrapolate that, due to Wright's success with one particular strain, there was a reasonable expectation of success for other avian strains. Affirmed.

▶ ANALYSIS

Wright reveals the tough balancing act that occurs when a single example is listed. If a patent is drawn too narrowly, others could make simple changes to the example and circumvent the patent. However, one that is broadly defined would provide a windfall to the inventor. Samuel Morse's telegraph patent application was similar to Wright's in that he attempted to not limit himself to the "specific machinery." The Supreme Court struck down his claim as invalid in *O'Reilly v. Morse*, 56 U.S. (15 How.) 62 (1854).

Quicknotes

35 U.S.C. § 112 Requires that patent applicants disclose how to make and use the invention and include a written description.

Pharmaceutical Resources, Inc. v. Roxane Laboratories, Inc.

Patent holder (P) v. Alleged infringer (D)

253 Fed. Appx. 26 (Fed. Cir. 2007).

NATURE OF CASE: Appeal from summary judgment declaring patent claims invalid.

FACT SUMMARY: Par (P) asserted broad claims in its patents '318 and '320, the generic version of the BMS Atzinger patent, related to stable flocculated suspension composition,. When it sued Roxane (D) for infringement, Roxane (D) argued the claims were invalid for lack of enablement.

🏛 RULE OF LAW
A patent application's specifications must enable a person skilled in the art to make the invention, so the claims cannot be so broad as to encompass unsuccessful examples in an unpredictable field.

FACTS: Bristol-Myers Squibb (BMS) patented a liquid pharmaceutical composition of megestrol acetate (the "Atzinger patent"). The Atzinger patent discloses one stable flocculated suspension composition using megestrol acetate and one particular wetting agent and one particular surfactant. Pharmaceutical Resources, Inc. and Par Pharmaceuticals, Inc. (collectively, "Par") (P) developed a generic version of BMS's product and patented it by using other wetting agents and surfactants. Par received the '318 and '320 patents. Par filed an infringement suit against Roxane Laboratories, Inc. (D) based on alleged infringement of claims of the '318 and '320 patents. Roxane (D) argued the claims were invalid and moved for summary judgment on the basis the claims lacked enablement. The district court determined Par (P) was not entitled to the broad claims asserted and granted summary judgment to Roxane (D). Par (P) appealed.

ISSUE: Must a patent application's specifications enable a person skilled in the art to make the invention, excluding claims encompassing unsuccessful examples in an unpredictable field?

HOLDING AND DECISION: (Moore, J.) Yes. A patent application's specifications must enable a person skilled in the art to make the invention, so the claims cannot be so broad as to encompass unsuccessful examples in an unpredictable field. 35 U.S.C. § 112 sets forth the enablement requirement for patents. This court set out the eight factors relevant to the analysis in *In re Wands*, 858 F.2d 731 (Fed. Cir. 1988): "(1) the quantity of experimentation necessary, (2) the amount of direction or guidance presented, (3) the presence or absence of working examples, (4) the nature of the invention, (5) the state of the prior art, (6) the relative skill of those in the art, (7) the predictability or unpredictability of the art, and (8) the breadth of the claims." Par's (P) specification must meet a rather high standard because of the breadth of its claims in an admittedly unpredictable field. Here, all record evidence supports a finding of an unpredictable field including the testimony of Par's (P) own witnesses and its argument in is prior litigation with BMS. The district court's finding that the field was unpredictable is correct. The district court also concluded Par's (P) claims were extraordinarily broad. The claims address any surfactant in any concentration, which includes hundreds of possible surfactants. Par's (P) specifications only include three working examples, which do not provide an enabling disclosure commensurate with the broad claims. Par's (P) experts testified about the criticality of the appropriate surfactant and concentration, which does not coincide with its broad specification claims failing to specify any particular surfactant and no concentration limitation. Par's (P) witnesses and the inventor did not provide evidence of enablement because of Par's (P) unsuccessful attempts to practice the subject matter within the claims' scope. Par (P) put forth only a scintilla of evidence that the claims were enabled and did not overcome its summary judgment burden. Each of the claims asserted in the '318 and '320 patents are invalid for lack of enablement. Affirmed.

▎ ANALYSIS

Experimentation is a permitted part of a patent specification, but the specification cannot be so broad as to include any possible permutation of the invention, even unsuccessful forms. The court does not intend to limit the patent to only the working examples shown in the specification but neither can it include any possible combination of the limitations of the invention. The patent is to be granted to the invention, not to all imaginary or impossible versions of the invention.

■═■

Quicknotes

35 U.S.C. § 112 Requires that patent applicants disclose how to make and use the invention and include a written description.

■═■

Vas-Cath Inc. v. Mahurkar

Medical product manufacturer (P) v. Product designer (D)

935 F.2d 1555 (Fed. Cir. 1991).

NATURE OF CASE: Appeal from partial final judgment finding patents invalid.

FACT SUMMARY: Mahurkar's (D) original application contained drawings of his catheter invention, and he later attempted to attach written descriptions.

🏛 RULE OF LAW
Drawings may be sufficient to provide the written description of the invention.

FACTS: Mahurkar (D) designed a double-lumen catheter that allowed blood to be removed from an artery and returned close to the place of removal. The invention made all other catheters obsolete. The design application was filed on March 8, 1982, and consisted of three somewhat detailed drawings, but it was abandoned on November 30, 1984. Mahurkar (D) received a Canadian patent on August 9, 1982. He then filed two utility applications including these same drawings, but with additional textual descriptions. Most significant was the description that one cylindrical portion must have a diameter substantially greater than one-half, but substantially less than one-half of the first cylindrical portion. Mahurkar 9D0 wanted the two utility applications, filed in 1984, to date back to the original 1982 filing date as continuations of the prior application. Vas-Cath (P) sued Mahurkar (D) for a declaratory judgment that its catheters did not infringe on Mahurkar's (D) utility patents, and Mahurkar (D) counterclaimed for infringement. The district court found the continuations did not date back since the original application's drawings failed to meet the "written description" requirement. Mahurkar (D) appealed.

ISSUE: May drawings be sufficient to provide the written description of the invention?

HOLDING AND DECISION: (Rich, J.) Yes. Drawings may be sufficient to provide the written description of the invention. Written description compliance is a question of fact, to be reviewed under the clearly erroneous standard. The purpose is broader than to merely explain how to "make and use." The applicant must also convey, with reasonable clarity to those skilled in the art, that, as of the filing date, he or she was in possession of the invention. The district court erred in its concern with "what the invention is." The claim before the court, and what Mahurkar (D) eventually patented, was exactly what the picture showed. More troubling is the textual explanations that may not follow inevitably from the diagrams. Mahurkar (D) provided expert testimony that one skilled in the arts would understand that the catheter must have the range specified in the claims, but the district court observed later patents to refute this. The district court must look solely to one skilled in the art on the date of filing, not afterwards. Therefore, the second issue must be resolved. Reversed and remanded.

▶ ANALYSIS

On remand, the court found that the drawings showed that Mahurkar (D) was in possession of the invention at the date of filing. Judge Easterbrook observed that the utility applications merely lay out what the designs show, and, if anything, they narrate the features of the drawing that are important, without adding anything. See *In re Mahurkar Patent Litigation*, 831 F. Supp. 1354 (N.D. Ill. 1993).

■■■

Quicknotes

35 U.S.C. § 112 Requires that patent applicants disclose how to make and use the invention and include a written description.

■■■

The Gentry Gallery, Inc. v. The Berkline Corp.

Furniture manufacturer (P) v. Furniture manufacturer (D)

134 F.3d 1473 (Fed. Cir. 1998).

NATURE OF CASE: Patent infringement suit.

FACT SUMMARY: Gentry (P) brought suit against Berkline (D) claiming patent infringement by Berkline's (D) manufacturing and selling of sectional sofas having two recliners facing in the same direction.

🏛 RULE OF LAW
Patent claims may be no broader than the supporting disclosure and, thus, a narrow disclosure will limit claim breadth.

FACTS: Gentry (P) owns the '244 patent to a sectional sofa in which two independent reclining seats face in the same direction. Gentry (P) filed suit alleging that Berkline (D) infringed its patent by manufacturing and selling sofas having two recliners facing in the same direction. The district court granted Berkline's (D) motion for summary judgment of noninfringement, but denied its motions for invalidity and unenforceability. The court concluded that Berkline's (D) sofas did not contain a fixed console and thus did not infringe Gentry's (P) patent.

ISSUE: May patent claims may be broader than the supporting disclosure?

HOLDING AND DECISION: (Lourie, J.) No. Patent claims may be no broader than the supporting disclosure and, thus, a narrow disclosure will limit claim breadth. Berkline (D) argued that because the patent only described the sofas having controls on the console, the claimed consoles were not described within the meaning of § 112. This court agrees that the patent's disclosure does not support claims in which the location of the recliner controls is other than on the console. Whether a specification complies with the written description requirement of § 112 is a question of fact to be reviewed for clear error on appeal. To fulfill the written description requirement, the patent specification must "clearly allow persons of ordinary skill in the art to recognize that [the inventor] invented what is claimed." This requirement is met if the written description describes the invention, with all its claimed limitations. While a claim need not be limited to a preferred embodiment, the scope of a right to exclude may be limited by a narrow disclosure. Here the original disclosure clearly identifies the console as the only possible location for the controls. Locating the controls anywhere but on the consoles is outside the stated purpose of the invention. Claims may be no broader than the supporting disclosure; thus, a narrow disclosure will limit claim breadth. The district court erred in finding that Gentry (P) was entitled to claims in which the recliner controls are not located on the console. Reversed.

▶ ANALYSIS

Gentry (P) relied on the position set forth in *Ethicon* that "an applicant . . . is generally allowed claims, when the art permits, which cover more than the specific embodiment shown." The court distinguishes that case from the present, however, indicating that while an applicant is free to draft claims broadly, within the restrictions imposed by the prior art, the inventor did so in *Ethicon* only because he did not, unlike Gentry (P), consider the element to be an essential part of his invention.

■ ═ ■

Quicknotes

INFRINGEMENT Conduct in violation of statute or that interferes with another's rights pursuant to law.

PATENT A limited monopoly conferred on the invention or discovery of any new or useful machine or process that is novel and nonobvious.

35 U.S.C. § 112 Requires that patent applicants disclose how to make and use the invention and include a written description.

■ ═ ■

Regents of the University of California v. Eli Lilly & Co.

Inventor (P) v. Alleged infringer (D)

119 F.3d 1559 (Fed. Cir. 1997).

NATURE OF CASE: Appeal of determination that a patent was invalid.

FACT SUMMARY: The University (P) sued Eli Lilly & Co. (D) for infringement. Eli Lilly & Co. (D) defended claiming that the patent was invalid because the specifications failed to provide an adequate written description of the subject matter.

🏛 RULE OF LAW

Claims for a DNA sequence will be considered invalid for failure to provide an adequate written description of the subject matter if a description of the DNA itself, which includes information pertaining to its relevant structure or physical characteristics, such as sequence information indicating which nucleotides constitute human cDNA, is not included.

FACTS: The University's (P) patent at issue involves recombinant DNA technology, which produces human insulin. Healthy people produce insulin in vivo via the terminal enzymatic cleavage of preproinsulin (PPI) to yield proinsulin (PI), a single amino acid chain. The patent's application was based upon the determination of the PI and PPI cDNA sequences found in rats. The patent specification mentions that the cDNA is part of the invention, provides only a general method for producing human insulin cDNA, and gives a description of the human insulin A and B chain amino acid sequences that cDNA encodes. The Regents of the University of California (The University) (P) sued Eli Lilly & Co. (D) for infringement and Eli Lilly & Co. (D) claimed that the patent was invalid. The district court ruled that the claims of the patent were invalid because the specification did not provide an adequate written description of the cDNA. The University (P) appealed.

ISSUE: Are Claims 1, 2, and 4 to 7 invalid for failing to provide an adequate written description?

HOLDING AND DECISION: (Lourie, J.) Yes. The claims are invalid for failing to provide an adequate written description. An adequate written description of a DNA requires more than a mere statement that it is part of the invention and reference to a potential method of isolating it; what is required is a description of the DNA itself. The claimed microorganism in Claim 5 requires human insulin-encoding cDNA. Example 6 provides only a general method for obtaining human cDNA. It does not provide a written description of the cDNA encoding human insulin, which is necessary to provide a written description of the subject matter of Claim 5. Information pertaining to cDNA's relevant structure or physical characteristics is necessary.

Sequence information indicating which nucleotides constitute human cDNA needs to appear in the patent. The specification therefore does not provide a written description of the invention of Claim 5. The patent specification provides only a general method for producing human insulin cDNA and a description of the human insulin A and B chain amino acid sequences that cDNA encodes. Claim 5 is therefore invalid for failure to provide an adequate written description. Furthermore, the remaining claims are also invalid because a description of rat insulin cDNA is not a description of the broad classes of vertebrate or mammalian insulin cDNA. A written description of an invention involving chemical genus requires a precise definition, such as by structure, formula, or chemical name of the claimed subject matter sufficient to distinguish it from other materials. In claims to genetic material, a generic statement such as "vertebrate insulin cDNA" or "mammalian insulin cDNA," without more, is not an adequate written description of the genus, because it does not distinguish the claimed genus from others, except by function. One skilled in the art, therefore, cannot visualize or recognize the identity of the members of the genus. A definition by function does not suffice to define the genus, because it is only an indication of what the gene does, rather than what it is. Therefore, naming a material generally known to exist, in the absence of knowledge as to what that material consists of, is not a description of that material. A definition of a cDNA requires a kind of specificity achieved by means of the recitation of the sequence of nucleotides that make up the cDNA. A description of a genus of cDNAs may be achieved by means of a representative number of cDNAs falling within the scope of the genus or of a recitation of structural features common to the members of the genus, which features constitute a substantial portion of the genus. Claims 1, 2, 4, 6 and 7 are therefore also invalid for failure to provide an adequate written description. Affirmed.

▶ ANALYSIS

The strict description requirement as set out in this case and the obviousness test as set forth in *In re Deuel*, 51 F.3d 1552, 34 U.S.P.Q.2d 1210 (Fed. Cir. 1995), are unique to U.S. patent law.

■=■

Enzo Biochem, Inc. v. Gen-Probe Inc.

[Parties not identified.]

296 F.3d 1316 (Fed. Cir. 2002).

NATURE OF CASE: Dissent from denial of rehearing en banc.

FACT SUMMARY: [Fact Summary not stated in casebook excerpt.]

 RULE OF LAW
[Rule of Law not stated in casebook excerpt.]

FACTS: [Facts not stated in casebook excerpt.]

ISSUE: [Issue not stated in casebook excerpt.]

HOLDING AND DECISION: [Holding and decision not stated.]

DISSENT: (Rader, J.) I dissent from the majority's opinion not to hear the case en banc. The majority's first mistake is its disregard of the statute that requires only that a written description assure that others can make and use the invention. The majority's second and greater mistake is its misapplication of our case law regarding written description. The origin and history of the written description requirement demonstrates that it was meant to enforce priority and it has no application to claims without priority problems. The court deviated from thirty years of practice in *Regents of the University of California v. Eli Lilly & Co.*, 119 F.3d 1559, 43 U.S.P.Q.2d 1398 (Fed. Cir. 1997), when it applied written description as a freestanding general disclosure requirement when no priority question was involved in place of the statutory standard of enablement. The patent disclosure in that case did indeed warrant rejection for lack of enablement, because the inventor did not show one of skill in the art how to make cDNA. A claim of vertebrate insulin cDNA scope far exceeds the patent's enabling disclosures. Rat insulin was the only thing the inventor had enabled. Instead of invalidating under the test for enablement however, the court created a new doctrine for adequacy of disclosure, written description. Written description had never before been a freestanding substitute for enablement. Enablement would have only required the inventor in *Lilly* to have specifications that show one of skill in the art how to acquire that sequence on his or her own. The written disclosure requirement in *Lilly* and this case threatens to disrupt the patent system further by replacing enablement, which is the statutory test for adequate disclosure, and imperils the integrity of the patent system. *Lilly* also prejudices those claims filed before it, because those inventors were not on notice of the *Lilly* written description requirement. It also prejudices small inventors who do not have the wherewithal to process every new invention to extract its nucleotide sequence.

CONCURRENCE: (Lourie, J.) The written description requirement is not a requirement for enablement but is its own separate requirement in addition to the enablement requirement. An invention must be described. Applying the written description requirement outside of the priority context is not precluded by statute or precedent. Moreover, the statute doesn't say that the written description is only for policing priority. It is incorrect that the mere appearance of vague claim language in an original claim necessarily satisfies the written description requirement.

▌ANALYSIS

No other country has a doctrine such as that articulated in *Regents of the University of California v. Eli Lilly & Co.*

■▬■

Chemcast Corp. v. Arco Industries Corp.

Grommet manufacturer (P) v. Competitor (D)

913 F.2d 923 (Fed. Cir. 1990).

NATURE OF CASE: Appeal from district court rejection of patent claim.

FACT SUMMARY: Rubright, an inventor for Chemcast (P), did not disclose his materials source for the dual durometer grommet in his specification but instead gave a list of generic potential materials.

🏛 RULE OF LAW
Specifications must satisfy a dual-pronged best mode inquiry: subjectively, whether the inventor knew of a better method than the one disclosed, and objectively, whether the disclosure is adequate to direct those skilled in the art in practicing the best mode.

FACTS: Rubright, an employee of Chemcast (P), filed an application for a dual durometer grommet made of PVC composite he obtained from a specific supplier, the formula being a trade secret of that supplier. Although the grommet had only successfully been made with this material, Rubright failed to indicate in the specification the name of the supplier and material brand and instead gave a list of generic potential materials. Rubright's supplier, Reynosol, had spent months and hundreds of hours developing the composite for Chemcast's (P) new grommet. Chemcast (P) subsequently sued Arco (D) for infringement of the grommet patent. The district court held that Chemcast (P) had violated the 35 U.S.C. § 112 best mode requirement for failing to disclose either the method of manufacture or the specific supplier of the preferred composite. Chemcast (P) appealed.

ISSUE: Must specifications satisfy a dual-pronged best mode inquiry: subjectively, whether the inventor knew of a better method than the one disclosed, and objectively, whether the disclosure is adequate to direct those skilled in the art in practicing the best mode?

HOLDING AND DECISION: (Mayer, J.) Yes. Specifications satisfy a dual-pronged best mode inquiry: subjectively, whether the inventor knew of a better method than the one disclosed, and objectively, whether the disclosure is adequate to direct those skilled in the art in practicing the best mode. 35 U.S.C. § 112 poses two separate issues. First, does the specification enable the practitioner of the art to perform the invention? Second, does the specification present the best mode the inventor knows of performance? Distinct from enablement, the best mode inquiry requires a subjective focus on the inventor's state of mind and whether he knows of a superior method to the one in the specification. Also, an objective inquiry must be made as to whether those versed in the art have the skill and understanding to

reproduce the best mode of performance from the text of the specification. If the inventor did know of a better mode and the specification does not direct practitioners to it, the best mode has been concealed, and the claim is invalid. Applying this two-pronged inquiry to the present case assumes that Chemcast's (P) preferred PVC composite is a trade secret of Reynosol. It is the only effective composite that Rubright was aware of. Yet Rubright's specification does not point others in Reynosol's direction but seeks to keep the source for Chemcast's (P) benefit. Inventors cannot be allowed to circumvent best mode requirements by protecting exclusive agreements with their preferred suppliers if that supplier possesses the key to the best mode of performance. In addition, the skill in the art is such that practitioners would have never known what Rubright's contemplated best mode was, nor would they have had the ability to carry it out. The best mode has been concealed. Affirmed.

▶ ANALYSIS

Note the distinction between 35 U.S.C. § 112 best mode and enablement inquiries as distinct. One way to consider the two is that a specification faulted for lack of enablement, with its undue experimentation standard, is unclear enough to be useful. Best mode difficulties arise when a specification is useful but does not provide the inventor's contemplated best use. In the above case, the amount of research needed to produce the PVC compound in question would give rise to an undue experimentation problem, if the solution were not a best mode issue.

■=■

Quicknotes

35 U.S.C. § 112 Requires that patent applicants disclose how to make and use the invention and include a written description.

■=■

Claims

Quick Reference Rules of Law

PAGE

1. **United States Peripheral Claiming Technique.**   Claims in utility applications that define   68
the invention entirely by reference to the specification and/or drawings can be rejected
under 35 U.S.C. § 112 ¶2. (Ex parte Fressola)

2. **Elemental Claim Structure.**   If the preamble phrase does not define the invention, recite   69
steps as important to the specification, or distinguish the invention from the prior art,
then the preamble does not limit the claim's scope. (Catalina Marketing International v.
Coolsavings.com, Inc.)

3. **Product-by-Process Claims.**   Process terms in product-by-process claims limit   70
infringement to products made by the claimed process only. (Atlantic Thermoplastics Co.
Inc. v. Faytex Corp.)

4. **Functional Claiming.**   A product or process that performs an identical function to a   71
patented invention may avoid literal infringement but still infringe under the doctrine of
equivalents. (Al-Site Corp. v. VSI International, Inc.)

5. **Functional Claiming.**   35 U.S.C. § 112 paragraph 6 requires patent applicants for a   72
means-plus-function limitation in a computer-implemented invention to disclose
the algorithm that transforms the general purpose computer to a special purpose
computer programmed to perform the claimed function. (Aristocrat Technologies
Australia Pty Ltd. v. International Game Technology)

6. **Claim Definiteness.**   A claim is valid under 35 U.S.C. § 112 if those skilled in the art would   74
understand what is claimed when the claim is read in light of the specification.
(Orthokinetics, Inc. v. Safety Travel Chairs, Inc.)

7. **Claim Definiteness.**   A patent's written description cannot include an undefined standard   75
for a component of the invention or the patent will be invalid for indefiniteness.
(Datamize, LLC v. Plumtree Software, Inc.)

Ex parte Fressola

N/A

27 U.S.P.Q. 2d 1608 (PTO 1993).

NATURE OF CASE: Appeal to the Board of an examiner's rejection of a claim.

FACT SUMMARY: Fressola used an omnibus claim, referring to specifications and drawings elsewhere in the application, and the Examiner rejected it.

> ## RULE OF LAW
> Claims in utility applications that define the invention entirely by reference to the specification and/or drawings can be rejected under 35 U.S.C. § 112 ¶2.

FACTS: Fressola sought a patent for a method and system of producing stereographic images of celestial objects. The invention required a digital computer under program control to be used with an input device and display device. It would take stereographic images and, using distance information, offset one of the two images on the display device. Fressola's Claim 42 read: "A system for the display of stereographic three-dimensional images of celestial objects as disclosed in the specification and drawings herein." The examiner rejected Claim 42 as failing to particularly point out and distinctly claim the subject matter. Fressola appealed.

ISSUE: Can claims in utility applications that define the invention entirely by reference to the specification and/or drawings be rejected under 35 U.S.C. § 112 ¶2?

HOLDING AND DECISION: (Serota, Chairman) Yes. Claims in utility applications that define the invention entirely by reference to the specification and/or drawings, so-called omnibus or formal claims can be rejected under 35 U.S.C. § 112 ¶2. Although historically these were allowed, the conversion from central definitions to peripheral definitions changed this. Modern claim interpretation requires that the claims particularly point out and distinctly claim the invention without reading in limitations from the specification. Claim 42 is indefinite and fails to particularly point out and distinctly claim what Fressola regards as his invention. The written description or specification is a different statutory requirement than the claim. The claims define the boundaries of the patent, and the metes and bounds of the invention must be clearly set forth in the claims so the public can evaluate what would infringe. Other points supporting a finding against the Fressola include the difficulty involved in interpreting such general phrases as "as disclosed in the drawings herein," and the fact that this application contains nineteen figures and 147 pages of specification. Affirmed.

▶ ANALYSIS

Each patent claim must be written as a single English sentence. This mandate was challenged in *Fressola v. Manbeck*, 36 U.S.P.Q.2d 1211 (D.D.C. 1995), as violating the Administrative Procedure Act. Fressola contended that the one-sentence requirement bore no reasonable relationship to the language of and policies of and policies of 35 U.S.C. § 112, which required that patent applications conclude with one or more claims particularly pointing out and distinctly claiming the invention. However, the court found there was no tension between the language of the 35 U.S.C. § 112 and the one-sentence rule. Of course, each patent may have multiple claims and claims can be asserted in combination against infringers in the United States' multiple claim system. Notably, the United Kingdom accepts omnibus claims.

■=■

Quicknotes

35 U.S.C. § 112 Requires that patent applicants disclose how to make and use the invention and include a written description.

■=■

Catalina Marketing International v. Coolsavings.com, Inc.

Inventor (P) v. Alleged infringer (D)

289 F.3d 801 (Fed. Cir. 2002).

NATURE OF CASE: Appeal of summary judgment of non-infringement.

FACT SUMMARY: Catalina (P) sued Coolsavings (D) for infringing on its patent for a coupon dispensing machine. Coolsavings (D) argued that there was no infringement, because Catalina's (P) patent application contained limiting language.

🏛 RULE OF LAW
If the preamble phrase does not define the invention, recite steps as important to the specification, or distinguish the invention from the prior art, then the preamble does not limit the claim's scope.

FACTS: Catalina's (P) patent claims a selection and distribution system for discount coupons. The system dispenses coupons to consumers at kiosk-like terminals located at predesignated sites such as consumer stores. During prosecution of the patent, the examiner twice rejected all of the claims as obvious. On its third attempt, Catalina (P) amended Claim 1 and submitted several declarations as to why it was nonobvious. The language pertaining to the location of the terminals was not amended; nor did Catalina (P) argue that the location of their terminals distinguished them from the location listed in another existing patent. Coolsavings (D) has a patent for a Web-based coupon system that monitors and controls the distribution of coupons from its website. Catalina (P) sued Coolsavings (D) alleging that Coolsavings' system infringed Catalina's (P) patent. The district court found on summary judgment that Coolsavings (D) did not infringe the claims of Catalina's (P) patent. The court construed the claim language "predesignated sites such as consumer stores" and held that Cool-savings (D) did not infringe, either literally or by equivalents, the construed language. Catalina (P) appealed.

ISSUE: Did the district court erroneously rely on non-limiting language in the preamble of Claim 1?

HOLDING AND DECISION: (Rader, J.) Yes. The district court erroneously relied on nonlimiting language in the preamble of Claim 1. The district court's analysis focused solely on the phrase "located at predesignated sites such as consumer stores." A preamble is nonlimiting where a patentee defines a structurally complex invention in the claim body and uses the preamble only to state a purpose or intended use for the invention. If the preamble phrase does not define the invention, recite steps as important to the specification, or distinguish the invention from the prior art, then the preamble does not limit the claim's scope. Preamble language merely extolling benefits of the claimed invention does not limit the claim scope without clear reliance on those benefits or features as patentability significant. In the present case, the claims, specification, and prosecution history of the patent demonstrate that the preamble phrase "located at predesignated sites such as consumer stores" is not a limitation of Claim 1. Catalina (P) did not rely on this phrase to define its invention nor is it essential to understand terms in the claim body. The specification does not make the location of the terminals an additional structure for the claimed terminals. Catalina (P) also did not rely on the preamble phrase to distinguish over a previous patent. Deletion of the location phrase also does not affect the structural definition or operation of the terminal itself. However, the use of this language in Claim 25 limits Claim 25, and therefore Coolsavings' (D) system does not literally satisfy the limitation of Claim 25. Affirmed in part and reversed in part.

▍ANALYSIS

The Jepson claim uses the preamble as a tool to recite structural claim limitations. Therefore, the preamble is admitted to be prior art unless it reflects the inventor's own work.

■=■

Atlantic Thermoplastics Co. Inc. v. Faytex Corp.

Shoe part manufacturer (P) v. Competitor (D

970 F.2d 834 (Fed. Cir. 1992).

NATURE OF CASE: Appeal from finding that infringement did not occur.

FACT SUMMARY: Faytex (D) sold innersoles identical to the ones covered in Atlantic's (P) patent, but created by a different process.

🏛 **RULE OF LAW**
Process terms in product-by-process claims limit infringement to products made by the claimed process only.

FACTS: Atlantic's (P) patent contained both a process and product-by-process claim for a shock absorbing shoe innersole. Faytex (D) distributed innersoles made by two different manufacturers, Surge and Sorbothane. Surge used the patented process, and there is no dispute that infringement occurred. However, Sorbothane's process was different, and the district court felt that it did not violate the process claim. Atlantic (P) argued that since the product was identical, it violated the claim in the patent. The district court found that the selling of Sorbothane-made soles did not violate Atlantic's (P) patent, and Atlantic (P) appealed. Faytex (D) cross-appealed from the award of lost profit damages for the sale of Surge and Sorbothane innersoles.

ISSUE: Do process terms in product-by-process claims limit infringement to products made by the claimed process only?

HOLDING AND DECISION: (Rader, J.) Yes. Process terms in product-by-process claims limit infringement to products made by the claimed process only. The Supreme Court has stated in a line of cases that an infringement inquiry into product claims with process limitations should focus on whether the accused product was made by the claimed process. A claim to a product by a specific process is not infringed by the same product made by a different process. The Patent and Trademark Office and the Court of Customs Patent Appeals recognize product-by-process claims, but state that they are the exception to the rule. As such, they limit claims to products created by the process. The lower court should rehear certain questions with the knowledge that product-by-process claims serve as limitations. The finding that Faytex (D) did not infringe in selling Sorbothane shoes is affirmed. Vacated in part, affirmed in part, and remanded.

▶ **ANALYSIS**

In some circumstances, a product cannot be defined other than by the process making it. Other times, an inventor claims a new product both by its structure and the process

making it. In these instances, the product-by-process claim specifies a product defined only by several process steps. The Federal Circuit in *Scripps Clinic & Research Fdn. v. Genentech, Inc.*, 927 F.2d 1565 (1991), seemed to state that although a product-by-process claim sets forth only one way of making a product, it covers all ways of making the product. In short, the product is covered as well. *Scripps* appears to be in direct contrast to the later *Atlantic Thermoplastics*. Notably, the *Scripps* court failed to address the Supreme Court precedent that the *Atlantic* court lengthily covered.

■■■

Quicknotes

35 U.S.C. § 112 Requires that patent applicants disclose how to make and use the invention and include a written description.

■■■

Al-Site Corp. v. VSI International, Inc.

Eyeglass manufacturer (P) v. Competitor (D)

174 F.3d 1308 (Fed. Cir. 1999).

NATURE OF CASE: Appeal from judgment in a patent infringement suit.

FACT SUMMARY: Magnivision (P) alleged that VSI (D) infringed its patent for technology for displaying eyeglasses on racks.

▥ RULE OF LAW
A product or process that performs an identical function to a patented invention may avoid literal infringement but still infringe under the doctrine of equivalents.

FACTS: Magnivision (P) sold non-prescription eyeglasses and obtained a patent for an eyeglass rack that allows consumers to try on glasses and return them to the rack without removing their display hangers. The hanger includes an extension that encircles the nose bridge of the glasses. VSI (D), a competitor, began using a similar rack that did not use this type of fastening means. Still, Magnivision (P) filed suit against VSI (D) for infringement. A district court jury found literal infringement on one claim and infringement under the doctrine of equivalents on other claims. However, both parties disagreed with the court's instructions on the scope of the patent claims and doctrine of equivalents.

ISSUE: May a product or process that performs an identical function to a patented invention avoid literal infringement but still infringe under the doctrine of equivalents?

HOLDING AND DECISION: (Rader, J.) Yes. A product or process that performs an identical function to a patented invention may avoid literal infringement but still infringe under the doctrine of equivalents. The test for determining equivalence under 35 U.S.C. § 112 is whether the differences between the structure in the accused device and any disclosed in the specification are insubstantial. Equivalents under § 112 narrows the application of broad literal claims, restricting a functional claim element to those means that are equivalent to the actual means shown in the specification. It thus informs the claim meaning for a literal infringement analysis. On the other hand, the doctrine of equivalents extends enforcement of claim terms beyond their literal reach in the event that there is equivalence between the elements of the accused product and the claimed elements of a patented invention. Although they have different purposes and administrations, a finding of a lack of literal infringement for lack of equivalent structure could preclude a finding of equivalence under the doctrine of equivalents. Therefore, if an accused product or process performs the identical function and yet avoids literal infringement for lack of a structural equivalent, it may avoid

infringing the same element under the doctrine. In the present case, the function of VSI's (D) eyeglass rack is identical to the function claimed in Magnivision's (P) patent and the jury found insubstantial structural differences. This finding is sufficient to support the inference that the jury found infringement even under the most restricted reading of the claims. Accordingly, any error in the trial court's determination of the claim scope did not affect the ultimate decision. Affirmed.

▸ ANALYSIS

In this case, the jury found that a chemical fastener used by VSI (D) was the equivalent of the mechanical fastener described in the Magnivision (P) patent claim. The decision allowed this rather broad interpretation by the jury. The mistake made by the trial court was in interpreting some of the claims as means-plus-function elements subject to § 112 limitations.

■▬■

Quicknotes

DOCTRINE OF EQUIVALENTS Rule that two inventions are the same for purposes of patent infringement if they achieve essentially the same result in the same manner despite trivial differences.

■▬■

Aristocrat Technologies Australia Pty Ltd. v. International Game Technology

Patent holder (P) v. Alleged infringer (D)

521 F.3d 1328 (Fed. Cir. 2008).

NATURE OF CASE: Appeal from district court ruling patent claims invalid for indefiniteness.

FACT SUMMARY: Aristocrat (P) patented a slot machine symbol combination invention and claimed IGT (D) infringed upon its patent. IGT (D) argued the patent claims were invalid for indefiniteness because Aristocrat (P) did not disclose the structure for producing the invention.

🏛 RULE OF LAW
35 U.S.C. § 112 paragraph 6 requires patent applicants for a means-plus-function limitation in a computer-implemented invention to disclose the algorithm that transforms the general purpose computer to a special purpose computer programmed to perform the claimed function.

FACTS: Aristocrat Technologies Australia Pty Ltd. (P) received patent '102 regarding an electronic slot machine allowing a player to select winning combinations of symbol positions. International Game Technology (D) manufactures and sells gaming machines, which Aristocrat (P) claimed infringed upon patent '102. Aristocrat (P) elected to claim pursuant to § 112 paragraph 6, which requires the disclosure of the structure used to implement the invention. The patent claims relate to the player's ability to define numerous different arrangements of symbols to increase potential winnings on the slot machine. The claim defined the structure as a general purpose, programmable microprocessor. The district court found that insufficient specificity and noted Aristocrat (P) failed to specify a specific algorithm to perform the invented function. The district court held all claims of patent '102 invalid for indefiniteness. Aristocrat (P) appealed.

ISSUE: Does 35 U.S.C. § 112 paragraph 6 require patent applicants for a means-plus-function limitation in a computer-implemented invention to disclose the algorithm that transforms the general purpose computer to a special purpose computer programmed to perform the claimed function?

HOLDING AND DECISION: (Bryson, J.) Yes. 35 U.S.C. § 112 paragraph 6 requires patent applicants for a means-plus-function limitation in a computer-implemented invention to disclose the algorithm that transforms the general purpose computer to a special purpose computer programmed to perform the claimed function. The issue here is the definiteness of the terms "game control means" or "control means" because Aristocrat (P) elected to claim pursuant to § 112 paragraph 6, which requires disclosure of the structure by which the invention is implemented. Here, the term is a means-plus-function term that must be specific or the entire claim is invalid for indefiniteness. Aristocrat (P) argued it disclosed a general purpose, programmable microprocessor that implemented the invention with "appropriate programming." The structure disclosed must be more than a general purpose computer or microprocessor or the application is attempting to patent pure function. Instructions for the algorithm or software used on the general purpose computer or microprocessor necessarily transform the general disclosure into a specific disclosure for a special purpose machine designed to carry out the particular function. Here, Aristocrat (P) admits the only structure description is that of a general purpose computer appropriately programmed. The specification does not include the type of programming that would result in the invention. The specification does not include an algorithm that would permit one skilled in the art to reproduce the invention although precedent states known mathematical equations need not be disclosed as they would be readily known by one skilled in the art. Aristocrat's (P) specification merely sets out examples that would result from the "appropriate programming." Aristocrat (P) argues that one skilled in the art could reproduce the invention, but that is confusing enablement requirement of § 112 paragraph 1 with the structure disclosure requirement of § 112 paragraph 6. The purpose of the structure disclosure is to limit the patent claim to the structure specified rather than prohibit all persons who use a general purpose computer from performing the claimed functions. Aristocrat (P) must at least specify the method used to transform the general purpose computer to a "special purpose computer programmed to perform the disclosed algorithm." Absent the necessary disclosure, Aristocrat's (P) claims are indefinite. Affirmed.

▶ ANALYSIS

The court did not require Aristocrat (P) to include detailed source code or a highly detailed disclosure of the algorithm, but required it to include some identifying algorithm. The court also did not require Aristocrat (P) to disclose readily known algorithms or basic mathematical equations. Aristocrat (P) merely needed to provide a middle-ground disclosure that identified the software element used to produce its invention. Patent applicants can avoid this

Continued on next page.

requirement by not identifying a software element in the claim or making a method claim instead of means-plus-function claim.

■━━■

Quicknotes

35 U.S.C. § 112 Requires that patent applicants disclose how to make and use the invention and include a written description.

■━━■

Orthokinetics, Inc. v. Safety Travel Chairs, Inc.

Wheelchair manufacturer (P) v. Competitor (D)

806 F.2d 1565 (Fed. Cir. 1986).

NATURE OF CASE: Appeal of grant of defense JNOV motion holding claims invalid.

FACT SUMMARY: Orthokinetics' (P) wheelchair patent's claims did not specify the sizes and types of automobiles which the wheelchair was to aid in entering and exiting.

RULE OF LAW
A claim is valid under 35 U.S.C. § 112 if those skilled in the art would understand what is claimed when the claim is read in light of the specification.

FACTS: Orthokinetics (P) received a patent for a collapsible pediatric wheelchair that facilitated the placing of wheelchair-bound persons in and out of automobiles. Orthokinetics (P) introduced the product in 1973, and in 1978, Safety Travel Chairs (STC) (D) began to sell similar chairs. Orthokinetics (P) sued for infringement. STC (D) argued that the patent was invalid since the claim language did not particularly point out and distinctly claim the invention. Specifically, the claim stated, "wherein said front leg portion is so dimensioned as to be insertable through the space between the doorframe of an automobile and one of the seats thereof." The jury found for Orthokinetics (P), but the district court granted STC's (D) motion for JNOV, holding claims invalid. The district court pointed out that an individual desiring to build a non infringing travel chair could not tell whether his chair would violate the patent until he had constructed a model and tested it on vehicles ranging from a Honda Civic to a Lincoln Continental. Orthokinetics (P) appealed.

ISSUE: Is a claim valid under 35 U.S.C. § 112 if those skilled in the art would understand what is claimed when the claim is read in light of the specification?

HOLDING AND DECISION: (Markey, C.J.) Yes. A claim is valid under 35 U.S.C. § 112 if those skilled in the art would understand what is claimed when the claim is read in light of the specification. In this case, the district court erred in requiring the claim "describe" the invention. That is the role of the disclosure portion of the specification, not the claims. Furthermore, the "full, clear, concise, and exact requirement" applies only to the disclosure portion, and not the claims. Orthokinetics' (P) witnesses, who were skilled in the art, testified that one skilled in the art could easily ascertain the dimensions, and the jury had the right to credit that testimony. Patent law does not require that all possible lengths corresponding to the spaces in hundreds of different automobiles be listed in the patent, let alone the claims. Reversed.

ANALYSIS

The *Orthokinetics* court stated that the term "so dimensioned" was as accurate as the subject matter permitted, automobiles being of various sizes. Use of words of degree, such as "about," "approximately," "close to," etc., are acceptable in certain applications, but can lead to rejection on definiteness in others. In *Andrew Corp. v. Gabriel Electronics*, 847 F.2d 819 (Fed. Cir. 1988), the court stated that such words were acceptable, "when serving reasonably to describe the claimed subject matter to those of skill in the field of the invention, and to distinguish the claimed subject matter from the prior art."

◼═◼

Quicknotes

35 U.S.C. § 112 Requires that patent applicants disclose how to make and use the invention and include a written description.

◼═◼

Datamize, LLC v. Plumtree Software, Inc.

Patent holder (P) v. Alleged infringer (D)

417 F.3d 1342 (Fed. Cir. 2005).

NATURE OF CASE: Appeal from summary judgment holding patent claims invalid for indefiniteness.

FACT SUMMARY: Datamize's (P) only independent claim in its '137 patent, requires the patented interface software to produce interface screens that are "aesthetically pleasing." Datamize (P) does not define "aesthetically pleasing" in its claims and the district court granted summary judgment to Plumtree (D) on the basis the claims were invalid for indefiniteness.

🏛 RULE OF LAW
A patent's written description cannot include an undefined standard for a component of the invention or the patent will be invalid for indefiniteness.

FACTS: Datamize, LLC (P) held the '137 patent related to a software program allowing a person to author user interfaces for electronic kiosks by selecting from limited options of interface screens. The only independent claim of the '137 patent requires the interface screens to be uniform and "aesthetically pleasing." Datamize (P) sued Plumtree Software, Inc. (D) for infringement of its '137 patent and Plumtree (D) moved for summary judgment on the grounds the claims of the '137 patent were invalid for indefiniteness. The district court granted Plumtree (D) summary judgment for the indefiniteness of the phrase "aesthetically pleasing." Datamize (P) appealed.

ISSUE: Can a patent's written description include an undefined standard for a component of the invention?

HOLDING AND DECISION: (Prost, J.) No. A patent's written description cannot include an undefined standard for a component of the invention or the patent will be invalid for indefiniteness. 35 U.S.C. § 112 paragraph 2 requires the patent specification's claims to distinctly claim the subject matter of the invention. The requirement is in place to differentiate the claim from prior art, and to inform the public of what is to be excluded from public domain in the future. Issued patents are entitled to an assumption of statutory validity unless the claim construction proves futile. The construction cannot be merely difficult but must prove fruitless with a showing of clear and convincing evidence of invalidity. Here, Datamize (P) correctly argues that "aesthetically pleasing" must be construed in the context of the '137 patent's only independent claim. The claim's written description, however, merely identifies components of the invention that must be aesthetically pleasing rather than a true definition for the phrase that would enable a person skilled in the art to know when the interface objectively has become aesthetically pleasing. Absent a definition, the requirement of "aesthetically pleasing" remains a purely subjective determination with no guidance on which colors are more pleasing than others, which button styles are more pleasing, and so forth. The district court appropriately awarded summary judgment to Plumtree (D) because the phrase "aesthetically pleasing" renders the entire '137 patent indefinite and thus invalid. Affirmed.

▶ ANALYSIS

Requiring the limitation "aesthetically pleasing" to be defined actually protects Datamize (P) as well as alleged infringers. The undefined term could be worked around by future patent applicants with the simple claim that their interface screens do not have to be "aesthetically pleasing" but consist of specific colors or styles. Objectives of the Patent Act are to protect the patent holders as well as accurately inform the public of the foreclosed invention's components. An undefined term in the patent specifications accomplishes neither.

■═■

Quicknotes

35 U.S.C. § 112 Requires that patent applicants disclose how to make and use the invention and include a written description.

■═■

Quick Reference Rules of Law

PAGE

1. **Continuing Application Practice.** A continuing application and the application on which   *78*
   it is based are considered part of the same transaction constituting one continuous
   application. (Transco Products Inc. v. Performance Contracting, Inc.)

2. **Inventorship.** (1) Testimony corroborated by sketches is sufficient to show clearly and   *79*
   convincingly co-invention. (2) A joint inventor as to even one claim enjoys a presumption of
   ownership in the entire patent. (Ethicon, Inc. v. United States Surgical Corp.)

3. **Inequitable Conduct: Intent.** Failure to withdraw a patent application when there is a suit   *81*
   for inequitable conduct does not alone constitute intent to deceive. (Kingsdown Medical
   Consultants, Ltd. v. Hollister Inc.)

4. **Inequitable Conduct: Materiality.** Data material to patentability must be disclosed with   *82*
   the specifications, or upon a showing of clear and convincing evidence of intent to
   deceive with regard to the material data, the patent will be unenforceable.
   (Aventis Pharma S.A. v. Amphastar Pharmaceuticals, Inc.)

5. **Double Patenting.** Analysis of double patenting requires determining whether the same   *84*
   invention is being claimed twice, and whether the claim is an obvious variation of an
   already disclosed invention. (In re Vogel)

6. **Double Patenting.** Patent claims may be similar but must be non-obvious and "patentably   *85*
   distinct" to earn patent protection. (In re Metoprolol Succinate Patent Litigation)

7. **Post-Grant Procedures: Reissue.** The failure to include narrower or dependent   *86*
   claims in a patent is not sufficient in itself to establish error warranting reissue under 35 U.S.C.
   § 251. (Hewlett-Packard Co. v. Bausch & Lomb, Inc.)

8. **International Prosecution.** Claims are entitled to the benefit of their foreign priority date   *87*
   under 35 U.S.C. § 119 only if the foreign priority application properly supports them
   as required by § 112. (In re Gosteli)

9. **International Prosecution.** The effective date of a United States patent used as a prior art   *88*
   reference is the date the application therefore was filed in the United States and not a
   foreign "convention" filing date to which the patentee of the reference is entitled by statute.
   (In re Hilmer)

Transco Products Inc. v. Performance Contracting, Inc.

[Parties not identified.]

38 F.3d 551, 32 U.S.P.Q.2d 1077 (Fed. Cir. 1994).

NATURE OF CASE: [Nature of case not stated in casebook excerpt.]

FACT SUMMARY: [Fact summary not stated in casebook excerpt.]

🏛 RULE OF LAW
A continuing application and the application on which it is based are considered part of the same transaction constituting one continuous application.

FACTS: [Facts not stated in casebook excerpt.]

ISSUE: Is a continuing application and the application on which it is based considered part of the same transaction constituting one continuous application?

HOLDING AND DECISION: [Judge not stated in casebook excerpt.] Yes. A continuing application and the application on which it is based are considered part of the same transaction constituting one continuous application. In addition to ordinary and provisional patent applications, an applicant may file a continuation, divisional, or continuation-in-part (CIP) application of a prior application. Continuation, divisional, and CIP applications are all continuing applications. A continuing application is one filed during the pendency of another application that contains at least part of the disclosure of the other application and names at least one inventor in common with that application. Continuation and divisional applications are based on the same disclosure as an earlier application, but they differ in what they claim. A continuation application claims the same invention claimed in the earlier application; divisional claims only one or more, but not all, of the independent inventions of the earlier application. A CIP application contains a portion or all of the disclosure of an earlier application together with added matter not present in that earlier application. The term "parent" is often used to refer to the immediately preceding application upon which a continuing application claims priority. The term "original" is used to refer to the first application in a chain of continuing applications.

▶ ANALYSIS

The excerpt of this case highlights the kinds of patent applications that may arise in addition to ordinary and provisional applications.

■■■

Ethicon, Inc. v. United States Surgical Corp.

Licensee (P) v. Alleged infringer (D)

135 F.3d 1456, 45 U.S.P.Q. 2d 1545 (Fed. Cir. 1998).

NATURE OF CASE: Appeal of judgment of non-infringement.

FACT SUMMARY: Ethicon (P) sued Surgical (D) for patent infringement. Surgical (D) defended by claiming that it had a license to use the patent from a co-inventor of the invention in the patent.

🏛 RULE OF LAW
(1) Testimony corroborated by sketches is sufficient to show clearly and convincingly co-invention.
(2) A joint inventor as to even one claim enjoys a presumption of ownership in the entire patent.

FACTS: Yoon (P) and his exclusive licensee, Ethicon (P), sued Surgical (D) for infringement of Yoon's (P) patent. The patent concerns trocars. A trocar is an essential tool for endoscopic surgery. It makes small incisions in the wall of a body cavity to admit endoscopic instruments. The patented trocar alleviates the danger of damage to internal organs by equipping the trocar with a blunt, spring-loaded rod that springs forward to precede the blade or springs back into a protective sheath and shields against injury. The patent also teaches the use of an electronic sensor in the end of the blade to signal to the surgeon at the moment of puncture. Choi (D), an electronics technician, worked without pay with Yoon (P), a medical doctor and inventor of numerous patented devices for endoscopic surgery, on a project for safety trocars. Their relationship ended after eighteen months of collaboration. That same year, Yoon (P) filed an application for a patent for the trocar, naming himself as the sole inventor, without Choi's (D) knowledge. Ethicon (P) filed suit against Surgical (D) for patent infringement. Choi (D) intervened and claimed to be an omitted co-inventor of the patent and to have granted Surgical (D) a retroactive license under the patent. The district court found Choi (D) to be an omitted co-inventor and granted Surgical's (D) motion to dismiss. Ethicon (P) appealed.

ISSUE:
(1) Did Choi (D) present sufficient evidence with sufficient corroboration to show co-invention of Claims 33 and 47 clearly and convincingly?
(2) Do the terms of the license agreement limit it to only that part of the invention to which Choi (D) contributed or to the entire part?

HOLDING AND DECISION: (Rader, J.)
(1) Yes. Choi (D) presented sufficient evidence with sufficient corroboration to show co-invention of Claims 33 and 47 clearly and convincingly. Each joint inventor must contribute to the conception of the invention. Each needs to perform only part of the task that produces the invention. Therefore, a contribution to one claim is sufficient to be considered a co-inventor. In the present case, Choi (D) conceived part of the invention recited in Claim 33. Figures 18 and 19 of the patent illustrate an embodiment of Claim 33. Choi (D) conceived of and contributed to two features contained in the embodiment, locating the blunt probe in the shaft and allowing it to pass through an aperture on the blade surface, and, thus, contributed to the subject matter of Claim 33. Claim 33 includes the elements that Choi (D) contributed. His contribution is evidenced by his testimony that it was his idea to extend the blunt probe through an aperture in the trocar blade. To corroborate his testimony, he produced a series of sketches he created while working with Yoon (P). Based on many circumstantial factors, such as Choi's (D) background in electronics and expert testimony that some of the sketches dealt with sophisticated concepts that only an electrical engineer or technician would understand, it is evident that Choi (D) was presenting ideas to Yoon (P) and not vice versa. Furthermore, Choi (D) also contributed to the conception of the subject matter of Claim 47. Figures 34–36 illustrate the invention in Claim 47. Choi (D) invented the rod detaining means disclosed in the specification. Oral testimony of the parties and Choi's (D) sketches evidence this.

(2) No. The terms of the license agreement do not limit it to only that part of the invention to which Choi (D) contributed, but rather Choi (D) enjoys a presumption of ownership in the entire part. A joint inventor as to even one claim enjoys a presumption of ownership in the entire patent. Yoon (P) must therefore share with Choi (D) ownership of all the claims, even those which he invented by himself. Thus, Choi (D) had the right to license rights in the entire patent. Choi (D) is a co-inventor and thus a joint-owner of the patent. He did not consent to a suit against Surgical (D). Therefore, the motion to dismiss is valid. Affirmed.

DISSENT: (Newman, J.) Whether or not Choi (D) made an inventive contribution to two of the 55 claims of the patent, he is not a joint owner of the other 53 claims. The law of joint invention does not so require, because it has nothing to do with patent ownership, but rather is concerned with the technical problems that arise with team research. The law of joint invention permits persons to be named on the patent document, whether as minor

Continued on next page.

contributors to a subordinate embodiment or as full part-
ners in the creation and development of the invention. It
does not automatically convey ownership of the entire
patent to everyone who could be named as an inventor,
whatever the contribution. Furthermore, the law of property does not require Choi (D) to be a joint owner of the
other 53 claims because all persons, however minor their
contributions, are not to be treated as full owners of the
entire property as a matter of law.

▶ *ANALYSIS*

Equity among joint owners seems to be disregarded by the
majority.

■══■

Quicknotes

35 U.S.C. § 116   Allows for joint inventors, even though the
inventors did not work together or make equal contributions to the invention.

■══■

Kingsdown Medical Consultants, Ltd. v. Hollister Inc.

Medical products manufacturer (P) v. Competitor (D)

863 F.2d 867 (Fed. Cir. 1988).

NATURE OF CASE: Appeal from judgment finding patent unenforceable.

FACT SUMMARY: Kingsdown (P) erroneously included a claim in its continuation application that had been rejected as indefinite in its original application. The included claim prevented Hollister (D) from marketing Hollister's (D) product and Hollister (D) claimed inequitable conduct as a defense to Kingsdown's (P) subsequent patent infringement case.

🏛 RULE OF LAW
Failure to withdraw a patent application when there is a suit for inequitable conduct does not alone constitute intent to deceive.

FACTS: Kingsdown (P) erroneously included a claim in its continuation application that had been rejected in the initial patent application. The claim was proper subject matter but had been rejected as indefinite. Kingsdown (P) included the claim in the application after viewing the Hollister (D) device in order to prevent him from marketing the product. Hollister (D) claimed inequitable conduct. Kingsdown's (P) attorney became aware of the mistake when it was pointed out by Hollister (D). Experts on each side testified that there was no evidence of deceitful intent. The district court found the patent unenforceable based on Kingsdown's (P) inequitable conduct. Kingsdown (P) appealed.

ISSUE: Does failure to withdraw a patent application when there is a suit for inequitable conduct alone constitute intent to deceive?

HOLDING AND DECISION: (Markey, C.J.) No. Failure to withdraw a patent application when there is a suit for inequitable conduct does not alone constitute intent to deceive. The district court's finding of intent must be upheld unless it is clearly erroneous. The district court determined that Kingsdown (P) intended to deceive based on the inclusion of an invalid claim in the continuation application. Although the inclusion of the claim constitutes negligence, it does not rise to the level of gross negligence necessary to find intent to deceive. There is nothing illegal in amending an application to exclude a competitor's product. Hollister's (D) contention that Kingsdown's (P) failure to withdraw the application constitutes bad faith in and of itself is erroneous. The court should not promulgate a rule dissuading patentees from defending against claims, and the courts should not adopt a rule encouraging inequitable conduct charges, as there are already far too many of these claims. The district court's finding of deceitful intent was clearly erroneous. Reversed and remanded.

▶ ANALYSIS

Notwithstanding its conclusion, the court reaffirmed the rule that a patent application is rendered unenforceable upon a finding of inequitable conduct during the prosecution of the patent. The ultimate question of whether inequitable conduct has occurred is equitable in nature. As an equitable issue, it is committed to the discretion of the trial court and therefore is reviewed under an abuse of discretion standard.

■═■

Quicknotes

35 U.S.C. § 112 Requires that patent applicants disclose how to make and use the invention and include a written description.

EQUITABLE Just; fair.

■═■

Aventis Pharma S.A. v. Amphastar Pharmaceuticals, Inc.

Patent holder (P) v. Alleged infringer (D)

525 F.3d 1334 (Fed. Cir. 2008).

NATURE OF CASE: Second appeal from finding of patent unenforceability due to inequitable conduct and intent to deceive.

FACT SUMMARY: Aventis (P) held a patent on a drug that it claimed had a significant improvement in half-life over a nearly identical drug covered by a European patent. Aventis (P) did not disclose that its half-life data arose from comparisons of the drug at different doses. When compared at the same dose, the half-life difference was insignificant. The district court held Aventis (P) had intent to deceive by failing to disclose the material information of the half-life dose comparisons and thus the issued patent was unenforceable for inequitable conduct.

🏛 RULE OF LAW
Data material to patentability must be disclosed with the specifications, or upon a showing of clear and convincing evidence of intent to deceive with regard to the material data, the patent will be unenforceable.

FACTS: Aventis Pharma S.A. (P) held the '618 patent, which was surrendered when Aventis (P) received the '743 patent. Both patents related to a composition comprising low molecular weight heparins. The drugs, marketed as Lovenox in the United States and Clexane in Europe, work to prevent blood clotting and minimize the possibility of hemorrhaging, particularly during high-risk surgery. The claimed advantage of the patented drugs is that they exhibit a longer half-life compared to heparin. Initially, the patent claims were rejected based on obviousness and anticipation because the prior art, particularly European Patent '144, taught a nearly identical product. Aventis (P) disputed the rejections on the basis the half-life of the new drugs was significantly longer, evidencing a difference in structure. Aventis (P) continued to rely on the difference in half-life in its subsequent appeals until the patent was allowed. Aventis (P) later sued Amphastar Pharmaceuticals, Inc. (D) for patent infringement in making and marketing generic versions of the drugs. In considering Amphastar's (D) argument that the patent was invalid, the district court held the half-life improvement to be material to patentability because that was the reason the examiner finally issued the patent. The district court found Aventis (P) had intent to deceive the examiner because Aventis (P) set forth no credible explanation for its reliance on an allegedly improved half-life when it had compared half-life at different doses but did not disclose this dosage information. When compared at the same doses, the half-life was nominally the same. The district court granted summary judgment to Amphastar (D) and declared the patent unenforceable for inequitable conduct, which was intent to deceive. Aventis

(P) appealed to this court on the grounds the dose information was not material to the patentability or the examiner would have requested it when she was presented with half-life data. Aventis (P) also claimed its expert, Dr. Andre Uzan, informed the examiner of the difference in dose when his declaration stated "it enables the same effect to be achieved with lower dosages." This court held Dr. Uzan's statement did not fully inform the examiner and the withholding of the dose information was a failure to disclose material information. The dose information was material to the issue of patentability. This court remanded, however, for the district court to determine intent to deceive if the different dose comparison was reasonable within the field and thus failure to disclose was inadvertent. On remand, the district court held a bench trial on the limited issue of intent to deceive and again found Aventis (P) had intent to deceive the examiner. Aventis (P) appealed again.

ISSUE: Must data material to patentability be disclosed with the specifications, or upon a showing of clear and convincing evidence of intent to deceive with regard to the material data, will the patent be unenforceable?

HOLDING AND DECISION: (Prost, J.) Yes. Data material to patentability must be disclosed with the specifications, or upon a showing of clear and convincing evidence of intent to deceive with regard to the material data, the patent will be unenforceable. Inequitable conduct's element of intent to deceive is satisfied by all the evidence, including evidence of good faith, indicating sufficient culpability requiring a finding of intent to deceive. This intent is often derived from a review of the surrounding facts and circumstances. On this second appeal, Aventis (P) argues Dr. Uzan compared the half-life at different doses to show a difference in property to address the obviousness rejection rather than a difference in composition to address the anticipation rejection. The dose comparison can differ to demonstrate a difference in property because it is more appropriate to use the clinically relevant dose of each compound. Aventis (P) therefore argues it was error for the district court to consider compositional differences as central to patentability and further error to find that Dr. Uzan's comparisons were intended to show compositional differences. Nothing indicates, however, the district court considered only the anticipation rejection when the court was clearly aware of the additional obviousness rejection and considered the half-life comparisons for both rejections. The court may have been mistaken in the believing anticipation remained as a rejection when the examiner ultimately withdrew that basis

Continued on next page.

for rejection, but the mistake was not critical because the court already found intent to deceive based on the specification example and Dr. Uzan's earlier declarations containing misleading dose information. Dr. Uzan's failure to disclose the dose information was not inadvertent, included in the example, or excused by his intent to disclose the information even though he failed to do so. Affirmed.

DISSENT: (Rader, J.) A finding of inequitable conduct is typically restricted to the most egregious cases and the evidence here does not rise to the level of clear and convincing evidence of intent to deceive. Inequitable conduct claims have become a litigation tactic and has resulted in a merging of intent to deceive with materiality of undisclosed information instead of focusing on the two prongs separately. Dr. Uzan should have disclosed the dose information as it was material to patentability, but the record hardly demonstrates intent to deceive. It was Dr. Uzan himself who revealed the error and the half-life data were apparently not relevant for patentability as the patent later reissued without the offending example. The finding of inequitable conduct should be reversed.

▌ANALYSIS

The majority inferred the intent to deceive element from Dr. Uzan's failure to disclose the material comparison data rather than requiring an explicit finding that Dr. Uzan intended to deceive the patent office. The dissent wished to revert back to a clearer delineation between the materiality of the data withheld and the actual demonstration of intent to deceive because of the increase in using inequitable conduct as a defense. Congress responded in part to the concerns addressed in the dissent by introducing the Patent Reform Act of 2007 which would make the defense of inequitable conduct more difficult to employ as a litigation tactic.

■━■

Quicknotes

CULPA Fault.

EQUITABLE Just; fair.

■━■

In re Vogel

N/A

422 F.2d 438, 164 U.S.P.Q. 619 (C.C.P.A. 1970).

NATURE OF CASE: Appeal from decision rejecting three claims on grounds of double patenting.

FACT SUMMARY: The Patent Office Board of Appeals ruled that Vogel's meat and beef processing claims double patented his earlier pork patent.

🏛 RULE OF LAW
Analysis of double patenting requires determining whether the same invention is being claimed twice, and whether the claim is an obvious variation of an already disclosed invention.

FACTS: Vogel filed a patent on January 16, 1964 of which three of its claims were rejected. Two claims, 7 and 10, were directed at a process of packaging meat generally. The third, Claim 11, was directed at a similar process for beef specifically. Vogel had already filed for a patent that was issued on March 10, 1964 and which claimed a similar method directed at pork. The Board rejected Vogel's claims as double patenting in light of his pork patent and in view of a reference patent, Ellies. Ellies taught the use of meat packaging material having the same oxygen permeability listed in Vogel's claims. Vogel's pork claim made no reference to the oxygen permeability of the packaging material, but the rejected claims suggested the use of the Ellies material in its process. Vogel appealed.

ISSUE: Does analysis of double patenting require determining whether the same invention is being claimed twice, and whether the claim is an obvious variation of an already disclosed invention?

HOLDING AND DECISION: (Lane, J.) Yes. Analysis of double patenting requires that first one ask if the same invention is being claimed twice, and if not, then is the claim an obvious variation of an already disclosed invention. As to the first test, same invention means identical subject matter. A good, objective test for this is whether one of the claims could be literally infringed without literally infringing the other. If it could, the claims are not to the same invention. The patent claims are to pork, but the application's claims are to meat and beef. Beef is not pork. As for the meat claims, they could be infringed by many processes that would not infringe the pork claims. The second question is: Does any claim in the application define merely an obvious variation of an invention disclosed and claimed in the patent? As to the beef claim, it is not an obvious variation, for there is no evidence that the spoliation characteristics of the two meats are similar. However, the meat claims are obvious variations. "Meat" reads literally on pork, and the only difference in the claims is the

mention of oxygen permeability ratios of the material. These can be found in the prior art of Ellies. Affirmed as to Claims 7 and 10; reversed as to Claim 11.

▶ ANALYSIS

Straight double patenting as analyzed in the first step of *Vogel* is supported by 35 U.S.C. § 101. The second step of *Vogel*'s test refers to obviousness-type double patenting, and it is a judicially created doctrine with a public policy rationale. The purpose is to outlaw patent term extensions even though there is no clear statutory basis. It allows the public to practice obvious variations of the invention after expiration of the patent. However, applicants may file terminal disclaimers that clarify the reach of the patent but do not extend the patent date. The *Vogel* court suggested that Vogel do this for his rejected claims.

■■■

Quicknotes

35 U.S.C. § 101 Whoever invents a new and useful process, machine or composition of matter may obtain a patent.

35 U.S.C. § 103 Denies patent if the invention of the subject matter would have been obvious to a person based on prior inventions.

■■■

In re Metoprolol Succinate Patent Litigation

Patent holders (P) v. Alleged infringers (D)

494 F.3d 1011 (Fed. Cir. 2007).

NATURE OF CASE: Appeal from finding of patent invalidity and grant of summary judgment to defendants.

FACT SUMMARY: Two pharmaceutical manufacturers patented extended release compounds with metoprolol succinate as an active ingredient. One of the manufacturers sued several generic manufacturers for patent infringement and the court held that manufacturer's patent invalid based on double-patenting.

> 🏛 **RULE OF LAW**
> Patent claims may be similar but must be non-obvious and "patentably distinct" to earn patent protection.

FACTS: Plaintiffs AstraZeneca AB, Aktiebolaget Hassle, and AstraZeneca L.P. (collectively "Astra") manufacture and market Toprol-XL, which is an extended release form of metoprolol succinate. An Astra employee in Sweden synthesized metoprolol succinate in 1971. In 1982, another Astra employee in Sweden synthesized metoprolol succinate, perhaps at the direction of two other employees, Appelgren and Eskilsson. In 1983, Appelgren and Eskilsson left Astra and joined Lejus Medical AB. Lejus filed a Swedish patent application for an extended release form of metoprolol succinate and listed Appelgren and Eskilsson as inventors. In 1985, Lejus filed for a U.S. patent, claiming priority from the Swedish patent. That same year, Astra commenced a transfer of ownership action on the Swedish patent based on their employee being the inventor in 1971. Lejus and Astra settled the ownership dispute with the settlement agreement terms assigning divided claims to Astra. Those claims included metoprolol succinate and pharmaceutical compounds in which metoprolol succinate was the active substance. Lejus retained the remaining claims of the '197 patent application. The Astra '897 Application was a continuation of the Lejus '197 Application and the continuation of the '897 Application resulted in the '154 Patent, which claimed only "Metoprolol succinate." At the same time, Lejus received the '318 Patent, which included a claim in which metoprolol succinate was an active ingredient for an extended release compound. Astra filed multiple suits in various district courts asserting that several defendants planned to manufacture and market generic versions of Toprol-XL and thus infringed Astra's patents. The defendants filed for summary judgment on the basis Astra's '154 Patent was invalid for double-patenting. The district court granted summary judgment to defendants and found '154 Patent invalid for double-patenting over the Lejus '318 Patent.

ISSUE: Must patent claims, although similar, be non-obvious and "patentably distinct" to earn patent protection?

HOLDING AND DECISION: (Gajarsa, J.) Yes. Patent claims may be similar but must be non-obvious and "patentably distinct" to earn patent protection. The judicially created doctrine of obviousness-type double patenting avoids extending patent protection to two inventions that may not be the "same" invention but are so alike as to be patentably indistinct. The '318 Patent claims a compound that releases metoprolol succinate. The '154 Patent claims the composition of metoprolol succinate itself. The district court found the '318 Patent to be the genus of the species claimed by the '154 Patent. The species claim came first, so the district court invalidated the '154 Patent claim for double-patenting as it was not patentably distinct. The claim comparison is correct so the issue becomes whether the claims were patentably distinct. Astra argues the genus/species relationship is inaccurate because the appropriate relationship is element/combination. This court has previously held that such semantics are irrelevant, so that argument fails. Astra next relies on three prior cases, but those cases are distinguishable or overcome by later case law. *In re Emert*, 124 F.3d 1458 (Fed. Cir. 1997), requires this court to affirm the invalidity of the '154 Patent. *Emert* invalidated a patent for double-patenting on the basis that patenting the element is obvious after reviewing a patent of a compound containing the element. Similarly here, the patent claim for metoprolol succinate is obvious from the patent on the delivery of metoprolol succinate and thus a double-patent wrongly issued. Affirmed in part.

DISSENT-IN-PART: (Schall, J.) The '154 Patent claim is patentably distinct from the '318 Patent claim. The compound metoprolol succinate has not been claimed twice. The '318 Patent claims a compound which may include the element, but the compound as a whole is what is claimed. The '154 Patent does not claim any type of compound at all. *Emert* does not control in this case because that case involved two claims to an oil-soluble dispersant. The district court decision should be reversed.

> ▶ *ANALYSIS*
>
> The double-patenting issue can be avoided by filing a "terminal disclaimer." The terminal disclaimer is appropriate when one inventor holds more than one patent on the same invention. The disclaimer states the later patent will expire at the same time as the first and is only enforceable if all patents are commonly owned. Here, however, the ownership dispute prevented such a filing and resulted in the invalidity of the patent.

■━■

Hewlett-Packard Co. v. Bausch & Lomb, Inc.

Paper plotter manufacturer (P) v. Competitor (D)

882 F.2d 1556, 11 U.S.P.Q.2d 1750 (Fed. Cir. 1989).

NATURE OF CASE: Appeal from final judgment holding claims added during reissue invalid.

FACT SUMMARY: Bausch & Lomb (D) submitted false affidavits declaring errors in an acquired patent in order to narrow the claims for an upcoming infringement action.

🏛 RULE OF LAW
The failure to include narrower or dependent claims in a patent is not sufficient in itself to establish error warranting reissue under 35 U.S.C. § 251.

FACTS: Yeiser invented an X-Y plotter described in the '950 patent, which was issued in 1973. The invention was commercialized briefly. In 1980 or 1981, Hewlett-Packard (HP) (P) introduced a moving paper X-Y plotter to great success. Bausch & Lomb (B&L) (D), a HP (P) competitor, discovered the '950 patent and bought it from the then-assignee for $30,000. B&L (D) was concerned that Claim 1, which arguably covers the HP (P) plotter, was overly broad, so B&L (D) filed a reissue application for three new claims, 10-12, that were narrower. The examiner rejected the claims as failing to specify an error warranting reissue or how the error occurred. B&L (D) overcame this rejection by submitting two affidavits from the original patent prosecutor, Fleming, stating that his claim was incorrect because he was unable to examine the invention or speak with the inventor for more than a brief period of time. Both affidavits were later found to be factually untrue. HP (P) then filed a declaratory judgment action asserting invalidity of all claims of the '684 patent containing the reissue application. B&L (D) counterclaimed, charging HP (P) with infringement, but the district court held the reissued claims invalid, because B&L (D) had filed blatantly inaccurate affidavits, and without the affidavits, B&L (D) failed to satisfy § 251. B&L (D) appealed.

ISSUE: Is the failure to include narrower or dependent claims in a patent sufficient in itself to establish error warranting reissue under 35 U.S.C. § 251?

HOLDING AND DECISION: (Nies, J.) No. The failure to include narrower or dependent claims in a patent is not sufficient in itself to establish error warranting reissue under 35 U.S.C. § 251. Section 251 requires two parts: (1) error in the patent and (2) error in conduct. The practice of allowing reissue for the purpose of including narrower claims as a hedge against possible invalidation of the broad claim is tacitly approved of in precedent. This would reach error in the patent, but it need not be decided since B&L (D) clearly did not meet the second part. The only evidence of error in conduct was in the Fleming affidavits, and these were shown to be factually untrue. Absent these, there was no error in conduct, and the reissue claims fail. However, it does not follow that Claims 1 to 9 must be held invalid merely because the reissue claims were. The original claims stand. Affirmed in part; vacated in part.

▶ ANALYSIS

Since it is quite difficult to determine what exactly constitutes error, and practitioners require certainty, there is a movement to abolish the error requirement. The 1992 Advisory Commission suggested that inconsistent interpretations of "error" by the courts mandated abolishment. The Advisory Commission pointed out the only public policy involved in limiting reissues to errors occurs in the case of deceptive intent. See the advisory commission on patent law reform, a report to the Secretary of Commerce 129 (1992).

■══■

Quicknotes

35 U.S.C. § 251 Allows for reissue of a patent when a patent is inoperative due to error.

■══■

In re Gosteli

N/A

872 F.2d 1008 (Fed. Cir. 1989).

NATURE OF CASE: Appeal from rejection of three claims in a patent application.

FACT SUMMARY: Gosteli attempted to antedate his U.S. patent filing date to the filing of his Luxembourg patent.

🏛 RULE OF LAW
Claims are entitled to the benefit of their foreign priority date under 35 U.S.C. § 119 only if the foreign priority application properly supports them as required by § 112.

FACTS: Gosteli's patent application for several compounds and subgenus chemical species used in the preparation of antibiotics was rejected as anticipated by the Menard patent. Gosteli's patent application was filed on May 4, 1978, and Menard's effective date was December 14, 1977. However, Gosteli had applied for a Luxembourg patent on May 9, 1977, and attempted to antedate his U.S. patent application to this filing date, thereby rendering Menard ineffective as a reference. The Luxembourg patent did not provide a written description of the entire subject matter of the claims claimed in the U.S. patent application, so the PTO Board of Patent Appeals rejected it as not covering the "same invention." Gosteli appealed.

ISSUE: Are claims entitled to the benefit of their foreign priority date under 35 U.S.C. § 119 only if the foreign priority application properly supports them as required by § 112?

HOLDING AND DECISION: (Bissell, J.) Yes. Claims are entitled to the benefit of their foreign priority date under 35 U.S.C. § 119 only if the foreign priority application properly supports them as required by § 112. The description in the foreign patent need not describe the subject matter exactly, but it must allow persons skilled in the ordinary art to recognize what Gosteli invented. The PTO Board has pointed out numerous differences, and Gosteli does not dispute that additional subject matter is present in his U.S. application. Therefore, the PTO Board's decision was not clearly erroneous. Gosteli's argument that the foreign patent establishes a constructive reduction to practice in this country under § 131 also fails, for he does not show any evidence of activity in this country. Affirmed.

▶ ANALYSIS

Gosteli's rejected claims concerned an expanded chemical genus, or Markush group. The *Gosteli* court declared that Gosteli's Luxembourg patent must literally describe these Markush groups. This may have been difficult given the format of Markush filing, which has been described as "provincial." Nevertheless, patent attorneys should always include claims that mimic earlier filed claims in order to antedate the priority of the later filed claim

■■■

Quicknotes

35 U.S.C. § 102(e) Disallows patents if the invention is subject of another patent or application.

■■■

In re Hilmer

N/A

359 F.2d 859 (C.C.P.A. 1966).

NATURE OF CASE: Appeal from a decision affirming a rejection of patent claims.

FACT SUMMARY: The decision affirming a rejection of Hilmer's patent claims involved a determination that a United States patent used as a prior art reference is considered effective as of its foreign "convention" filing date and not the date that the United States patent application was filed.

🏛 RULE OF LAW
The effective date of a United States patent used as a prior art reference is the date the application therefore was filed in the United States and not a foreign "convention" filing date to which the patentee of the reference is entitled by statute.

FACTS: Hilmer's patent claims were rejected on the ground that the invention was disclosed in an existing United States patent. On appeal, the primary question which arose was whether the effective date of a reference patent is the date that the United States application was filed or a foreign "convention" filing date to which the patentee is entitled by statute. The Patent Office Board of Appeals held that the effective date was the foreign "convention" filing date and affirmed the decision rejecting Hilmer's claims.

ISSUE: Is the effective date of a United States patent used as a prior art reference the date that the United States application therefore was filed and not a foreign "convention" filing date?

HOLDING AND DECISION: (Rich, J.) Yes. When a United States patent is to be used as a prior art reference, its effective date is the date the United States application therefore was filed and not a foreign "convention" filing date to which the patentee of the reference is entitled by statute. The *Milburn* case accorded a United States patent effect as a reference as of its United Slates filing date, but it did not involve a foreign "convention" filing date. Nonetheless, that doctrine was codified in Section 102(e) of the 1952 Patent Act and should be considered in deciding this case. Over and above this, the Patent Office pursued a uniform policy for over 26 years which regarded the effective date of a United States reference patent as the date the United States application was filed. For these reasons, the holding of the Board was improper. Reversed and remanded.

▶ ANALYSIS

Section 102(a) of the Patent Act provides that a patent will not issue where the invention was patented in this or any foreign country before the invention thereof by the applicant for patent. Use of the words "in this country" seems to indicate that the United States filing date would be the one used and not a foreign "convention" date to which the United States patentee was entitled.

■≡■

Quicknotes

■≡■

Infringement

Quick Reference Rules of Law

PAGE

1. **Infringement.** Claim interpretation is required to determine infringement and such interpretation arises from a review of the claim language, specification, drawings, and file wrapper. (Autogiro Co. of America v. United States) — 91

2. **Literal Infringement.** The construction of a patent, including terms of art within its claim, is a matter to be decided by the court rather than a jury. (Markman v. Westview Instruments, Inc.) — 92

3. **Literal Infringement.** Claim construction is solely a question of law subject to de novo review. (Cybor Corp. v. FAS Technologies, Inc.) — 93

4. **Literal Infringement.** A term in a claim of a patented invention should not be restricted to corresponding structures disclosed in the specification, or their equivalents, where the term's plain meaning can be given effect without such limitation. (Phillips v. AWH Corporation) — 94

5. **Literal Infringement.** A patentee later cannot argue infringement when the allegedly infringing invention claim unambiguously was disavowed during prosecution. (Computer Docking Station Corp. v. Dell, Inc.) — 96

6. **The Doctrine of Equivalents or Non-Textual Infringement.** The doctrine of equivalents is applied to mechanical or chemical equivalents in compositions or devices. (Graver Tank v. Linde Air Products Co.) — 97

7. **The Doctrine of Equivalents or Non-Textual Infringement.** The determination of equivalence should be applied as an objective inquiry on each individual element of the claim, rather than the process as a whole. (Warner-Jenkinson Company v. Hilton Davis Chemical Co.) — 98

8. **Limitations on the Doctrine of Equivalents: The "All Elements" Rule.** If an accused device has the equivalent to another patent's claim limitation somewhere in the device, then it is an infringing device. (Corning Glass Works v. Sumitomo Electric USA, Inc.) — 99

9. **Limitations on the Doctrine of Equivalents: Prosecution History Estoppel.** A narrowing amendment made to satisfy any requirement of the Patent Act may give rise to estoppel. Estoppel does not, however, bar the patentee from asserting infringement against any equivalent to the narrowed element. The patentee bears the burden of showing that the amendment does not surrender the particular equivalent in question. (Festo Corp. v. Shoketsu Kinzoku Kogyo Kabushiki Co., Ltd.) — 100

10. **Limitations on the Doctrine of Equivalents: The Dedication Doctrine.** A patentee cannot apply the doctrine of equivalents to cover unclaimed subject matter disclosed in the specification. (Johnson & Johnston Associates Inc. v. R.E. Service Co., Inc.) — 102

11. Limitations on the Doctrine of Equivalents: Prior Art Limitations. If the scope of equivalency necessary to find infringement would cover prior art, there can be no infringement. (Wilson Sporting Goods Co. v. David Geoffrey & Associates) *103*

12. Indirect Infringement. Contributory infringement requires proof of a direct nexus to a specific act of direct infringement and inducement to infringe requires knowledge and specific intent that one's actions will induce actual infringement. (DSU Medical Corporation v. JMS Company, Ltd.) *104*

13. Indirect Infringement. For used, refurbished, single-use cameras whose first sale was in the United States with a patentee's authorization, and for which the alleged violators activities were limited to the steps of removing the cardboard cover, cutting open the plastic casing, inserting new film and a container to receive the film, replacing the winding wheel for certain cameras, replacing the battery for flash cameras, resetting the counter, resealing the outer case, and adding a new cardboard cover; the totality of these procedures are permissible repair and not prohibited reconstruction. (Jazz Photo Corp. v. International Trade Comm.) *106*

14. Infringement Analyses Overseas: Europe. Claim language should be interpreted by determining what the ordinary person skilled in the art understands the claim to cover, which may involve a literal reading of the claim language or application of the drawings and description. (Kirin-Amgen Inc. and Others v. Hoechst Marion Roussel Limited and Others) *107*

15. Infringement Analyses Overseas: Europe. An accused product that is somewhat different from a patented product will be said to be equivalent with the patented product if the differing elements are not essential; if when the differing elements are interchanged the objective of the patented invention can be achieved; if by interchanging an artisan could have arrived at the accused product; if the accused product could not have easily been conceived by an artisan at the time of manufacture of the patent; and if the accused was not intentionally excluded from the scope of the claim during patent prosecution. (Tsubakimoto Seiko Co. Ltd. v. Thk K.K.) *108*

Autogiro Co. of America v. United States

[Parties not identified.]

384 F.2d 391 (Ct of Cl. 1967).

NATURE OF CASE: [Nature of Case not stated in casebook excerpt.]

FACT SUMMARY: [Fact Summary not stated in casebook excerpt.]

🏛 RULE OF LAW
Claim interpretation is required to determine infringement and such interpretation arises from a review of the claim language, specification, drawings, and file wrapper.

FACTS: [Facts not stated in casebook excerpt.]

ISSUE: Is claim interpretation required to determine infringement?

HOLDING AND DECISION: [Judge not stated in casebook excerpt.] Yes. Claim interpretation is required to determine infringement and such interpretation arises from a review of the claim language, specification, drawings, and file wrapper. The claims provide the formal patent definition. Courts may be tempted to confine themselves to the language of the claim, but a clear and unambiguous claim is a rare occurrence. Words exist to describe a thing rather than things being invented to support a word. The result is that words are often lagging behind invention and the inventor becomes the lexicographer. Courts might assume a word means what it has always meant when the inventor is using that word in an entirely new way. Thus courts should look at the entirety of the patent claim, including the specification, drawings, and file wrapper. [Decision not included in the casebook.]

▶ ANALYSIS

Autogiro, as excerpted, merely is dicta on claim interpretation. The warning to courts is to avoid complacency. Inventors, who typically are not wordsmiths, trying to put a machine or process into words may be left with less-than-ideal language that a court easily could misconstrue absent considering the patent application as a whole.

■■■■

Quicknotes

35 U.S.C. § 271 Codifies legal decisions on infringement.

■■■■

Markman v. Westview Instruments, Inc.

Dry cleaning system inventor (P) v. Competitor (D)

517 U.S. 370 (1996).

NATURE OF CASE: On certiorari from court of appeals' affirmation of judgment of noninfringement.

FACT SUMMARY: Markman (P) claimed that Westview (D) had infringed upon his patent for a device to monitor inventory in dry-cleaning establishments.

🏛 RULE OF LAW
The construction of a patent, including terms of art within its claim, is a matter to be decided by the court rather than a jury.

FACTS: Markman (P) patented a device that involved attaching bar code labels to every article of clothing as they came into a dry-cleaner, then monitoring the progress of each article using optical sensors located throughout the establishment. Westview (D) then sold an inventory control system that also created bar-coded tickets for each item of laundry. However, the Westview (D) system only kept track of transactions, and was not designed to monitor the progress of each item, nor detect additions or deletions from expected inventory. A jury found that Westview (D) had infringed upon Markman's (P) design for an inventory control system. The district court then stated that the construction of Markman's (P) patent claim, particularly the term "inventory," was a matter for the court and not the jury. Defining "inventory" for purposes of the claim as articles of clothing, and not simply transaction totals, the judge granted Westview's (D) motion for judgment as a matter of law. The court of appeals upheld the judgment, and the Supreme Court granted review.

ISSUE: Is the construction of a patent claim a question of law for the court?

HOLDING AND DECISION: (Souter, J.) Yes. The construction of a patent, including terms of art within its claim, is a matter to be decided by the court rather than a jury. The Seventh Amendment preserves the right of jury trial as it existed at common law when the Amendment was adopted in 1791. Patent infringement cases were tried to a jury in the 18th century, and must still be tried to a jury. However, although the jury must resolve the ultimate dispute, within the trial there may be questions of law for the court. Modern claim practice did not exist at the time of the passage of the Seventh Amendment. The closest 18th century analogue was the specification, and there is no evidence to show that construction of the specification was a jury issue. As to Markman's (P) claim that terms of art within the claim must be submitted to a jury, neither history nor functional considerations support his argument. The judge, vested with the duty of interpreting the patent as a whole, is in the best position to determine which definition of terms contained in the patent fits best within the overall structure. Finally, treating such interpretive issues as matters of law promotes consistency and predictability between and among courts. The judgment is affirmed.

▶ ANALYSIS

The question of interpretation here has traditionally been regarded as a mixed question of fact and law. Justice Souter concluded that the question of claim construction was properly a question of law for the court, and that the meaning of terms of art in a patent claim should be resolved by the judicial exercise of judgment rather than by majority vote.

◼▬◼

Quicknotes

CONSTRUCTION The examination and interpretation of statutes.

◼▬◼

Cybor Corp. v. FAS Technologies, Inc.

Alleged infringer (D) v. Patent holder (P)

138 F.3d 1448 (Fed. Cir. 1998).

NATURE OF CASE: Appeal from finding of patent infringement.

FACT SUMMARY: FAS (P) claimed Cybor (D) infringed its patent. On appeal, Cybor (D) argued the district court erred in claim construction.

 RULE OF LAW
Claim construction is solely a question of law subject to de novo review.

FACTS: FAS Technologies, Inc. (P) filed an infringement suit against Cybor Corp. (D) claiming Cybor (D) infringed its '837 Patent. The district court held Cybor (D) had infringed the patent. Cybor (D) appealed, claiming the district court erred in the claim construction.

ISSUE: Is claim construction solely a question of law subject to de novo review?

HOLDING AND DECISION: (Archer, J.) Yes. Claim construction is solely a question of law subject to de novo review. An infringement analysis involves two steps: first, determining the scope and meaning of the asserted patent claims; and next, comparing the properly construed claims to the allegedly infringing device. The U.S. Supreme Court unanimously affirmed this Court's en banc holding in *Markman v. Westview Instruments, Inc.*, 52 F.3d 967 (Fed. Cir. 1995) (*Markman I*), in which this Court held claim construction is a purely legal issue. The Supreme Court in *Markman II* stated claim construction is a "mongrel practice" falling between law and fact, but determined the judge will be a better arbiter of claim construction than a jury. The Supreme Court further examined the role of expert testimony in claim construction, finding that a jury is a better examiner of witness credibility but credibility plays a rare role in construction. The expert witness helps the court determine the patent claim in light of the patent as a whole. The standard of review enunciated in *Markman I* was not changed by *Markman II*, so claim construction, including related fact-based questions, is subject to de novo review. All other case law suggesting otherwise is hereby disavowed. Affirmed.

CONCURRENCE: (Bryson, J.) Determining that claim construction is subject to de novo review does not mean this court will ignore the district court's conclusion.

DISSENT: (Rader, J.) *Markman I* deviates from standard litigation procedure in many respects, but the central deviation affects the trial court's discretion to use expert testimony. It is perverse for the court to permit a trial court to use an expert to understand the claim but not to interpret it. *Markman I* was intended to provide certainty in claim construction because the parties could present expert testimony and rely on the judicial determination of the claim interpretation. Now, the appellate court has unfettered review of that interpretation. This creates a distinct problem because the trial court has the ability to fully understand the complexities of the claim, employ expert witnesses to understand the claim, spend hours reading source materials, and are not bound by the prepared record. The appellate court has no such advantages. The appellate court should defer to the claim interpretation of the trial court.

▶ ANALYSIS

Scholars immediately began clamoring for the Supreme Court to intervene and offer a final resolution to the issue of claim interpretation. The *Cybor Corp.* decision appeared to take away from the importance of the trial court in claim interpretation and thus the patent process. The Supreme Court, however, denied certiorari to several cases that could have presented the issue. In 2006, the Federal Circuit indicated a willingness to revisit *Cybor Corp.* and perhaps limit its application. The case stands, however, as the standard of review.

■=■

Quicknotes

CONSTRUCTION The examination and interpretation of statutes.

DE NOVO The review of a lower court decision by an appellate court, which is hearing the case as if it had not been previously heard and as if no judgment had been rendered.

INTERPRETATION The determination of the meaning of a statute.

■=■

Phillips v. AWH Corporation

Patent holder (P) v. Alleged infringer (D)

415 F.3d 1303 (Fed. Cir. 2005).

NATURE OF CASE: En banc rehearing of appeal from summary judgment order of patent noninfringement.

FACT SUMMARY: Phillips (P), who sued AWH Corp. (AWH) (D) for patent infringement, contended that the term "baffles" in claim 1 of his patented invention (the '798 patent) was not used in a restrictive manner so as to exclude structures that extend at a 90-degree angle from walls, and that the term should be given its plain meaning, rather than limiting the term to corresponding structures disclosed in the patent's specification, or their equivalents.

> 🏛 **RULE OF LAW**
> A term in a claim of a patented invention should not be restricted to corresponding structures disclosed in the specification, or their equivalents, where the term's plain meaning can be given effect without such limitation.

FACTS: Phillips (P) invented, and obtained a patent on, modular, steel-shell panels that could be welded together to form vandalism-resistant walls. Phillips (P) brought a patent infringement action against AWH Corp. (AWH) (D). Claim 1 of his patent (the '798 patent) stated: "further means disposed inside the shell for increasing its load bearing capacity comprising internal steel baffles extending inwardly from the steel shell walls." The district court found that the allegedly infringing product did not contain "baffles" as that term was used in claim 1, and, therefore, granted summary judgment of noninfringement. On appeal, the original court of appeals panel concluded that the patent used the term "baffles" in a restrictive manner so as to exclude structures that extend at a 90-degree angle from the walls. That panel noted that the specification repeatedly referred to the ability of the claimed baffles to deflect projectiles and that it described the baffles as being "disposed at such angles that bullets which might penetrate the outer steel panels are deflected." The panel also noted that the patent nowhere disclosed a right-angle baffle, and that baffles oriented at 90 degrees to the wall were found in the prior art. The panel added that the patent specification "is intended to support and inform the claims, and here it makes it unmistakably clear that the invention involves baffles angled at other than 90 [degrees]." The dissenting judge argued that the panel had improperly limited the claims to the particular embodiment of the invention disclosed in the specification, rather than adopting the "plain meaning" of the term "baffles." The court of appeals agreed to rehear the appeal en banc.

ISSUE: Should a term in a claim of a patented invention be restricted to corresponding structures disclosed in the specification, or their equivalents, where the term's plain meaning can be given effect without such limitation?

HOLDING AND DECISION: (Bryson, J.) No. A term in a claim of a patented invention should not be restricted to corresponding structures disclosed in the specification, or their equivalents, where the term's plain meaning can be given effect without such limitation. The issue of claim interpretation is framed by § 112 of the Patent Act (35 U.S.C. § 112). The second paragraph of that section directs the court to look to the language of the claims to determine what "the applicant regards as his invention." On the other hand, the first paragraph requires that the specification describe the invention set forth in the claims. The principal question presented, therefore, is the extent to which the court should resort to and rely on a patent's specification in seeking to ascertain the proper scope of its claims. First, it is a "bedrock principle" of patent law that "the claims of a patent define the invention to which the patentee is entitled the right to exclude." In addition, the words of a claim are given their ordinary and customary meaning, which is the meaning that the term would have to a person of ordinary skill in the art in question at the time of the invention. Importantly, the person of ordinary skill in the art is deemed to read the claim term not only in the context of the particular claim in which the disputed term appears, but in the context of the entire patent, including the specification. Where the ordinary meaning of claim language is readily apparent even to lay judges, general application dictionaries may be helpful. However, where such meaning is not apparent, the court must look to those sources available to the public that show what a person of skill in the art would have understood disputed claim language to mean. Those sources include the words of the claims themselves, the remainder of the specification, the prosecution history, and extrinsic evidence concerning relevant scientific principles, the meaning of technical terms, and the state of the art. Claims must be read in view of the specifications of which they are a part. Extrinsic evidence may comprise technical dictionaries and experts. However, an approach of claim language construction that places greater emphasis on technical dictionaries and encyclopedias than on the specification and prosecution history is inconsistent with rulings that the specification is the single best guide to the meaning of a disputed term and that the specification acts as a dictionary when it expressly defines terms used in the claims or when it defines terms by implication. The main problem with elevating the dictionary to such prominence is that it focuses the inquiry on the abstract meaning of words rather than on the

Continued on next page.

meaning of claim terms within the context of the patent. Properly viewed, the "ordinary meaning" of a claim term is its meaning to the ordinary artisan after reading the entire patent. The problem is that if the district court starts with the broad dictionary definition in every case and fails to fully appreciate how the specification implicitly limits that definition the error will systematically cause the construction of the claim to be unduly expansive. The risk of systematic over-breadth is greatly reduced if the court focuses at the outset on how the patentee used the claim term in the claims, specification, and prosecution history, rather than starting with a broad definition and whittling it down. In cases in which it will be hard to determine whether a person of skill in the art would understand the embodiments to define the outer limits of the claim term or merely to be exemplary in nature, attempting to resolve that problem in the context of the particular patent is likely to capture the scope of the actual invention more accurately than either strictly limiting the scope of the claims to the embodiments disclosed in the specification or divorcing the claim language from the specification. Applying these principles, it is clear from claim 1 that the baffles must be made of steel, must be a part of the load-bearing means for the wall section, and must be pointed inward from the walls. Both parties stipulate that "baffles" refers to objects that check, impede, or obstruct the flow of something. The other claims of the '798 patent and the specification support the conclusion that persons of ordinary skill in the art would understand the baffles recited in the patent to be load-bearing objects that serve to check, impede, or obstruct flow. At several points, the specification discusses positioning the baffles so as to deflect projectiles. While the patent makes clear the invention envisions baffles that serve that function, it does not imply that in order to qualify as baffles within the meaning of the claims, the internal support structures must serve the projectile-deflecting function in all the embodiments of all the claims. The specification discusses several other purposes served by the baffles, e.g., providing structural support. The specification also provides for "overlapping and interlocking the baffles to produce substantially an intermediate barrier wall between the opposite [wall] faces" to create insulation compartments. The fact that the written description of the '798 patent sets forth multiple objectives to be served by the baffles recited in the claims confirms that the term "baffles" should not be read restrictively to require that the baffles in each case serve all of the recited functions. Here, although deflecting projectiles is one of the advantages of the baffles, the patent does not require that the inward extending structures always be capable of performing that function. Accordingly, a person of skill in the art would not interpret the disclosure and claims of the '798 patent to mean that a structure extending inward from one of the wall faces is a "baffle" if it is at an acute or obtuse angle, but is not a "baffle" if it is disposed at a right angle. Remanded.

▶ *ANALYSIS*

The effect of this case has been to limit exclusive reliance on dictionaries as an "objective" and presumptive source for meanings of claim terms. After *Phillips,* courts may still use dictionaries in conjunction with the specification, especially where there is no intrinsic evidence in the specification as to a term's specialized meaning, but the specification must be referenced to the extent possible.

■■■■

Quicknotes

INFRINGEMENT Conduct in violation of statute or that interferes with another's rights pursuant to law.

PATENT A limited monopoly conferred on the invention or discovery of any new or useful machine or process that is novel and nonobvious.

SUMMARY JUDGMENT Judgment rendered by a court in response to a motion by one of the parties, claiming that the lack of a question of material fact in respect to an issue warrants disposition of the issue without consideration by the jury.

■■■■

Computer Docking Station Corp. v. Dell, Inc.

Patentee (P) v. Alleged infringer (D)

519 F.3d 1366 (Fed. Cir. 2008).

NATURE OF CASE: Appeal from summary judgment granted to defendants.

FACT SUMMARY: Computer Docking Station Corp. (CDSC) (P) unambiguously disavowed computers with built-in keyboards or displays when distinguishing its "portable computer" from laptops. CDSC (P) then sued various laptop computer manufacturers for patent infringement.

🏛 RULE OF LAW
A patentee later cannot argue infringement when the allegedly infringing invention claim unambiguously was disavowed during prosecution.

FACTS: Computer Docking Station Corp. (CDSC) (P) submitted a patent application for a "portable computer microprocessing system" or "portable computer" that had keyboard and display options that could be coupled with it. The examiner initially rejected the claims as anticipated and obvious in light of the '128 patent to Herron disclosing a laptop computer and docking module. In appealing the rejection and amending its claims, CDSC (P) repeatedly disavowed computers with built-in keyboards or displays. CDSC (P) subsequently received the assigned '645 patent. Then CDSC (P) filed suit against Dell, Inc. (D) and other computer manufacturers on an infringement claim, arguing that Dell's (D) laptops and docking stations infringed upon the '645 patent. Dell (D) moved for summary judgment which the district court granted. CDSC (P) appealed.

ISSUE: Can a patentee later argue infringement when the allegedly infringing invention claim unambiguously was disavowed during prosecution?

HOLDING AND DECISION: (Rader, J.) No. A patentee later cannot argue infringement when the allegedly infringing invention claim unambiguously was disavowed during prosecution. Claim language defines the patented invention, so the court should consider the claim itself, the specification, and prosecution history in interpreting the claim language. The specification might limit the claim to a particular structure even though the claim language itself appears broader. Further, prosecution disclaimer may limit the claim but only if the disclaimer is unambiguous. Here, CDSC (P) repeatedly and unambiguously disclaimed laptops, or any computers with built-in keyboards or displays, when it fought to distinguish its invention from the prior art. CDSC (P) cannot now argue that its patent claim covers laptops when it asserts an infringement claim against Dell (D). The prosecution history is clear that CDSC (P) does not intend its patent to cover Dell's (D) machines. Affirmed.

► ANALYSIS

Claim interpretation is complicated, detailed, and technical, so all available information should help a judge lacking the expertise to evaluate the invention claims on his or her own. Discerning a prosecution disclaimer, however, can be equally complicated and technical because of the detailed prosecution history that accompanies patent infringement cases. Finding a prosecution disclaimer allows for a more narrow reading of a claim but also serves as grounds for reversal if the appellate court determines the disclaimer was not "unambiguous."

Quicknotes

SUMMARY JUDGMENT Judgment rendered by a court in response to a motion by one of the parties, claiming that the lack of a question of material fact in respect to an issue warrants disposition of the issue without consideration by the jury.

Graver Tank v. Linde Air Products Co.

Electric welder manufacturer (D) v. Competitor (P)

339 U.S. 605 (1950).

NATURE OF CASE: Writ of certiorari in patent infringement suit finding infringement.

FACT SUMMARY: Linde (P) alleged that Graver (D) had infringed its patent even though Graver (D) substituted an equivalent chemical for the one expressed in the patent.

🏛 RULE OF LAW
The doctrine of equivalents is applied to mechanical or chemical equivalents in compositions or devices.

FACTS: Linde (P) obtained an improvement patent on an electric welding composition or flux, its claims specifying essentially a combination of alkaline earth metal silicate and calcium fluoride. Graver (D) began production of its own composition that substituted silicates of manganese, not an alkaline earth metal, for the silicates of magnesium, which is an alkaline earth metal, used by Linde (P). Although Linde (P), which charged Graver (D) with infringement, had mentioned manganese in its specifications, it was not within the specific claims of the patent. Nevertheless, the courts found there was infringement, and Graver (D) appealed.

ISSUE: Does the doctrine of equivalents apply to chemical equivalents in compositions or devices?

HOLDING AND DECISION: (Jackson, J.) Yes. The doctrine of equivalents applies to mechanical or chemical equivalents in compositions or devices in the same way it applies where there is equivalence in mechanical components. It offers protection to the patentee against a device, process, or composition which performs substantially the same function as the patented device, process, or composition in substantially the same way to obtain the same result. The expert testimony in this case is the basis on which the courts below found that silicates of manganese, used by Graver (D), were the "equivalent" of the silicates of magnesium used in Linde's (P) patented composition under the doctrine of equivalents. Thus, the infringement finding must stand. Affirmed.

DISSENT: (Black, J.) The Court has impermissibly and incomprehensibly sterilized the Acts of Congress with its opinion. The petitioners here are not engaged in the malevolent acts referenced by the Court.

▶ ANALYSIS

The doctrine of equivalents can also work against a patentee. For example, an infringer's device may fall within the literal words of the patent claims but be so far changed in principle from the patented article that it performs the same or similar function in a substantially different way. In such a case, the doctrine can be applied to defeat an infringement claim.

◼▬◼

Quicknotes

DOCTRINE OF EQUIVALENTS Rule that two inventions are the same for purposes of patent infringement if they achieve essentially the same result in the same manner despite trivial differences.

◼▬◼

Warner-Jenkinson Company v. Hilton Davis Chemical Co.

Dye manufacturer (D) v. Competitor (P)

520 U.S. 17 (1997).

NATURE OF CASE: Appeal from affirmed finding of infringement.

FACT SUMMARY: After its method of removing impurities from dyes was found to have infringed on Hilton's (P) patent under the doctrine of equivalents, Warner-Jenkinson (D) petitioned for writ of certiorari.

🏛 RULE OF LAW
The determination of equivalence should be applied as an objective inquiry on each individual element of the claim, rather than the process as a whole.

FACTS: Warner-Jenkinson (D) petitioned for certiorari, and the Supreme Court accepted, noting that there were three separate dissents shared by five of the twelve judges. Hilton Davis (P) and Warner-Jenkinson (D) manufactured dyes. To meet stringent food and drug requirements, manufacturers must remove all impurities from the dyes, and the Hilton (P) patent concerned a filtration method using osmosis to separate components by drawing the solution through a membrane. The patent referred to a membrane with pore sizes of 5-15 Angstroms, a hydrostatic pressure from 200 to 400 p.s.i.g., and a pH from 6.0 to 9.0. Warner (D) developed its process independently from Hilton (P). Hilton (P) sued Warner (D) for infringement. At trial, Hilton (P) showed evidence that Warner's (D) method operated at a pressure from 200 to 500 p.s.i.g. and at a pH of lower than 5.0. The jury found infringement under the doctrine of equivalents, and Warner (D) appealed. The appellate court affirmed, concluding that there was no literal infringement, but there was "equivalence" between Warner's (D) method and the claimed elements of Hilton's (P) patented method.

ISSUE: Should the determination of equivalence be applied as an objective inquiry on each individual element of the claim, rather than the process as a whole?

HOLDING AND DECISION: (Thomas, J.) Yes. The determination of equivalence should be applied as an objective inquiry on each individual element of the claim, rather than the process as a whole. Warner's (D) argument that the doctrine of equivalents is inconsistent with the 1952 revision of the Patent Act is incorrect. The 1952 Act is not materially different than the 1870 Act as it relates to Warner's (D) arguments, and Congress did not implicitly reject the doctrine of equivalents. However, the doctrine of "prosecution history estoppel" is not superseded, and it is still available as a defense to infringement for a limited set of reasons. Under that doctrine, any surrender of subject matter during patent prosecution precludes recapturing any part of that subject matter, unless the patent-holder demonstrates that an amendment required during prosecution had a purpose unrelated to patentability. As for the doctrine of equivalents, the linguistic question of whether the proper test is function-way-results or insubstantial differences is not important. The simple question is whether the accused product or process contains elements identical or equivalent to each claimed element of the invention in the patent. Whether application of the doctrine of equivalents is a task for the judge or jury is irrelevant to the questions presented in this case, so it will not be addressed. Because the Federal Circuit did not consider the requirements related to prosecution history estoppel and the preservation of some meaning for each element of a claim, further proceedings are required. Reversed and remanded.

▶ ANALYSIS

On remand, the Federal Circuit found for Hilton Davis (P) again in finding the pH of 5.0 was equivalent to the claimed pH of 6.0. In their opinion, the Federal Circuit seemed to take issue with the Supreme Court's remand. The Supreme Court noted that a difference of 1.0 in pH levels represents a tenfold difference in acidity, but the Federal Circuit corrected this assumption. In a footnote, the Federal Circuit noted that a difference of 1.0 in pH is instead a tenfold difference in hydrogen ion concentration, not acidity. The Federal Circuit once again reiterated that the Hilton Davis (P) process would work at a pH as low as 2.0; this seemed to imply that they had not failed to overlook the original meaning of each claim element as the Supreme Court indicated in its instructions on remand.

■=■

Quicknotes

35 U.S.C. § 112 Requires that patent applicants disclose how to make and use the invention and include a written description.

DOCTRINE OF EQUIVALENTS Rule that two inventions are the same for purposes of patent infringement if they achieve essentially the same result in the same manner despite trivial differences.

ESTOPPEL An equitable doctrine precluding a party from asserting a right to the detriment of another who justifiably relied on the conduct.

■=■

Corning Glass Works v. Sumitomo Electric USA, Inc.

Telecommunication parts manufacturer (P) v. Alleged infringer (D)

868 F.2d 1251 (Fed. Cir. 1989).

NATURE OF CASE: Appeal from finding defendant liable for patent infringement.

FACT SUMMARY: Sumitomo's (D) S-3 fibers accomplished the same purpose as Corning's (P) fiber optics. Corning (P) claimed infringement.

🏛 RULE OF LAW
If an accused device has the equivalent to another patent's claim limitation somewhere in the device, then it is an infringing device.

FACTS: Prior fiberoptics only permitted short-distance communications and efforts began to develop long-distance options. Corning (P) then patented a fiberoptic composite consisting of a doped silica core and a fused silica cladding (doping optional) whose purpose was to function specifically as an optical waveguide over long distances (the '915 patent). Sumitomo (D) later patented its S-3 fibers, which accomplished the same objective as the fibers in the '915 patent. The district court held the S-3 fibers infringed upon the '915 patent claims and the '915 claims were not invalid. Sumitomo (D) appealed.

ISSUE: If an accused device has the equivalent to another patent's claim limitation somewhere in the device, then is it an infringing device?

HOLDING AND DECISION: (Nies, J.) Yes. If an accused device has the equivalent to another patent's claim limitation somewhere in the device, then it is an infringing device. No dispute exists that the S-3 fibers perform the same function as Corning's (P) fibers. The issue is whether the function is performed in "substantially the same way." Here, Corning (P) admits its claims do not literally read on the S-3 fibers but asserts the S-3 fibers perform in an equivalent fashion to its claimed invention, thus meeting the Graver Tank test. The district court found the S-3 fiber substitution of "fluorine dopant" negatively altering the "index of refraction of fused silica [ ] in the cladding" was the equivalent to the Corning (P) dopant which positively altered the index of refraction of fused silica. Sumitomo (D) argues the "All Elements" rule applies, but the equivalent limitation need not appear in a corresponding component such that each element is equivalent, just equivalent somewhere in an accused device. Corning (P) argues the question is whether adding a positive dopant to the core is the equivalent to adding negative dopant to the cladding. The district court agreed that the two were equivalent and this court does not find error in that holding. This Court has never developed a rigid test and employs the function/way/result equivalency analysis in accord with *Graver Tank*. Affirmed.

▶ ANALYSIS

The doctrine of equivalents prohibits an invention receiving patent protection by changing a limitation description when the limitation is substantially the same as another patent's claim limitation. The language does not need to be the same so long as the function or result of the claimed invention is substantially is the same.

■▬■

Quicknotes

DOCTRINE OF EQUIVALENTS Rule that two inventions are the same for purposes of patent infringement if they achieve essentially the same result in the same manner despite trivial differences.

■▬■

Festo Corp. v. Shoketsu Kinzoku Kogyo Kabushiki Co., Ltd.

Inventor (P) v. Competitor (D)

535 U.S. 722 (2002).

NATURE OF CASE: Appeal of judgment of non-infringement.

FACT SUMMARY: Festo (P) sued Shoketsu (D) for patent infringement. Shoketsu (D) argued that by narrowing claims to obtain its patents, Festo (P) surrendered all equivalents to the amended claims.

🏛 RULE OF LAW

A narrowing amendment made to satisfy any requirement of the Patent Act may give rise to estoppel. Estoppel does not, however, bar the patentee from asserting infringement against any equivalent to the narrowed element. The patentee bears the burden of showing that the amendment does not surrender the particular equivalent in question.

FACTS: Festo (P) owns two patents for a magnetic rodless cylinder, a piston-driven device that relies on magnets to move objects in a conveying system. The prosecution history reveals that in response to rejection, both patent applications were amended to reference prior art and new limitations. The new limitations were that (1) the inventions contain a pair of sealing rings, each having a lip on one side, and (2) that the outer shell of the device, the sleeve, be made of a magnetizable material. Shoketsu (D) subsequently entered the market with a similar device that had a single sealing ring with a two-way lip and a sleeve made of nonmagnetizable alloy. Festo (P) sued for infringement claiming that although there was not literal infringement, the devices were so similar that Shoketzu's (D) device infringed under the doctrine of equivalents. Shoketsu (D) defended arguing that Festo (P) was estopped from making this argument because of the prosecution history of the patents. The district court held that Festo's (P) amendments were not made to avoid prior art and therefore did not give rise to estoppel. The court of appeals reversed and held that by narrowing a claim to obtain a patent, the patentee surrenders all equivalents to the amended claim element. Previous decisions had held that prosecution history estoppel constituted a flexible bar, foreclosing some, but not all, claims of equivalence, depending on the purpose of the amendment and the alterations in the text. Festo (P) appealed.

ISSUE: Did the court of appeals err in holding that: (1) estoppel can be applied to every amendment made to satisfy the requirements of the Patent Act and not just to amendments made to avoid pre-emption by an earlier invention; and (2) when estoppel arises it bars every suit against every equivalent to the amended claim element?

HOLDING AND DECISION: (Kennedy, J.)

(1) No. The court of appeals did not err in holding that a narrowing amendment made to satisfy any requirement of the Patent Act may give rise to an estoppel. The scope of a patent is not limited to its literal terms but instead embraces all equivalents to the claims described. Prosecution history estoppel requires that the claims of a patent be interpreted in light of the proceedings in the PTO during the application process. When the patentee originally claims the subject matter alleged to infringe but then narrowed the claim in response to a rejection, he may not argue that the surrendered territory comprised unforeseen subject matter that should be deemed equivalent to the literal claims of the issued patent. To forgo an appeal of a rejection and submit an amended claim is a concession that the invention as patented does not reach as far as the original claim. The patentee is thus surrendering certain subject matter as a condition of receiving a patent. A narrowing amendment made to satisfy any requirement of the Patent Act may give rise to an estoppel. A number of statutory requirements must be sustained before a patent can issue. Estoppel arises when an amendment is made to secure the patent and the amendment narrows the patent's scope. If an amendment just concerns the form of the application and not the subject matter of the invention, then it would not narrow the patent's scope or raise an estoppel. If such an amendment is necessary and narrows the patent's scope, even if only for the purpose of better description, estoppel may apply.

(2) Yes. The court of appeals erred in holding that estoppel bars the inventor from asserting infringement against any equivalent to the narrowed element. It was an error to adopt a complete bar. The reach of prosecution estoppel requires an examination of the subject matter surrendered by the narrowing amendment. A complete bar would avoid this inquiry. The narrowing amendment may demonstrate what the claim is not, but it may still fail to capture what the claim is and therefore equivalents may still exist. The amended claim is not so perfect in description that no one could devise an equivalent. The patentee should bear the burden of showing that the amendment does not surrender the particular equivalent in question. There are some cases where the amendment cannot reasonably be viewed as surrendering a particular equivalent. The equivalent may have been unforeseeable at the time of the application or the rationale underlying the amendment may bear no more than a tangential

Continued on next page.

relation to the equivalent in question. The patentee must show that at the time of the amendment, one skilled in the art could not reasonably have been expected to have drafted a claim that would literally have encompassed the alleged equivalent. In this case, Festo (P) did not rebut the presumption that estoppel applies, and the equivalents have been surrendered. The limitations were made in response to rejection. The question then becomes what territory the amendments surrendered, or whether they did surrender the equivalents at issue. Vacated and remanded.

▶ *ANALYSIS*

This was probably the most important commercial case of the Supreme Court's 2002–2003 term.

■■■■

Quicknotes

DOCTRINE OF EQUIVALENTS Rule that two inventions are the same for purposes of patent infringement if they achieve essentially the same result in the same manner despite trivial differences.

ESTOPPEL An equitable doctrine precluding a party from asserting a right to the detriment of another who justifiably relied on the conduct.

■■■■

Johnson & Johnston Associates Inc. v. R.E. Service Co., Inc.

Inventor (P) v. Alleged infringer (D)

285 F.3d 1046 (Fed. Cir. 2002).

NATURE OF CASE: Appeal of infringement judgment.

FACT SUMMARY: Johnston (P) sued R.E. Service Co., Inc. and Mark Frater (collectively, "RES") (D) for infringement. RES (D) defended by claiming that Johnston (P) did not claim steel substrates, but limited its patent scope to aluminum substrates, thus dedicating to the public this unclaimed subject matter.

RULE OF LAW
A patentee cannot apply the doctrine of equivalents to cover unclaimed subject matter disclosed in the specification.

FACTS: Johnson (P) has a patent for the manufacturing of printed circuit boards. The patent claims an assembly that prevents damage caused by manual handling of the sheets of copper foil during manufacturing. The invention adheres the fragile copper foil to a stiffer substrate sheet of aluminum. RES (D) subsequently began making new laminates for manufacture of printed circuit boards. Its products joined copper foil to a sheet of steel as the substrate, instead of a sheet of aluminum. Johnson (P) sued RES (D) alleging infringement of its patent. On cross-motions for summary judgment, the district court ruled that the patent did not dedicate the steel substrate to the public. A jury found infringement under the doctrine of equivalents. The court of appeals ordered en banc rehearing of the doctrine of equivalents issue. On appeal, RES (D) argued Johnston (P) did not claim steel substrates, but limited its patent scope to aluminum substrates, thus dedicating to the public this unclaimed subject matter and therefore the district court should have ordered summary judgment in its favor.

ISSUE: Can a patentee apply the doctrine of equivalents to cover unclaimed subject matter disclosed in the specification?

HOLDING AND DECISION: (Per curiam) No. A patentee cannot apply the doctrine of equivalents to cover unclaimed subject matter disclosed in the specification. Thus, RES (D) could not have infringed Johnson's (P) patent under the doctrine of equivalents. Claims define the scope of patent protection and give notice thereof. The claim requirement presupposes that a patent applicant defines his invention in the claims, not in the specification. The law of infringement compares the accused product with the claims as construed by the court and not with embodiments in the specifications. When a patent drafter discloses but declines to claim subject matter, this action dedicates that unclaimed subject matter to the public. The doctrine of equivalents extends the right to exclude beyond the literal claims. Application of the doctrine of equivalents to recapture subject matter deliberately left unclaimed would conflict with the primacy of the claims in defining the scope of the patentee's exclusive right. A patentee therefore cannot narrowly claim an invention to avoid prosecution scrutiny by the PTO, and then after patent issuance use the doctrine of equivalents to establish infringement because the specification discloses equivalents. In the present case, Johnston's (P) patent specifically limited the claims to a sheet of aluminum and the aluminum sheet. The specification, however, included other metals, such as stainless steel or nickel alloy, that might be used. Having disclosed without claiming the steel substrates, Johnson (P) cannot now invoke the doctrine of equivalents to extend its aluminum limitation to encompass steel. A patentee can, however, remedy the situation by filing, within two years from the grant of the original patent, a reissue application or by filing a separate application. Reversed.

CONCURRENCE: (Rader, J.) I would offer the alternative reasoning that the doctrine of equivalents does not capture subject matter that the patent drafter reasonably could have foreseen during the application process and included in the claims. This will serve both the predominant notice function of the claims by making them the sole definition of the inventions scope in all foreseeable circumstances and the protective function of the doctrine of equivalents. In the present case, Johnston's (P) patent disclosure expressly admits that it foresaw other metals serving as substrates, yet the patent did not claim anything beyond aluminum. Forseeability thus bars Johnston (P) from recapturing as an equivalent subject matter not claimed but disclosed.

ANALYSIS

This case was decided during the time the Supreme Court was drafting *Festo Corp. v. Shoketsu Kinzoku Kogyo Kabushiki Co., Ltd.*, 535 U.S. 722 (2002).

Quicknotes

DOCTRINE OF EQUIVALENTS Rule that two inventions are the same for purposes of patent infringement if they achieve essentially the same result in the same manner despite trivial differences.

ESTOPPEL An equitable doctrine precluding a party from asserting a right to the detriment of another who justifiably relied on the conduct.

Wilson Sporting Goods Co. v. David Geoffrey & Associates

Golf ball maker (P) v. Golf ball distributor (D)

904 F.2d 677 (Fed. Cir. 1990).

NATURE OF CASE: Appeal from jury finding of infringement.

FACT SUMMARY: Wilson (P) won an infringement suit concerning the design patent on its golf balls, and Dunlop (D) and David Geoffrey & Associates (D) appealed.

🏛 RULE OF LAW
If the scope of equivalency necessary to find infringement would cover prior art, there can be no infringement.

FACTS: Wilson (P) sued both Dunlop (D) and David Geoffrey & Associates (DGA) (D) for infringement on its golf ball patent. The patent concerned the placement of dimples on the golf ball. The patent divided the ball into an icosahedron (20 triangles) and then drew lines between the midpoints of each triangle, so there were 80 triangles. The 80 dimples were then arranged so no dimple was on a line. This process was described in Wilson's Claim 1 and the other twenty-six claims were dependent on it. The prior art was the British Pugh patent and several Uniroyal patents. Both considered dividing the ball into a polygon, including an icosahedron, and either subdividing the ball into 320 triangles or placing the dimples based on the icosahedron's lines. The jury found for Wilson (P), and Dunlop (D) and DGA (D) appealed, arguing the prior art covered their inventions, so it could not infringe.

ISSUE: If the scope of equivalency necessary to find infringement would cover prior art, can there be infringement?

HOLDING AND DECISION: (Rich, J.) No. If the scope of equivalency necessary to find infringement would cover prior art, there can be no infringement. Since prior art limits what an inventor could have claimed, it limits the possible range of permissible equivalents of a claim. To simplify analysis, imagine a hypothetical patent that literally covers the accused product. The question then becomes whether the Patent and Trademark Office would have allowed the hypothetical patent over the prior art. The burden is upon the patent owner, or Wilson (P), to prove the range of equivalents it seeks would not ensnare the prior art. The hypothetical claim, similar to Wilson's (P) Claim 1 but sufficient to cover the Dunlop (D) balls, would not have been patentable given the Uniroyal prior art. The dependent claims must be examined separately, but they are not infringed either. Reversed.

▶ ANALYSIS

Wilson clearly put the burden on the patentees to both create and prove the validity of the hypothetical claim.

There was widespread criticism of this, and the Federal Circuit in *Key Manufacturing Group, Inc. v. Microdot, Inc.*, 925 F.2d 1444, 17 U.S.P.Q.2d 1806 (Fed. Cir. 1991), pointed out the hypothetical claim analysis was not "obligatory" in every doctrine of equivalents determination. Indeed, the *Wilson* court had only characterized the hypothetical claim analysis as "helpful," not necessary.

■══■

Quicknotes

DOCTRINE OF EQUIVALENTS Rule that two inventions are the same for purposes of patent infringement if they achieve essentially the same result in the same manner despite trivial differences.

■══■

DSU Medical Corporation v. JMS Company, Ltd.

Patentee (P) v. Alleged infringer (D)

471 F.3d 1293 (Fed. Cir. 2006).

NATURE OF CASE: Appeal from damage award for patent infringement.

FACT SUMMARY: DSU (P) patented a device that closed over a needle set. ITL (D) manufactured a clamshell design device that could close but did not include a needle set. JMS (D) sold the ITL (D) device but sold it as a closed device over a needle set. DSU (P) sued for patent infringement.

🏛 RULE OF LAW
Contributory infringement requires proof of a direct nexus to a specific act of direct infringement and inducement to infringe requires knowledge and specific intent that one's actions will induce actual infringement.

FACTS: DSU Medical Corporation (P) patented a guarded, winged-needle assembly that reduced the risk of accidental needle-sticks (the '311 and '072 patents). ITL Corporation Pty, Limited (ITL) (D) manufactures the Platypus needle guard, which does not include a needle. JMS Company, Ltd. (D) entered into a distribution agreement with ITL (D) to sell the Platypus worldwide. Prior to distributing the Platypus to customers, JMS (D) would close the needle guards around needle sets. DSU (P) filed suit against JMS (D) and ITL (D), asserting patent infringement of the '311 patent and that the two defendants induced each other to infringe the '311 patent. The trial court granted defendants summary judgment on several issues because it held they did not infringe upon Claim 1 of the '311 patent when the trial court interpreted "slidably enclosing" to require a permanently enclosed cover and the presence of a needle. The Platypus was a closeable clamshell configuration without a needle. The trial court also interpreted "slot" in Claim 46 as not requiring a defined width. The Platypus jaws accommodate any wing thickness, so it would not infringe if the '311 patent required only the width necessary to accommodate its minor thickness wings. The width not defined, however, meant the Platypus was infringing on the '311 patent. Thus, when the Platypus is sold in its closed-shell configuration, it has a slot and literally infringes when closed over a needle set. The jury found JMS (D) liable for contributory infringement, but found noninfringement in favor of ITL (D). DSU (P) appealed the jury verdict in favor of ITL (D).

ISSUE: Does contributory infringement require proof of a direct nexus to a specific act of direct infringement and does inducement to infringe require knowledge and specific intent that one's actions will induce actual infringement?

HOLDING AND DECISION: (Rader, J.) Yes. Contributory infringement requires proof of a direct nexus to a specific act of direct infringement and inducement to infringe requires knowledge and specific intent that one's actions will induce actual infringement. DSU (P) argues on appeal that ITL (D) contributed to JMS (D) infringement of the '311 patent. DSU (P) had to demonstrate contributory infringement by showing that ITL (D) manufactured and sold the Platypus with no substantial noninfringing uses when in the closed position, and made U.S. sales that contributed to an act of JMS's (D) direct infringement. The trial court found all elements present except a direct nexus to a specific act of direct infringement. This court agrees because the record does not show that ITL (D) sold its Platypus in the U.S. in the closed-shell configuration but only shipped the open-shell device to JMS (D). The trial court further found that ITL (D) did not intend JMS (D) to infringe by closing the shell for sales. Thus, ITL's (D) actions did not directly contribute to JMS's (D) specific act of direct infringement. Affirmed.

HOLDING AND DECISION: (En banc) The en banc court considers the intent requirement for a claim of induced infringement as advanced by DSU (P). Induced infringement requires the alleged infringer to know or should have known that actions would induce actual infringement as well as knowledge of the patent. Specific intent and action must be shown; it is insufficient to show knowledge of possible inducement or knowledge of the direct infringer's activities. The evidence at trial demonstrated ITL's (D) lack of intent to induce infringement. The jury was within its rights to find in favor of ITL (D). Affirmed.

▶ ANALYSIS
The de novo review standard requires parties to submit complete, detailed records on appeal or face what this court deemed "inferences" of evidence supporting the claims. The court will not infer infringing behavior but must find actual intent within the appellate record.

■=■

Quicknotes
DE NOVO The review of a lower court decision by an appellate court, which is hearing the case as if it had not been previously heard and as if no judgment had been rendered.

Continued on next page.

EN BANC The hearing of a matter by all the judges of the court, rather than only the necessary quorum.

INFRINGEMENT Conduct in violation of a statute or contract that interferes with another's rights pursuant to law.

INTENT The state of mind that exists when one's purpose is to commit a criminal act.

■━━■

Jazz Photo Corp. v. International Trade Comm.

Infringer (D) v. Federal agency (P)

264 F.3d 1094 (Fed. Cir. 2001).

NATURE OF CASE: Appeal of judgment of infringement and violation of the Tariff Act.

FACT SUMMARY: The Commission (P) alleged that Jazz (D) had infringed patents owned by Fuji and violated the Tariff Act by purchasing Fuji's used patented product, refurbishing it, and importing it into the United States.

RULE OF LAW
For used, refurbished, single-use cameras whose first sale was in the United States with a patentee's authorization, and for which the alleged violators activities were limited to the steps of removing the cardboard cover, cutting open the plastic casing, inserting new film and a container to receive the film, replacing the winding wheel for certain cameras, replacing the battery for flash cameras, resetting the counter, resealing the outer case, and adding a new cardboard cover; the totality of these procedures are permissible repair and not prohibited reconstruction.

FACTS: Fuji has several patents for a single-use camera, known as lens-fitted film packages (LFFPs). Several of the patents are directed at specific components of LFFPs. Discarded LFFPs were purchased and refurbished by Jazz (D), who would then import them. Jazz (D) refurbished them by removing the cardboard cover, cutting open the plastic casing, inserting new film and a container to receive the film, replacing the winding wheel for certain cameras, replacing the battery for flash cameras, resetting the counter, resealing the outer case, and adding a new cardboard cover. The refurbished cameras contain all of the elements of all or most of the claims of Fuji's patents. Jazz (D) was found by the Commission (P) to have infringed Fuji patents and to have violated the Tariff Act by importing the used and refurbished LFFPs. The Commission (P) found that the refurbishment of the used cameras was prohibited reconstruction as opposed to permissible repair. Jazz (D) appealed.

ISSUE: Were Jazz's (D) actions prohibited reconstruction or permissible repair?

HOLDING AND DECISION: (Newman, J.) Jazz's (D) actions were permissible repair. For used cameras whose first sale was in the United States with Fuji's authorization, the steps Jazz (D) took to refurbish them does not satisfy the standards required by precedent for prohibited reconstruction, but rather are permissible repair. Patented articles when sold become the private individual property of the purchasers and are no longer specifically protected by the patent laws. The rights of ownership, however, do not include the right to construct an essentially new article on the template of the original. However, the right to preserve the useful life of the original article is included in the ownership rights. The right of repair also accompanies the article to succeeding owners. The disassembly and cleaning of patented articles accompanied by replacement of unpatented parts that have become worn or spent in order to preserves the utility for which the article was originally intended is thus considered repair. In the present case, the acts of inserting new film and a new film container, resetting the film counter, and resealing the broken case are more akin to repair. Consideration of the remaining useful capacity of the article and the nature and role of the replaced parts in achieving that useful capacity is to be made. Fuji's unilateral intent does not bar reuse of the patented article or convert repair into reconstruction. The replacement of unpatented parts having a shorter life than is available from the combination of the whole is characteristic of repair. On the totality of the circumstances, the changes made by Jazz (D) all relate to replacement of the film, the LFFP otherwise remaining as originally sold. Several of the patents are directed to specific components of LFFPs. The ruling of reconstruction as to these patents is incorrect because the remanufacturing process simply reuses the original components, such that there is no issue of replacing parts that were separately patented. If the claimed component is not replaced but simply reused, this component is neither repaired nor reconstructed. Affirmed in part, reversed in part, and remanded.

ANALYSIS

Most cases that address the distinction between repair and reconstruction find that the defendant's activities constituted repair.

■═■

Quicknotes

INFRINGEMENT Conduct in violation of a statute or contract that interferes with another's rights pursuant to law.

■═■

Kirin-Amgen Inc. and Others v. Hoechst Marion Roussel Limited and Others

Patentee (P) v. Alleged infringer (D)

[2004] UKHL 46 Session 2003-04, [2002] EWCA Civ 1096 Thursday 21st October, 2004.

NATURE OF CASE: Appeal from finding of non-infringement.

FACT SUMMARY: Amgen (P) held a patent on DNA recombination and argued its patent was general enough to cover any method of developing a particular sequence.

🏛 RULE OF LAW

Claim language should be interpreted by determining what the ordinary person skilled in the art understands the claim to cover, which may involve a literal reading of the claim language or application of the drawings and description.

FACTS: Kirin-Amgen Inc. (P) held a patent on homologous DNA recombination and argued its claim included any DNA sequence, whether endogenous or exogenous, to secure EPO expression in a "host cell." It filed an infringement suit against multiple defendants claiming infringement. The trial court determined the patented invention was the discovery of the EPO gene sequencing and related information. The patent specification was general enough therefore to include any method of making EPO even if new technology arose years later. The trial court found the defendants had infringed. The court of appeals determined the invention was a way of making EPO, which would allow others to make EPO in a different method using different or new technology. The court of appeals reversed the trial court's finding of infringement. Amgen (P) appealed.

ISSUE: Should claim language be interpreted by determining what the ordinary person skilled in the art understands the claim to cover, which may involve a literal reading of the claim language or application of the drawings and description?

HOLDING AND DECISION: (Hoffmann, Lord) Yes. Claim language should be interpreted by determining what the ordinary person skilled in the art understands the claim to cover, which may involve a literal reading of the claim language or application of the drawings and description. Patent protection in European states is determined by Article 69 which relies on the claim language, which may be interpreted by the description and drawings included with the patent application. This is the historical United Kingdom method, which differed from that in Germany or the Netherlands. The difference in claim language importance led to the adoption of "Protocol on the Interpretation of Article 69," which requires claims to be read in their strict, literal meaning with use of the description and drawings to resolve ambiguities. United Kingdom infringement law incorporates both Article 69 and the Protocol, but UK courts typically deviate from strict, literal readings of claims and focus on what the addressee would understand the words to mean. In patent claims, the notional addressee is the person of ordinary skill in the art, so claim interpretation began to focus on what the person of ordinary skill would have understood the claim to cover. The Americans avoided the narrow, literal interpretation by developing the doctrine of equivalents and extended protection to equivalent claims that simply used different language. The UK abandoned literalism, but does not go too far outside the claim language. Here, Amgen (P) argues its claim 1 includes endogenous and exogenous coding although the terms are not literally in the claim language. The trial court heard expert testimony and determined an ordinary person skilled in the art would not have thought the DNA sequencing claim to include endogenous coding. The trial court called its interpretation "literal" and proceeded to evaluate the claim under the Protocol. The Protocol is inapplicable here, however, because no one would misunderstand "exogenous DNA sequence coding" to include "endogenous DNA sequence coding" but the ordinary person skilled in the art might understand the invention was so general as to render exogenous versus endogenous irrelevant. Amgen (P) argues the claim includes gene activation although that was not known when the patent was issued. The court of appeals, however, disagreed and found the claim language was not general enough to include technology previously unknown. This Court agrees. The claim only includes exogenous DNA sequence coding and defendants thus did not infringe. Appeal dismissed.

▶ ANALYSIS

This case confirms prior United Kingdom case law limiting the interpretation of claim language. The United States expanded its protection to include equivalent inventions while the United Kingdom expects its patent applicants to delineate the protection sought. If the patent should be general enough to cover new technologies, then the drafter should use general language such that the ordinary person skilled in the art understands it to include the new technologies. The claim will otherwise be interpreted more narrowly.

■━■

Tsubakimoto Seiko Co. Ltd. v. Thk K.K.

[Parties not identified.]

Japan Sup. Ct., 1994 (o) 1083 (1998).

NATURE OF CASE: Patent infringement suit.

FACT SUMMARY: A patented invention and one similar are discussed in regards to their differences and similarities in order to determine when infringement would occur.

🏛 RULE OF LAW
An accused product that is somewhat different from a patented product will be said to be equivalent with the patented product if the differing elements are not essential; if when the differing elements are interchanged the objective of the patented invention can be achieved; if by interchanging an artisan could have arrived at the accused product; if the accused product could not have easily been conceived by an artisan at the time of manufacture of the patent; and if the accused was not intentionally excluded from the scope of the claim during patent prosecution.

FACTS: The accused product literally meets all limitations except for the outer cylinder limitation and the thin wall portion limitation. As to the outer cylinder limitation, the patented product has a U-shaped cross section and annular circumferentially directed grooves. The corresponding elements on the accused product are a semicircular cross-section and cylindrical portion. As to the thin wall portion limitation, the patented product retainer is an integral structure providing the functions of guiding balls to move in endless circulation, retaining balls when the spline shaft is withdrawn and forming a recessed portion for guiding the rib portions of the spline shaft. The accused product has a cooperative action of three members, the upper edge portions of the ribs formed between the load bearing ball-guiding grooves of the outer cylinder, a plate-like member, and a return cap. The lower court found that the accused product is substantially the same as that shown in the patent with respect to the solution for the technical problem, the basic technical idea, and the effects obtained.

ISSUE: When will an accused product that is somewhat different from a patented product infringe on the patented product?

HOLDING AND DECISION: [Judge not stated in casebook excerpt.] An accused product that is somewhat different from a patented product will be said to be equivalent to the patented product if the differing elements are not essential; if when the differing elements are interchanged the objective of the patented invention can be achieved; if by interchanging an artisan could have arrived at the accused product; if the accused product could not have easily been conceived by an artisan at the time of manufacture of the

patent; and if the accused was not intentionally excluded from the scope of the claim during patent prosecution. It is very difficult to describe claims to cover all possible infringing embodiments of the patented invention. Without such a rule of infringement, a competitor can escape from patent enforcement by simply replacing some claimed elements with means or material developed after the patent application. The incentive for innovation would be reduced, which would conflict with the goal of the patent system, which is to contribute to the industrial development through the protection and encouragement of inventions. Remanded.

▶ ANALYSIS

Up until the time of this decision, Japan had been criticized for awarding patent claims with too narrow scopes. Further, the doctrine of equivalents did not exist in Japan.

▆▅▆

Quicknotes

DOCTRINE OF EQUIVALENTS Rule that two inventions are the same for purposes of patent infringement if they achieve essentially the same result in the same manner despite trivial differences.

▆▅▆

CHAPTER 12

Additional Defenses

Quick Reference Rules of Law

PAGE

1. **Experimental Use.** The limited use of a patented drug for testing and investigation strictly related to FDA drug approval requirements during the last 6 months of the term of the patent constitutes a use which, unless licensed, the patent statute makes actionable. (Roche Products, Inc. v. Bolar Pharmaceutical Co., Inc.) — *110*

2. **Experimental Use.** The experimental use defense does not apply to use that is in furtherance of the user's legitimate business and is not solely for amusement, to satisfy idle curiosity, or strictly philosophical inquiry. (Madey v. Duke University) — *111*

3. **Misuse.** Patent misuse charges should be evaluated under antitrust principles, and there is no antitrust prohibition against a patent owner's using price discrimination to maximize his income. (USM Corp. v. SPS Technologies, Inc.) — *112*

4. **Laches and Estoppel.** Principles of laches and equitable estoppel are legitimate defenses to patent infringement suits. (A.C. Aukerman Co. v. R.L. Chaides Construction Co.) — *113*

5. **Shop Rights.** Whether an employer has "shop rights" to patented subject matter requires a look at the totality of the circumstances to determine whether principles of equity and fairness demand a finding that a "shop right" exists. (McElmurry v. Arkansas Power & Light Co.) — *114*

Roche Products, Inc. v. Bolar Pharmaceutical Co., Inc.

Patentee (P) v. Alleged infringer (D)

733 F.2d 858 (Fed. Cir. 1984).

NATURE OF CASE: Appeal from finding of non-infringement.

FACT SUMMARY: Roche (P) had a patent that was set to expire in a few months. Bolar (D) sought to develop a generic version of the compound covered by Roche's (P) patent and began experiments prior to the expiration of the patent. Roche (P) sued for infringement and a restraining order.

🏛 RULE OF LAW
The limited use of a patented drug for testing and investigation strictly related to FDA drug approval requirements during the last 6 months of the term of the patent constitutes a use which, unless licensed, the patent statute makes actionable.

FACTS: Roche Products, Inc. (P) was the assignee of the '053 patent for a chemical compound, flurazepam hcl, which was the active ingredient in the popular sleeping pill Dalmane. The '053 patent was set to expire in 1984 and Bolar Pharmaceutical Co., Inc. (D) began investigating the manufacture of a generic version of Dalmane in early 1983. The generic approval process took two years so Bolar (D) intended to begin testing of the generic for FDA approval prior to the expiration date of the '053 patent. Roche (P) filed suit for infringement and sought an injunction against Bolar's (D) use of flurazepam hcl for any purpose. The trial court granted Roche (P) a temporary restraining order, granted Bolar (D) a change of venue, and the new district court consolidated Roche's (P) motion for a permanent restraining order with a trial on the merits. The district court denied Roche's (P) permanent restraining order on the basis Bolar's (D) use was de minimis and experimental. Roche (P) appealed.

ISSUE: "Does the limited use of a patented drug for testing and investigation strictly related to FDA drug approval requirements during the last 6 months of the term of the patent constitute a use which, unless licensed, the patent statute makes actionable?"

HOLDING AND DECISION: (Nichols, J.) Yes. The limited use of a patented drug for testing and investigation strictly related to FDA drug approval requirements during the last 6 months of the term of the patent constitutes a use which, unless licensed, the patent statute makes actionable. Bolar (D) argues its use falls within the experimental use exception or a new exception crafted out of public policy preference for the development of generic drugs. The long-standing rule is that no infringement exists if the use of the patented article is for a de minimis purpose. Bolar (D) concedes its use does not fall within the traditionally narrow interpretation of the experimental use exception, which is fatal to its defense. Tests, such as those conducted by Bolar (D), do not fall within experimental use and are thus infringements on the patent. Bolar (D) did not intend its use for amusement, idle curiosity, or philosophical inquiry. This Court will not expand the experimental use exception to include other uses. Bolar (D) next argues that the Drug Amendments of 1962 caused a substantial increase in the approval process timeline for generic drugs. This, Bolar (D) argues, extends the patent protection an additional two years unless manufacturers are allowed to begin drug testing and investigation prior to the patent expiration. It is not within this Court's province to rewrite the patent statute because of the effect of a later statute. Reversed and remanded.

▶ ANALYSIS

Congress responded to the *Roche* decision by amending the law to permit patent practice in furtherance of an application for FDA approval for a pending drug. The patent practice does not fall within the experimental use defense but is a limited allowed use pursuant to the new law.

■=■

Quicknotes

DE MINIMIS Insignificant; trivial; not of sufficient significance to require legal action.

FOOD AND DRUG ADMINISTRATION (FDA) A federal agency responsible for establishing safety and quality standards for foods, drugs, and cosmetics.

■=■

Madey v. Duke University

Patentee (P) v. Alleged infringer (D)

307 F.3d 1351 (Fed. Cir. 2002).

NATURE OF CASE: Appeal from summary judgment granted to defendant.

FACT SUMMARY: Madey (P) sued Duke (D) for patent infringement for using his lab equipment. Duke (D) claimed its use fell within the experimental use exception.

🏛 RULE OF LAW
The experimental use defense does not apply to use that is in furtherance of the user's legitimate business and is not solely for amusement, to satisfy idle curiosity, or strictly philosophical inquiry.

FACTS: Dr. John M.J. Madey (P) moved his successful lab with substantial lab equipment from Stanford to Duke University (D). Madey (P) had sole ownership of two patents practiced by some of the lab equipment. Duke (D) eventually removed Madey (P) as lab director but continued to use the lab equipment. Madey (P) resigned and then sued Duke (D) for patent infringement based on Duke's (D) continued use of the equipment. Duke (D) argued its use fell within the experimental use exception. Madey (P) argued Duke's (D) use was for commercial purposes. Duke (D) relied on its patent policy preamble, which stated Duke (D) did not engage in research or development for primarily commercial purposes. The district court agreed with Duke (D) and required Madey (P) to demonstrate Duke's (D) use was for "definite, cognizable, and not insubstantial commercial purposes." The district court also held the defense applied to experimental, non-profit purposes. The district court granted Duke's (D) summary judgment motion. Madey (P) appealed.

ISSUE: Does the experimental use defense apply to use that is in furtherance of the user's legitimate business and is not solely for amusement, to satisfy idle curiosity, or strictly philosophical inquiry?

HOLDING AND DECISION: (Gajarsa, J.) No. The experimental use defense does not apply to use that is in furtherance of the user's legitimate business and is not solely for amusement, to satisfy idle curiosity, or strictly philosophical inquiry. Madey (P) argues the district court improperly shifted the burden to him to prove Duke's (D) use was not experimental. This court agrees because Duke (D) must put forth and prove that defense. It is not, however, an affirmative defense that must be pled or lost. The district court also impermissibly broadened the defense to include experimental, non-profit purposes. The experimental use defense is narrow and does not apply when the use is even slightly commercial in nature. The profit or non-profit status is irrelevant. Here, Duke's (D) use was in furtherance of its legitimate business, which includes research advancement to gain grants and recognition. On remand, the district court should consider Duke's (D) legitimate business and not its non-profit status. Reversed in part and remanded.

▶ ANALYSIS

Educational institutions objected vociferously to this opinion on the charge it took away academic freedoms and scientific advancement. The opinion, however, marked no significant change in patent law. The experimental use exception was always intended to be narrowly applied and the court merely reiterated its literal application of the exception.

■▬■

USM Corp. v. SPS Technologies, Inc.

Industrial fastener maker (P) v. Competitor (D)

694 F.2d 505 (7th Cir. 1982).

NATURE OF CASE: Appeal from order finding patent invalid.

FACT SUMMARY: SPS (D) allowed USM (P) to license out its patented product, but charged a higher fee if USM (P) sublicensed with certain companies.

🏛 RULE OF LAW
Patent misuse charges should be evaluated under antitrust principles, and there is no antitrust prohibition against a patent owner's using price discrimination to maximize his income.

FACTS: SPS (D) manufactured industrial fasteners and owned a patent on a patch-type self-locking industrial fastener. USM (P) sold a similar product. As part of a settlement of a previous case, SPS (D) granted USM (P) a license that allowed USM (P) to continue using the patent, but required USM (P) to pay royalties to SPS (D). The agreement required USM (P) to pay SPS (D) 25% of any royalties it obtained from sublicensing the patent. However, if USM (P) should sublicense to any one of four companies that SPS (D) had previously licensed directly, USM (P) had to remit 75% of the royalties obtained. In 1974, three years after the settlement, USM (P) filed suit seeking to invalidate SPS's (D) patent and get back the royalties paid. The district court dismissed on summary judgment the charge of patent misuse, and USM (P) appealed.

ISSUE: Should patent misuse charges be evaluated under antitrust principles?

HOLDING AND DECISION: (Posner, J.) Yes. Patent misuse charges should be evaluated under antitrust principles, and there is no antitrust prohibition against a patent owner's using price discrimination to maximize his income. Patent misuse has been described as an equitable concept designed to prevent use of a patent contrary to public policy. However, this definition is too formal. Examination of previous patent misuse cases reveals an overlap between misuse and antitrust principles. Apart from the conventional applications of patent misuse, (such as tying in unpatented products or resale price maintenance), there are no cases where standards different from those of antitrust law were actually applied to yield different results. Thus, antitrust principles are applied. The price discrimination practice complained of herein is not prohibited by antitrust law, and USM (P) failed to present any evidence of anticompetitive effect as required to satisfy a rule of reason antitrust determination. Reversed in part and affirmed in part.

▶ ANALYSIS

As Judge Posner indicated in *USM*, the line between patent misuse and antitrust law is blurry at best. Notably, the Federal Circuit does not have exclusive jurisdiction over patent-antitrust cases, but recall that patent misuse only arises as an equitable defense to a charge of patent infringement. Therefore, the standards determining patent misuse are a matter solely controlled by the Federal Circuit.

Quicknotes

ANTITRUST Body of federal law prohibiting business conduct that constitutes a restraint on trade.

EQUITABLE Just; fair.

A.C. Aukerman Co. v. R.L. Chaides Construction Co.

Highway barrier maker (P) v. Contractor (D)

960 F.2d 1020 (Fed. Cir. 1992).

NATURE OF CASE: Rehearing en banc to reconsider principles of laches and equitable estoppel applicable to a patent infringement suit.

FACT SUMMARY: Chaides (D) had actual notice of Aukerman's (P) patents and potential infringement claims. It refused to license the slip-form molds that potentially infringed Aukerman's (P) patents. After several years of communication attempts and license offers, Aukerman (P) filed an infringement suit.

> ## 🏛 RULE OF LAW
> Principles of laches and equitable estoppel are legitimate defenses to patent infringement suits.

FACTS: A.C. Aukerman Company (P) is the assignee of two patents relating to forming concrete highway barriers. Aukerman (P) entered into an agreement as part of a litigation settlement with Gomaco Corporation. Gomaco became a licensee and notified Aukerman (P) of purchasers of the adjustable slip-form molds it sold to form the barriers. R.L. Chaides Construction Co. (D) purchased a slip-form and Gomaco notified Aukerman (P). Aukerman (P) then sent a letter to Chaides (D) informing it that use of the slip-form may raise an infringement question. The parties continued communications and Aukerman (P) eventually informed Chaides (D) that it would waive past infringement if Chaides (D) agreed to license the form from Aukerman (P). Chaides (D) refused and communication between the parties ceased for approximately eight years. Chaides (D) then developed a second slip-form mold which Aukerman (P) claimed was an infringement. After additional fruitless attempts at communication and a licensing offer, Aukerman (P) filed suit against Chaides (D) for patent infringement. The district court granted Chaides (D) summary judgment.

ISSUE: Are principles of laches and equitable estoppel legitimate equitable defenses to patent infringement suits?

HOLDING AND DECISION: (Nies, C.J.) Yes. Principles of laches and equitable estoppel are legitimate defenses to patent infringement suits. Laches is cognizable under 35 U.S.C. § 282 as an equitable defense to a claim for patent infringement and may bar the patentee's claim for damages. Laches has two elements: (1) the patentee's delay in bringing suit was unreasonable and inexcusable; and (2) the alleged infringer suffered material prejudice attributable to the delay. A presumption of laches arises if the patentee delayed bringing suit for six years after the patentee knew or should have known about the alleged infringement. The presumption has the effect of shifting the burden of going forward with the evidence, not the burden of persuasion.

Equitable estoppel is also cognizable under 35 U.S.C. § 282 as an equitable defense. Equitable estoppel has three elements: (1) the patentee through misleading conduct led the alleged infringer to reasonably infer that the patentee did not intend to enforce the patent; (2) the alleged infringer relied upon the conduct of the patentee; and (3) because of its reliance, the alleged infringer would be materially prejudiced if the patentee may proceed with its claim. Reversed.

▶ ANALYSIS

There has been a noticeable increase in the use of equitable defenses centering upon the conduct of the patentee. While a patent is presumed to be valid, presumption can be shifted by the types of equitable defenses explained in the case. In effect, the patentee must come to court with clean hands in order to acquire judicial relief.

■═■

Quicknotes

LACHES An equitable defense against the enforcement of rights that have been neglected for a long period of time.

EQUITABLE ESTOPPEL A doctrine that precludes a person from asserting a right to which he or she was entitled due to his or her action, conduct or failing to act, causing another party to justifiably rely on such conduct to his or her detriment.

■═■

McElmurry v. Arkansas Power & Light Co.

Electrostatic precipitator inventor (P) v. Power company (D)

995 F.2d 1576 (Fed. Cir. 1993).

NATURE OF CASE: Appeal from grant of summary judgment for defendant finding no infringement.

FACT SUMMARY: Bowman invented a level detector while working at AP & L (D), but the assignee of the patent, White River Technologies (WRT) (P), claimed that AP & L (D) could not hire others to install the invention.

🏛 RULE OF LAW
Whether an employer has "shop rights" to patented subject matter requires a look at the totality of the circumstances to determine whether principles of equity and fairness demand a finding that a "shop right" exists.

FACTS: AP & L (D) hired Bowman, the patentee, in 1980 to assist in the installation and operation of electrostatic precipitators. An electronic precipitator removes granular ash particles from gasses emitted by coal-fired boilers to generate steam. Bowman, with another AP & L (D) employee, Roberts, improved upon the system that detected the level of fly ash in the hoppers. They designed and tested it in 1982. When it proved successful, AP & L (D) ordered it placed on the 128 hoppers at their White Bluff plant. Bowman later joined with McElmurry (P) to form White Rivers Technology, Inc. (WRT) (P) and patented the invention. Before leaving AP & L (D), Bowman assisted an employee in installing the detector at the Independence Steam Electric Station (ISES). Eventually, 142 level detectors were installed at ISES, but WRT (P) only received the contract on sixty-four of these. WRT (P) brought suit against AP & L (D) for infringement. The district court granted AP & L's (D) motion for summary judgment, concluding that AP & L (D) had "shop rights." WRT (P) appealed.

ISSUE: Does determination of whether an employer has "shop rights" require a look to the totality of the circumstances on a case-by-case basis to determine whether principles of equity and fairness demand such a finding?

HOLDING AND DECISION: (Rich, J.) Yes. Determination of whether an employer has "shop rights" requires a look to the totality of the circumstances on a case-by-case basis to determine whether principles of equity and fairness demand a finding that a "shop right" exists. Courts vary between labeling shop rights a type of implied license, a form of equitable estoppel, or a combination of both. It is closer to a combination and the proper test is as stated. One should look to such factors as the circumstances surrounding the development of the invention and the inventor's activities to determine whether fairness and equity demand the employer be allowed to use that invention in

his business. Since the district court used the proper analysis, there is no reason for reversal. AP & L (D) acquired a "shop right" to the patented level detector, but Bowman still retains the right to exclude all others besides AP & L (D). Affirmed.

▶ ANALYSIS

The general rule is that, absent a contract stating otherwise, an independent discovery is the employee's unless he was acting within the scope and purpose of his employment at the time. The "shop right" is the exception, and it was a remedy created at common law. However, it applies only to the employer; others are not allowed free use of the invention. Bowman argued that AP & L's (D) dissemination of the detector information rendered his invention worthless. But as the court pointed out, this is not infringement, and other companies besides AP & L (D) are not free to install the detector without WRT's (P) consent.

■■■

Quicknotes

EQUITABLE ESTOPPEL A doctrine that precludes a person from asserting a right to which he or she was entitled due to his or her action, conduct or failing to act, causing another party to justifiably rely on such conduct to his or her detriment.

SHOP RIGHTS The right of an employer to utilize the patented invention of an employee, devised and completed during working hours and with the employer's facilities and equipment, without the payment of royalties.

■■■

CHAPTER 13

Remedies

Quick Reference Rules of Law

PAGE

1. **Injunctions.**   The traditional four-part equitable test for injunctive relief applies to Patent   *116*
Act cases. (eBay Inc. v. MercExchange, L.L.C.)

2. **Injunctions.**   A preliminary injunction is appropriate upon satisfaction of reasonable   *117*
likelihood of success on the merits, irreparable harm absent the injunction, balance
of hardships in the moving party's favor; and the public's interest is served by the injunction.
(Sanofi-Synthelabo v. Apotex, Inc.)

3. **Damages: Basic Principles.**   A patent owner must receive from the infringer   *118*
damages adequate to compensate for the infringement. (Panduit Corp. v. Stahlin Bros. Fibre
Works, Inc.)

4. **Damages: Basic Principles.**   (1) If a particular injury was or should have been reasonably   *119*
foreseeable by an infringing competitor in the relevant market, broadly defined, that
injury is generally compensable. (2) The "entire market value rule" requires that
the unpatented component must function together with the patented component in some
manner to produce a desired end. (Rite-Hite Corp. v. Kelley Co.)

5. **Damages: The Market Share Rule.**   If the patentee's and the infringer's products are   *120*
not substitutes in a competitive market, the *Panduit* test to determine lost profits is
improper. (BIC Leisure Products, Inc. v. Windsurfing International, Inc.)

6. **Damages: Reasonable Royalties.**   The amount of damages for patent infringement is   *121*
based upon the value of a reasonable royalty for use of the patent. (Georgia-Pacific
Corp. v. United States Plywood Corp.)

7. **Enhanced Damages and Attorney Fees.**   A patentee must show objective recklessness   *122*
to recover enhanced damages on proof of willful infringement and a defendant no
longer has an affirmative duty to obtain a legal opinion prior to action. (In re Seagate
Technology, LLC)

8. **Marking.**   (1) Implied licensees are required to mark the invention under 35 U.S.C. § 287.   *124*
(2) For purposes of § 287(a), notice must be of the infringement, not merely notice
of the patent's existence or ownership. (Amsted Industries Inc. v. Buckeye Steel Castings Co.)

eBay Inc. v. MercExchange, L.L.C.

Alleged infringer (D) v. Patentee (P)

547 U.S. 388 (2006).

NATURE OF CASE: Appeal from denial of permanent injunction.

FACT SUMMARY: eBay (D) and MercExchange (P) could not agree on a license for MercExchange's (P) patent. When eBay (D) proceeded with its website, MercExchange (P) sued for patent infringement and won damages arising out of eBay's (D) liability. MercExchange (P) also sought a permanent injunction.

> **🏛 RULE OF LAW**
> The traditional four-part equitable test for injunctive relief applies to Patent Act cases.

FACTS: MercExchange, L.L.C. (P) held a business method patent for an electronic sales market using a central authority. It attempted to license its patent to eBay Inc. (D), but the parties could not reach an agreement. eBay (D) proceeded with its website which allowed private sellers to list goods for sale at auction or at a fixed price. MercExchange (P) filed suit for patent infringement. A jury found the patent valid and awarded damages to MercExchange (P) for eBay's (D) infringement. MercExchange (P) filed a motion for a permanent injunction, but the district court denied it. MercExchange (P) appealed and the Federal Circuit reversed based on the general rule that courts will grant permanent injunctions in patent infringement "absent exceptional circumstances." eBay (D) filed its petition for a writ of certiorari, which the Supreme Court granted to determine the appropriateness of the general rule on permanent injunctions in patent infringement cases.

ISSUE: Does the traditional four-part equitable test for injunctive relief apply to Patent Act cases?

HOLDING AND DECISION: (Thomas, J.) Yes. The traditional four-part equitable test for injunctive relief applies to Patent Act cases. A party seeking an injunction traditionally must establish four elements: (1) it has suffered an irreparable injury; (2) it has no adequate remedy at law; (3) an equitable remedy is warranted after balancing the hardships between plaintiff and defendant; and (4) a permanent injunction serves the public interest. These principles also apply to the Patent Act. The district court and the court of appeals failed to apply these principles when considering the appropriateness of a permanent injunction in this case. The district court impermissibly broadened the scope of the elements while the court of appeals applied a "general rule" for patent infringement cases. The district court must apply the four-part test in patent cases as well as other equitable cases. Vacated.

CONCURRENCE: (Roberts, C.J.) Courts historically have granted injunctive relief in patent cases but that history does not guarantee a right to injunctive relief. The four-part test must still be applied to determine the appropriateness of relief.

CONCURRENCE: (Kennedy, J.) The four-part test is appropriate. Many companies now use patent protection as a means to secure licensing fees and the threat of injunctive relief as a means to secure exorbitant licensing fees. Courts should take the availability of money damages into account when considering injunctive relief.

▌ *ANALYSIS*

The Court considered MercExchange's (P) history of licensing the patent in determining that money damages were appropriate rather than injunctive relief. In 2008, after several years of litigation, the parties reached a settlement wherein MercExchange (P) assigned its patents to eBay (D).

■■■

Quicknotes

CERTIORARI A discretionary writ issued by a superior court to an inferior court in order to review the lower court's decisions; the Supreme Court's writ ordering such review.

INJUNCTION A court order, requiring a person to do or prohibiting that person from doing, a specific act.

INJUNCTIVE RELIEF A court order issued as a remedy, requiring a person to do, or prohibiting that person from doing, a specific act.

■■■

Sanofi-Synthelabo v. Apotex, Inc.

Patentee (P) v. Alleged infringer (D)

470 F.3d 1368 (Fed. Cir. 2006).

NATURE OF CASE: Appeal from grant of preliminary injunction.

FACT SUMMARY: Apotex (D) sought to manufacture and market a generic version of Sanofi's (P) patented drug. Sanofi (P) sought and was granted a preliminary injunction.

🏛 RULE OF LAW
A preliminary injunction is appropriate upon satisfaction of reasonable likelihood of success on the merits, irreparable harm absent the injunction, balance of hardships in the moving party's favor; and the public's interest is served by the injunction.

FACTS: Sanofi-Synthelabo (P) holds the '265 patent to the active ingredient in its marketed drug, Plavix. Apotex (D) filed an Abbreviated New Drug Application (ANDA) because it sought to manufacture and sell a generic version. In the ANDA, Apotex (D) claimed the '265 patent was invalid. Sanofi (P) sued Apotex (D) on the basis that the ANDA was infringement. The suit triggered a 30-month stay of the ANDA, which was granted upon expiration of the stay. Apotex (D) then launched the generic version of Plavix and Sanofi (P) filed for a preliminary injunction. The district court granted the injunctive relief and ruled on Apotex (D) defenses. Apotex (D) appealed the preliminary injunction.

ISSUE: Is a preliminary injunction appropriate upon satisfaction of reasonable likelihood of success on the merits, irreparable harm absent the injunction, balance of hardships in the moving party's favor; and the public's interest is served by the injunction?

HOLDING AND DECISION: (Lourie, J.) Yes. A preliminary injunction is appropriate upon satisfaction of reasonable likelihood of success on the merits, irreparable harm absent the injunction, balance of hardships in the moving party's favor; and the public's interest is served by the injunction. Here, Apotex (D) conceded infringement and Apotex's (D) appeal of the district court's findings as to its defenses fails. Sanofi (P) asserted it would suffer irreparable harm including Plavix clinical trials, layoffs, and irreversible price erosion. The balance of hardships favors Sanofi (P) because Apotex (D) chose to engage in its risky behavior in launching its product pre-judgment. Finally, Apotex (D) appeals the bond amount as insufficient to secure its potential losses. The bond is set at the district court's discretion and nothing indicates it considered impermissible evidence. Apotex's (D) points on appeal fail. Affirmed.

▶ ANALYSIS

Sanofi (P) fought hard to protect its multi-billion dollar revenue drug Plavix. Other countries sought to eliminate Plavix's patent protection in their countries as a method to permit the manufacture and sale of generic versions. In 2008, the Federal Circuit affirmed the trial court's denial of Apotex's (D) validity challenge.

Quicknotes

INJUNCTION A court order requiring a person to do, or prohibiting that person from doing, a specific act.

INJUNCTIVE RELIEF A court order issued as a remedy, requiring a person to do, or prohibiting that person from doing, a specific act.

Panduit Corp. v. Stahlin Bros. Fibre Works, Inc.

Electric wiring duct maker (P) v. Competitor (D)

575 F.2d 1152 (6th Cir. 1978).

NATURE OF CASE: Appeal from judgment of district court adopting special master's award of damages.

FACT SUMMARY: Panduit (P) appealed a damages award of 2½% royalty given for infringement of its electrical duct patent.

🏛 RULE OF LAW
A patent owner must receive from the infringer damages adequate to compensate for the infringement.

FACTS: In 1962, Panduit (P) obtained the rights to the Walch patent for covering ducts for electrical control systems. Stahlin (D) manufactured and sold the "Lok-Slot" and "Web-Slot" ducts in 1957 and continued to do so after Panduit (P) acquired the patent. In 1969, the district court held the patent valid and infringed, enjoined Stahlin (D) from further infringement, and ordered an accounting. In 1971, the district court held Stahlin (D) in contempt and appointed a special master to render a report on damages. The court adopted the report, which recommended damages of $44,709.60 based on a 2½% reasonable royalty rate. Panduit (P) appealed the damages, seeking $808,003 in lost profits due to lost sales or, in the alternative, a 35% reasonable royalty rate. Panduit (P) also sought $4,069,000 lost on its own sales due to a price cut by Stahlin (D).

ISSUE: Must a patent owner receive from the infringer damages adequate to compensate for the infringement?

HOLDING AND DECISION: (Markey, C.J.) Yes. A patent owner must receive from the infringer damages adequate to compensate for the infringement. The question is: had the infringer not infringed, what would the patentee have made? To obtain lost sales, a patent owner must prove: (1) a demand for the patented product, (2) absence of acceptable non-infringing substitutes, (3) capability to exploit the demand, and (4) the amount of profit he would have made. Panduit (P) established elements 1 and 3, and the court erred in holding Panduit (P) did not establish element 2. However, Panduit (P) lacked evidence on its fixed costs, so element 4 was not satisfied. The district court's denial of lost sales is affirmed. When, as here, lost profits cannot be proved, the patent owner is entitled to a reasonable royalty. A reasonable royalty is an amount that a person desiring to make and sell the product would be willing to pay as a royalty and yet be able to make a profit. The special master made several errors in computing this figure. Factors that should have been considered include: (1) the lack of acceptable non-infringing substitutes, (2) Panduit's (P) unvarying policy of not licensing the patent, (3) the future business and profit Panduit (P) would expect to lose by licensing a competitor, and (4) the fact that the infringed patent gave the entire market to Panduit (P). Reversed and remanded.

▶ ANALYSIS

The four-part test of *Panduit* has been referred to by its acronym, the DAMP test. It is not, however, the exclusive test for determining whether lost profits should be awarded. Lost profits may also be inferred from lost revenues in those situations where the patent holder and the infringer are the only entities supplying the product. Since lost profits were not available in this case, Panduit (P) also sought a reasonable royalty. This is not unusual. Although a reasonable royalty is typically less than lost profits, this may not always be the case.

■■■

Quicknotes

35 U.S.C. § 284 Requires that an infringer pay damages adequate to compensate patent owner for the infringement.

LOST PROFITS The potential value of income earned or the potential value of goods that are the subject of the contract; may be used in calculating damages where the contract has been breached.

ROYALTY Payment to the owner of property for the use or sale of such property either as a percentage of profits or per unit sold.

■■■

Rite-Hite Corp. v. Kelley Co.

Parts manufacturer (P) v. Competitor (D)

56 F.3d 1538 (Fed. Cir. 1995).

NATURE OF CASE: Appeal from award of damages for infringement.

FACT SUMMARY: Rite-Hite (P) was awarded damages for lost sales of products not covered in the patent.

🏛 RULE OF LAW
(1) If a particular injury was or should have been reasonably foreseeable by an infringing competitor in the relevant market, broadly defined, that injury is generally compensable.
(2) The "entire market value rule" requires that the unpatented component must function together with the patented component in some manner to produce a desired end.

FACTS: Rite-Hite (P) held the patent on a device for securing a vehicle to a loading dock to prevent the vehicle from separating during loading and unloading. Rite-Hite (P) sued Kelley (D) for patent infringement and won. The district court awarded damages for the lost sales of the patented product, and Kelley (D) did not contest. However, the district court also awarded damages for Rite-Hite's (P) lost sales of its ADL-100 restraints, a similar device that was not covered by the patent, and for Rite-Hite's (P) lost sales of its dock levelers, a bridging platform sold with the restraints and used to bridge the edges of a vehicle and dock. Kelley (D) appealed the latter two awards.

ISSUE:
(1) If a particular injury was or should have been reasonably foreseeable by an infringing competitor in the relevant market, is that injury generally compensable?
(2) Does the "entire market value rule" require that the unpatented component function together with the patented component in some manner to produce a desired end?

HOLDING AND DECISION: (Lourie, J.)
(1) Yes. If a particular injury was or should have been reasonably foreseeable by an infringing competitor in the relevant market, broadly defined, that injury is generally compensable. Kelley (D) has not provided any statute, precedent, policy, or logic to limit the compensability of lost sales of a patentee's device that directly competes with the infringing device if it is proven that those lost sales were caused in fact by the infringement. Rite-Hite's (P) ADL-100 sales were reasonably foreseeable, and, thus, the award of damages for lost ADL-100 sales is affirmed.
(2) Yes. The "entire market value rule" requires that the unpatented component must function together with the patented component in some manner to produce a

desired end. If an unpatented component does so, then the entire value market rule permits recovery of damages based on the value of the patentee's entire apparatus. In this case, the dock levelers were sold only for marketing reasons; they did not operate together to achieve one result. The damages award based on the lost sales of the dock leveler is vacated.

DISSENT IN PART: (Nies, J.) Diversion of ADL-100 sales is not an injury to Rite-Hite's (P) property rights granted by the patent. Damages should be limited to the lost MDL-55 sales.

CONCURRENCE AND DISSENT: (Newman, J.) There is no law or policy served by eliminating recovery of actual damages when patents are involved. Damages for the dock levelers should be granted.

▶ ANALYSIS

Note that both dissents also concur in part, and moreover, completely contradict each other. Judge Nies found for Kelley (D) on both appealed claims, but Judge Newman found for Rite-Hite (P) on both. Judge Newman felt the marketing interdependence of the product was far more significant than "functionality." Judge Nies backed his argument with case law and a policy argument that the incentive to invest in patented products would be dulled if a new product's patent protected both the status quo and lost profits for old.

Quicknotes

35 U.S.C. § 284 Requires that an infringer pay damages adequate to compensate patent owner for the infringement.

MARKET VALUE The price of particular property or goods that a buyer would offer and a seller accept in the open market, following full disclosure.

PROFIT An amount gained above those monies or value paid in the form of costs.

BIC Leisure Products, Inc. v. Windsurfing International, Inc.

Sailboard Maker (D) v. Competitor (P)

1 F.3d 1214 (Fed. Cir. 1993).

NATURE OF CASE: Appeal from amount of damages awarded in infringement action.

FACT SUMMARY: Windsurfing (P) was awarded damages based upon its market share, but BIC's (D) boards were targeted at a different segment of the sailboard market.

RULE OF LAW
If the patentee's and the infringer's products are not substitutes in a competitive market, the *Panduit* test to determine lost profits is improper.

FACTS: Windsurfing (P) was awarded damages from BIC (D) for lost profits from March 8, 1983 to September 30, 1985. Windsurfing (P) primarily manufactured its patented "One-Design Class." Despite the rising popularity of faster and more versatile boards in the early 1980s, Windsurfing (P) continued with the slower, less maneuverable "One-Design Class." Windsurfing (P) also failed to adopt the new blow molding process, and stuck with the rotomolding process. Consequently, Windsurfing's (P) market dropped from 29.2% to 13.6% from 1983 to 1985. BIC's (D) sailboards differed from Windsurfing's (P), and BIC (D) sold its boards cheaply, targeting the entry-level sailboard market. Conversely, Windsurfing (P) priced its boards at the upper end of the spectrum. BIC's (D) average price over the three-year period was $351.33, while Windsurfing's (P) was $610. The district court modified the test set forth in *Panduit Corp. v. Stahlin Bros. Fibre Works,* 575 F.2d 1152 (6th Cir. 1978), to presume that Windsurfing (P) would capture a share of BIC's (D) sales in proportion to Windsurfing's (P) share of the market. BIC (D) appealed. The district court also refused to award lost profits based on price erosion, and Windsurfing (P) appealed.

ISSUE: If the patentee's and the infringer's products are not substitutes in a competitive market, is the *Panduit* test to determine lost profits proper?

HOLDING AND DECISION: (Rader, J.) No. If the patentee's and the infringer's products are not substitutes in a competitive market, the *Panduit* test to determine lost profits is improper. To recover lost profits, a patent owner must prove that "but for" the infringement, it would have made the infringer's sales. Both the first *Panduit* factor, demand for the patented product, and the second, absence of acceptable, non-infringing alternatives, assume the patent owner and infringer sell substantially the same product, and therefore do not meet the "but for" test. If the products are not sufficiently similar, the infringer's customers would not necessarily transfer their demand to the patent owner's product. Without BIC (D) in the market,

BIC's (D) customers would have likely sought boards in the same price range and not then purchased Windsurfing (P) boards. As for the price erosion decision, the record shows that other market forces besides BIC (D) led to Windsurfing (P) lowering its board costs. Reversed in part, affirmed in part.

ANALYSIS

The price erosion doctrine was created to compensate a plaintiff who lost profits because the infringement forced the plaintiff to reduce his prices. In Windsurfing (P), the facts revealed several other factors that probably led to Windsurfing (P) lowering its costs. However, when 3M and Johnson & Johnson engaged in vigorous price competition over equivalent products that caused a steady decline in prices, a price erosion award was found to be acceptable. See *Minnesota Mining & Manufacturing Co. v. Johnson & Johnson Orthopaedics Inc.,* 976 F.2d 1559, 24 U.S.P.Q.2d 1321 (Fed. Cir. 1992).

Quicknotes

PANDUIT TEST a damages test explained in *Panduit Corp. v. Stahlin Bros. Fibre Works,* 575 F.2d 1152 (6th Cir. 1978).

Georgia-Pacific Corp. v. United States Plywood Corp.

[Parties not identified.]

318 F. Supp. 1116, *modified*, 446 F.2d 295 (S.D.N.Y. 1971).

NATURE OF CASE: [Nature of Case not stated in casebook excerpt.]

FACT SUMMARY: [Fact Summary not stated in casebook excerpt.]

> **RULE OF LAW**
> The amount of damages for patent infringement is based upon the value of a reasonable royalty for use of the patent.

FACTS: [Facts not stated in casebook excerpt.]

ISSUE: Is the amount of damages for patent infringement based upon the value of a reasonable royalty for use of the patent?

HOLDING AND DECISION: (Tenney, J.) Yes. The amount of damages for patent infringement is based upon the value of a reasonable royalty for use of the patent. The reasonable royalty value can be determined by an examination of a variety of evidentiary facts. Such evidence may include royalties received, established profitability of the product, and opinion testimony of qualified experts. Conflicting evidence calls for the exercise of the district court's judicial discretion. [Decision not stated in casebook excerpt.]

▶ ANALYSIS

The measure of damages used in the *Georgia-Pacific Corp.* case, the reasonable royalty measure, is the one most commonly used. If, as is the case here, there are no existing licenses, the court will determine what a reasonable royalty rate would be, as it did here. Other methods of determining damages are to base them on the profits made by the infringer, or the losses sustained by the patentee as a result of the infringement.

■≡■

Quicknotes

ROYALTY Payment to the owner of property for the use or sale of such property either as a percentage of profits or per unit sold.

■≡■

In re Seagate Technology, LLC

Alleged infringer (D)

497 F.3d 1360 (Fed. Cir. 2007).

NATURE OF CASE: Writ of mandamus.

FACT SUMMARY: The trial court held Seagate (D) waived its attorney-client privilege and work product protection for in-house, trial, and opinion counsel communications concerning the infringement, invalidity, and enforceability of Convolve patents. Seagate (D) sought a writ of mandamus to vacate the trial court's orders for document production.

🏛 RULE OF LAW
A patentee must show objective recklessness to recover enhanced damages on proof of willful infringement and a defendant no longer has an affirmative duty to obtain a legal opinion prior to action.

FACTS: Convolve, Inc. sued Seagate Technology, LLC (D) for willful violation of several patents. Just prior to the lawsuit, Seagate (D) hired opinion counsel, Gerald Sekimura, to evaluate the Convolve patents. Sekimura issued three opinion letters. Seagate (D) notified Convolve of its intent to rely on the opinion letters as a defense, disclosed his work product, and produced him for deposition. Convolve then moved for disclosure of work product of all counsel, including trial counsel. The trial court held Seagate (D) waived attorney-client privilege concerning infringement, invalidity, and enforceability of the Convolve patents. It ordered the production of documents and testimony and provided for in camera review of trial strategy documents. Finally, the trial court held work product protection was waived. Seagate (D) moved for a stay and certification of an interlocutory appeal, which the trial court denied. Seagate (D) petitioned the federal court for a writ of mandamus to order the trial court to vacate its discovery production orders. The federal court sua sponte ordered en banc review.

ISSUE: Must a patentee show objective recklessness to recover enhanced damages on proof of willful infringement and does a defendant still have an affirmative duty to obtain a legal opinion prior to action?

HOLDING AND DECISION: (Mayer, J.) Yes and no. A patentee must show objective recklessness to recover enhanced damages on proof of willful infringement and a defendant no longer has an affirmative duty to obtain a legal opinion prior to action. A writ of mandamus is appropriate for a party who has no other method of obtaining the relief requested and the right to the writ is "clear and indisputable." In a discovery dispute regarding claims of privilege, mandamus is appropriate when: (1) an important issue of first impression is raised; (2) a delay until final judgment means the loss of the privilege; (3) immediate resolution avoids doctrine development that would undermine the

privilege. This case meets the criteria. Convolve can only obtain enhanced damages upon showing willful infringement. *Underwater Devices Inc. v. Morrison-Knudsen Co.,* 717 F.2d 1380 (Fed. Cir. 1983) set forth the analysis for willful infringement and enhanced damages. A potential infringer on actual notice of another's patent rights has the affirmative duty to obtain legal advice prior to initiating potentially infringing action. Thus developed the advice of counsel defense where alleged infringers claim reliance on legal opinions. "Willful" in *Underwater Devices,* however, is less stringent, more akin to negligence, than willful in the civil context and thus does not comply with Supreme Court precedent. *Underwater Devices* is overruled, a showing of objective recklessness is required, and the alleged infringer has no affirmative duty of due care. No duty to obtain legal opinion exists. Convolve argues it is improper to consider "willfulness" here but the proper legal standard informs the discovery scope, so this opinion is neither advisory nor hypothetical. Next, this Court considers the attorney-client privilege waiver. The attorney-client privilege is meant to encourage frank communication and can only be waived by the client. The scope of a client's waiver has no bright-line rule. Here, trial counsel and opinion counsel serve vastly different functions and the Supreme Court has recognized the need to protect trial counsel's thoughts and strategy. Further, a claim of willfulness requires a good faith basis that the alleged infringer's pre-filing conduct was willful infringement. Thus, trial counsel's communications are not relevant to the pre-litigation willfulness. A claim of post-litigation willfulness can be addressed via a motion for preliminary injunction. Finally, a similar analysis applies to the waiver of work production protection. The waiver may be extended to trial counsel in some circumstances, but the general rule should be that waiver for reliance on opinion counsel work product as a defense to willful infringement does not extend to trial counsel. Writ granted.

▶ ANALYSIS

This case set off waves in the patent litigation community because it nullified the affirmative duty to act with due care in willfulness cases. Prior to this opinion, defendants often waived the attorney-client privilege to establish the advice-of-counsel defense and the scope of the waiver was highly litigated. Now the prosecution of willful infringement becomes more difficult and the waiver issue less complicated.

▬▭▬

Continued on next page.

Quicknotes

AFFIRMATIVE DUTY An obligation to undertake an affirmative action for the benefit of another.

ATTORNEY-CLIENT PRIVILEGE A doctrine precluding the admission into evidence of confidential communications between an attorney and his client made in the course of obtaining professional assistance.

DISCOVERY Pretrial procedure during which one party makes certain information available to the other.

DUE CARE The degree of care that can be expected from a reasonably prudent person under similar circumstances; synonymous with ordinary care.

EN BANC The hearing of a matter by all the judges of the court, rather than only the necessary quorum.

INTERLOCUTORY APPEAL The appeal of an issue that does not resolve the disposition of the case, but is essential to a determination of the parties' legal rights.

OBJECTIVE STANDARD A standard that is not personal to an individual, but is dependent on some external source.

PRELIMINARY INJUNCTION A judicial mandate issued to require or restrain a party from certain conduct; used to preserve a trial's subject matter or to prevent threatened injury.

RECKLESSNESS Conduct that is conscious and that creates a substantial and unjustifiable risk of harm to others.

STAY An order by a court requiring a party to refrain from a specific activity until the happening of an event or upon further action by the court.

SUA SPONTE An action taken by the court by its own motion and without the suggestion of one of the parties.

WILLFULLY An act that is undertaken intentionally, knowingly, and with the intent to commit an unlawful act without a justifiable excuse.

WORK PRODUCT Work performed by an attorney in preparation of litigation that is not subject to discovery.

WRIT OF MANDAMUS A court order issued commanding a public or private entity, or an official thereof, to perform a duty required by law.

■≡■

Amsted Industries Inc. v. Buckeye Steel Castings Co.

Railroad parts manufacturer (P) v. Competitor (D)

24 F.3d 178 (Fed. Cir. 1994).

NATURE OF CASE: Appeal from award of damages in infringement action.

FACT SUMMARY: Amsted (P) sent several letters notifying others it had acquired a patent and not to infringe.

🏛 RULE OF LAW
(1) Implied licensees are required to mark the invention under 35 U.S.C. § 287. (2) For purposes of § 287(a), notice must be of the infringement, not merely notice of the patent's existence or ownership.

FACTS: The '269 patent was entitled "Combined Body Bolster Center Filler and Center Plate for Railway Cars." It referred to a center plate in combination with several other components that formed a railroad car underframe structure. The patent was assigned to Dresser Industries until 1985, at which time it sold the patent and trademark to Amsted (P). On January 10, 1986, Amsted (P) sent letters to several companies, including Buckeye (D) that noted that Amsted (P) had acquired the patent. It warned the companies to "acquaint" themselves with the patent, so they would not infringe. Buckeye (D) knew it was infringing the patent at the time it received the letter. On January 27, 1989, Amsted (P) wrote another letter to Buckeye (D) informing Buckeye (D) that it was infringing the patent with center plate. The district court awarded damages from January 16, 1986, but limited Amstead's (P) recovery because the patented articles were not marked. Buckeye (D) appealed, claiming damages should be computed from the date of the second letter, since the 1986 letter did not constitute a notice of infringement under Section 287. Amsted (P) cross-appealed, claiming marking of its device was not necessary since it was an implied licensee.

ISSUE:
(1) Are implied licensees of a patented invention required to mark the invention under 35 U.S.C. § 287?
(2) For purposes of § 287(a), must notice be of the infringement, and not merely notice of the patent's existence or ownership?

HOLDING AND DECISION: (Lourie, J.)
(1) Yes. Implied licensees of a patented invention are required to mark the invention under 35 U.S.C. § 287. Such marking fulfills the policy goal of notifying the public concerning the patent status of items in commerce. Amsted (P) or its implied licensees were required to mark, and because they did not do so, Amsted (P) is precluded from recovering damages prior to the date of notification of infringement.

(2) Yes. For purposes of § 287(a), notice must be of the infringement, not merely notice of the patent's existence or ownership. Actual notice requires the affirmative communication of a specific charge of infringement by a specific accused device. It is irrelevant whether Buckeye (D) was aware that it was infringing when the first letter was sent in 1986. The correct approach focuses on the actions of the patentee. Damages toll from the date of the second letter. Damages must be recalculated from the date of the 1989 letter. Reversed and remanded.

▶ ANALYSIS

The Patent Act provides incentive for inventors to mark their inventions, for if no marking is made, damages can only be calculated from the date of notice. Occasionally, an applicant may choose not to mark a product, so it can sue after a competitor has invested in production facilities. 35 U.S.C. § 292 also provides remedies for false marking.

■=■

Quicknotes

35 U.S.C. § 287 Provides an incentive for patentees to mark their inventions with a motive of patent rights.

■=■

The Hatch-Waxman Act

Quick Reference Rules of Law

PAGE

1. **The Bolar Exemption.**   35 U.S.C. § 271(e)(1) exempts uses of patented inventions in preclinical research from infringement even when the research results are not ultimately included in a submission to the FDA. (Merck KGaA v. Integra Lifesciences I, Ltd.) — *126*

2. **ANDA Litigation.**   An applicant filing an Abbreviated New Drug Application must certify if the new generic drug will infringe upon a patent which triggers a deadline for the patentee to file suit and receive a stay of FDA approval of the ANDA. (Mylan Pharmaceuticals, Inc. v. Thompson) — *127*

3. **The Orange Book.**   The FDA's role with regard to the accuracy of the Orange Book is purely ministerial. (aaiPharma Inc. v. Thompson) — *128*

4. **Declaratory Judgment Jurisdiction.**   Article III's limitation of federal courts' jurisdiction reflected in the Declaratory Judgment Act does not require a patent licensee to terminate or be in breach of its license agreement before it can seek a declaratory judgment that the underlying patent is invalid, unenforceable, or not infringed. (MedImmune, Inc. v. Genentech, Inc.) — *130*

5. **Declaratory Judgment Jurisdiction.**   A party does not have to have a reasonable apprehension of imminent suit before a federal court has jurisdiction over a declaratory judgment action so long as all the circumstances show judicial relief can redress an actual or imminent injury through declaratory judgment. (Teva Pharmaceuticals USA, Inc. v. Novartis Pharmaceuticals Corp.) — *131*

6. **Authorized Generics.**   The FDA is not empowered to prohibit the sale of an authorized generic during the 180-day exclusivity period granted to the first ANDA applicant to file. (Mylan Pharmaceuticals, Inc. v. U.S. Food and Drug Administration) — *133*

Merck KGaA v. Integra Lifesciences I, Ltd.

Alleged infringer (D) v. Patentee (P)

545 U.S. 193 (2005).

NATURE OF CASE: Writ of certiorari to review appellate court construction of § 271(e)(1).

FACT SUMMARY: Merck (D) used compounds covered by Integra's (P) patents in experiments and research without providing the results to the FDA. Integra (P) claimed infringement and Merck (D) defended with § 271(e)(1).

🏛 RULE OF LAW
35 U.S.C. § 271(e)(1) exempts uses of patented inventions in preclinical research from infringement even when the research results are not ultimately included in a submission to the FDA.

FACTS: Integra Lifesciences I, Ltd. (P) owns five patents related to RGD peptide. Merck KGaA (D) began research into angiogenesis and the research eventually included RGD peptides. The primary researcher used RGD peptides in experiments and developed cyclic RGD peptides. Integra (P) sued Merck (D) alleging willful infringement and inducement to infringe. Merck (D) defended with a research exemption and § 271(e)(1). A jury awarded damages to Integra (P), the appellate court upheld the ruling that Integra's (P) patents covered the cyclic peptides and § 271(e)(1) did not apply. The Supreme Court granted certiorari review to review the court of appeals' construction of § 271(e)(1).

ISSUE: Does 35 U.S.C. § 271(e)(1) exempt uses of patented inventions in preclinical research from infringement even when the research results are not ultimately included in a submission to the FDA?

HOLDING AND DECISION: (Scalia, J.) Yes. 35 U.S.C. § 271(e)(1) exempts uses of patented inventions in preclinical research from infringement even when the research results are not ultimately included in a submission to the FDA. § 271(e)(1) permits patented inventions to be used when the information is to be developed and submitted pursuant to a federal law. The statute is broad and does not contemplate only certain information or certain submissions. The parties concede its breadth, but Integra (P) argues the FDA is not interested in preclinical information other than safety and any research into other information is outside the scope of the exemption. The FDA, however, does not limit its inquiry and neither will this Court. The appellate court concluded § 271(e)(1) did not apply here because Merck (D) was not using the patented RGD peptides to gather information for submission to the FDA but to determine the best drug candidate for future clinical testing. The court also concluded not all experimental activity that might lead to a future FDA submission qualifies for the exemption. This Court agrees with the latter statement but not the first.

Scientific experiments are trial and error and not every experiment will lead to an FDA submission. Congress exempted all uses "reasonably related" to the process of information development. The experiments are thus protected so long as there is a reasonable basis for believing they will lead to submissible relevant information. Vacated and remanded.

▌ ANALYSIS

The Federal Circuit tried to narrow the safe harbor exemption for research activities but the Supreme Court confirmed the breadth of the statute. The Court did not distinguish between preclinical and clinical trials. It now increases the likelihood that defendants will argue that every potentially infringing action was done in anticipation of future submission to the FDA regardless of the actual submission.

∎═∎

Quicknotes

FOOD AND DRUG ADMINISTRATION (FDA) A federal agency responsible for establishing safety and quality standards for foods, drugs, and cosmetics.

∎═∎

Mylan Pharmaceuticals, Inc. v. Thompson

[Parties not identified.]

268 F.3d 1323 (Fed. Cir. 2001).

NATURE OF CASE: [Nature of Case not stated in casebook excerpt.]

FACT SUMMARY: [Fact Summary not stated in casebook excerpt.]

> 🏛 **RULE OF LAW**
> An applicant filing an Abbreviated New Drug Application (ANDA) must certify if the new generic drug will infringe upon a patent which triggers a deadline for the patentee to file suit and receive a stay of FDA approval of the ANDA.

FACTS: [Facts not stated in casebook excerpt.]

ISSUE: Must an applicant filing an Abbreviated New Drug Application certify if the new generic drug will infringe upon a patent which triggers a deadline for the patentee to file suit and receive a stay of FDA approval of the ANDA?

HOLDING AND DECISION: (Mayer, C.J.) Yes. An applicant filing an Abbreviated New Drug Application must certify if the new generic drug will infringe upon a patent which triggers a deadline for the patentee to file suit and receive a stay of FDA approval of the ANDA. The ANDA came about to expedite approval for generic drug manufacturers while inducing name brand manufacturers to continue research and develop under patent protection. ANDA filers cannot seek to market generic drugs prior to patent expiration but the mere application process does not trigger a patentee's right to sue for infringement. The ANDA applicant must certify the patents implicated in the generic drug manufacture; these certifications are traditionally Paragraph I, II, III or IV certification. Paragraph IV certification requires notice to the patentee and details for the assertion that the patent is invalid, unenforceable, or not infringed. The patentee then has 45 days to file suit for infringement, which initiates the stay on ANDA approval. The ANDA applicant also cannot file declaratory judgment action until after the expiration of the 45-day patentee review period. The patentee thus has time to file suit as well as delay the ANDA approval. [Decision not stated in casebook excerpt.]

▶ ANALYSIS

The Hatch-Waxman Act attempted to balance the interests of brand name patentees with the public's interest in generic drug manufacturers. Generic drug manufacturers achieved significant gains with the Act. Patentees gained patent protection extension while the FDA approval process proceeds.

Quicknotes

FOOD AND DRUG ADMINISTRATION (FDA) A federal agency responsible for establishing safety and quality standards for foods, drugs, and cosmetics.

■■■

aaiPharma Inc. v. Thompson

Third-party patentee (P) v. Secretary of Health and Human Services (D)

296 F.3d 227 (Fed. Cir. 2002).

NATURE OF CASE: Appeal from rejection of challenge under Administrative Procedure Act.

FACT SUMMARY: AaiPharma (P) wanted its patent included in the Orange Book as a patent related to the brand name drug Prozac. The patentee, as the NDA holder, refused to list the aaiPharma (P) patent and the FDA did not force it. AaiPharma (P) lost out on the notification required of ANDA applicants because its patent was not listed in the Orange Book.

🏛 RULE OF LAW
The FDA's role with regard to the accuracy of the Orange Book is purely ministerial.

FACTS: Pioneer (i.e., brand name) drug manufacturers must submit a New Drug Application (NDA) to the FDA for approval. NDA applicants must provide the FDA a listing of all patents that claim the approved drug or method to use that drug. The FDA, once it approves the NDA, then publishes the list in the "Approved Drug Products with Therapeutic Equivalence Evaluations" also known as the "Orange Book." The Hatch-Waxman Act created an opportunity for generic drug manufacturers to enter the market without investing the significant funds in clinical studies to demonstrate the generic's safety and efficacy. The generic manufacturer can submit an Abbreviated New Drug Application (ANDA), which relies on the pioneer drug manufacturer's clinical studies. The NDA applicant must supplement its Orange Book list about new patents that issue while approval is pending or within 30 days of new patents issued after approval. An ANDA applicant reviews the Orange Book patents and makes one of four certifications with its ANDA: (I) no pioneer drug patent information submitted to FDA; (II) the patent has expired; (III) patent will expire on a certain date; or (IV) patent is invalid or will not be infringed. A paragraph IV certification requires notice to the patentee and the NDA holder, which triggers a 45-day review period in which the patentee could file suit for infringement. If suit is filed, the ANDA is automatically stayed for thirty months. If the patent is not listed in the Orange Book, the ANDA applicant does not have to file a paragraph IV certification. AaiPharma, Inc. (P) received a patent on a variant of the active drug in Prozac. It sought to have its patent included in the Orange Book because the patent of Eli Lilly & Co., the Prozac patentee and NDA holder, was about to expire and several generic manufacturers planned to launch generic versions immediately. The inclusion of the aaiPharma (P) patent would require the generic manufacturers to give notice to aaiPharma (P) and trigger the review and potential stay periods. Only the NDA holders can submit patents for listing in the Orange Book, so aaiPharma (P)

asked Lilly to submit. The patentee refused and aaiPharma (P) asked the FDA (D) to intervene. The FDA (D) followed procedure and requested Lilly confirm the correctness of its Orange Book listing. When aaiPharma (P) did not get its patent listed, it sued the FDA (D) under the Administrative Procedure Act hours before the FDA (D) was to approve the generic manufacturer's ANDAs. The district court denied relief and aaiPharma (P) appealed.

ISSUE: Is the FDA's role with regard to the accuracy of the Orange Book purely ministerial?

HOLDING AND DECISION: (Michael, J.) If the aaiPharma (P) patent claims Prozac, then Lilly has an obligation to list the patent in the Orange Book. Enforcement mechanisms are unclear, however. Precedent shows that a generic drug manufacturer cannot sue an NDA holder to delist a patent, so it follows that a third-party patentee cannot force an NDA holder to list a patent. AaiPharma (P) thus sued the FDA (D) instead of Lilly. The FDA argues it plays a purely ministerial role in publishing the Orange Book with no responsibility to evaluate the accuracy of patent listings. AaiPharma (P) asserts the FDA (D), once notified of a failure to list a patent, must do more than request the NDA holder list the patent. The *Chevron* analysis applies here. The first step is whether Congress has spoken to the controlling issue. The FDA (D) and aaiPharma (P) assert different provisions of 21 U.S.C. § 355 to support each position and this Court finds the provisions conflict. Congress has thus failed to express its clear intent on whether the FDA (D) has an obligation to ensure the accuracy of the Orange Book. The next step is to determine if the FDA's (D) construction is permissible. The construction certainly is reasonable, but might be undermined by the subsections (d)(6) and (e)(4). Subsection (d) (6) requires the FDA (D) to refuse an NDA that fails to include the patent information. AaiPharma (P) interprets this to mean that the FDA (D) must evaluate the list to ensure accuracy. The more modest reading, however, is that the FDA (D) must reject the NDA if the list is omitted entirely. This is the better reading. Subsection (e)(4) requires the FDA (D) to withdraw NDA approval if the NDA holder does not file the list of patents within thirty days of notice from FDA (D) that the list was omitted. AaiPharma (P) argues this subsection permits the FDA (D) to withdraw NDA approval if it notifies the NDA holder that a patent was omitted from the list and the holder refuses to amend. The better reading is that this permits NDA holders, granted approval prior to the passage of the Hatch-Waxman Act, thirty days from notice to file the list. Thus, the FDA's (D) construction of § 355 is permissible.

Continued on next page.

Congress must act to fill the enforcement gap in the statute. Affirmed.

▶ *ANALYSIS*

The FDA has no obligation to ensure the accuracy of the patent information listed in the Orange Book but can rely solely on the self-report of the NDA holder. The statute is written in mandatory terms, but no enforcement mechanisms exist to ensure compliance. Congress has yet to address this oversight.

■═■

Quicknotes

FOOD AND DRUG ADMINISTRATION (FDA) A federal agency responsible for establishing safety and quality standards for foods, drugs, and cosmetics.

■═■

MedImmune, Inc. v. Genentech, Inc.

Drug manufacturer (P) v. Patentee (D)

549 U.S. 118 (2007).

NATURE OF CASE: Appeal of dismissal.

FACT SUMMARY: MedImmune (P), Genentech's (D) licensee, feared an infringement suit filed by Genentech (D). It filed a declaratory judgment action to declare Genentech's (D) new patent invalid.

🏛 **RULE OF LAW**
Article III's limitation of federal courts' jurisdiction reflected in the Declaratory Judgment Act does not require a patent licensee to terminate or be in breach of its license agreement before it can seek a declaratory judgment that the underlying patent is invalid, unenforceable, or not infringed.

FACTS: Genentech, Inc. (D) licensed an existing patent and a pending patent to drug manufacturer MedImmune, Inc. (P). The pending patent matured into a patent and Genentech (D) notified MedImmune (P) it would owe royalties on the new patent. MedImmune (P) believed the new patent was invalid and not infringed by its drug, so no royalties were owed. MedImmune (P) did not want to risk the results of an infringement suit, so it paid the royalties under protest and filed a declaratory judgment action against Genentech (D). The district court dismissed the suit on the grounds that the existence of the license agreement "obliterates any reasonable apprehension" of an infringement suit. Genentech (D) successfully argued that MedImmune (P) had failed to meet the justiciability "case or controversy" requirement of Article III jurisdiction over declaratory judgment actions. MedImmune (P) appealed.

ISSUE: Does Article III's limitation of federal courts' jurisdiction reflected in the Declaratory Judgment Act require a patent licensee to terminate or be in breach of its license agreement before it can seek a declaratory judgment that the underlying patent is invalid, unenforceable, or not infringed?

HOLDING AND DECISION: (Scalia, J.) No. Article III's limitation of federal courts' jurisdiction reflected in the Declaratory Judgment Act does not require a patent licensee to terminate or be in breach of its license agreement before it can seek a declaratory judgment that the underlying patent is invalid, unenforceable, or not infringed. A declaratory judgment action is appropriate when the dispute is definite, concrete, and touches the legal relations of parties having adverse legal interests. Here, if MedImmune (P) had refused to pay the royalties, all elements would be met. There is no imminent threat of harm, however, because MedImmune (P) paid the royalties and Genentech (D) would not file the infringement suit.

The issue then becomes whether the party must first expose itself to liability. A party facing government threat can bring a declaratory judgment action before imminent prosecution occurs, so this Court must consider whether the same principles apply to a party facing threat from another private party. This Court in *Altvater v. Freeman*, 319 U.S. 359 (1943), permitted a declaratory judgment action where royalties were paid under protest because the payor preserved its right to recover the royalties or challenge the claim. Genentech (D) argues that its license agreement with Medimmune (P) immunizes MedImmune (P) from an infringement suit so long as MedImmune (P) pays royalties and does not challenge the patents. The license agreement does not state that, however. Royalty payments do not guarantee abstention from a patent validity challenge. Further, the argument that MedImmune (P) cannot sue for invalidity while also enjoying the benefits of the license fails because MedImmune (P) is not disputing the license agreement's validity. Genentech's (D) arguments that jurisdiction is not found fail. Genentech (D) also requests this Court dismiss the lawsuit on discretionary grounds, but this is the first time this issue has been raised and the lower court can consider that on remand. Reversed and remanded.

▶ **ANALYSIS**

This case reversed long-settled Federal Circuit precedent, so similar cases may work through the system soon. Licensees may have felt obligated to continue to pay royalties to avoid the potentially bankrupting damages award of an infringement suit or face breach of the license agreement in failure to pay royalties. This opinion permits licensees an opportunity to dispute the patent validity while maintaining their business pursuant to the license.

■■▪

Quicknotes

DECLARATORY JUDGMENT ACT Allows prospective defendants to sue for a declaration of their rights.

JUSTICIABILITY An actual controversy that is capable of determination by the court.

LICENSE A right that is granted to a person allowing him or her to conduct an activity that without such permission he or she could not lawfully do, and which is unassignable and revocable at the will of the licensor.

ROYALTY Payment to the owner of property for the use or sale of such property either as a percentage of profits or per unit sold.

■■▪

Teva Pharmaceuticals USA, Inc. v. Novartis Pharmaceuticals Corp.

Generic drug manufacturer (P) v. Pioneer drug manufacturer (D)

482 F.3d 1330 (Fed. Cir. 2007).

NATURE OF CASE: Appeal from dismissal of declaratory judgment action.

FACT SUMMARY: Novartis (D) sued Teva (P) for patent infringement of one of its five patents. Teva (P) sued Novartis (D) in a declaratory judgment action requesting "patent certainty" on the validity of the remaining four patents. The district court dismissed for lack of subject matter jurisdiction because Teva (P) did not face the imminent threat of an infringement suit on the four remaining patents.

🏛 RULE OF LAW

A party does not have to have a reasonable apprehension of imminent suit before a federal court has jurisdiction over a declaratory judgment action so long as all the circumstances show judicial relief can redress an actual or imminent injury through declaratory judgment.

FACTS: Novartis Pharmaceuticals Corp. (D) holds the New Drug Application (NDA) for three strengths of Famvir. Its NDA lists five patents related to Famvir, including the '937 patent. Teva Pharmaceuticals USA, Inc. (P) filed its Abbreviated New Drug Application (ANDA) for a generic version of Famvir. Its application included a paragraph IV certification that Novartis's (D) patents were invalid. Novartis (D) filed an infringement suit against Teva (P) on the '937 patents but not the four remaining. Teva (P) then filed a declaratory judgment action on the four remaining patents for a finding that the patents were invalid. Novartis (D) moved to dismiss on the grounds that Teva (P) had no imminent threat of an infringement suit for the remaining patents, so the district court had no jurisdiction in a declaratory judgment action. The district court dismissed, applying the Federal Circuit's two-prong *Pfizer* test. Teva (P) appealed.

ISSUE: Must a party have a reasonable apprehension of imminent suit before a federal court has jurisdiction over a declaratory judgment action so long as all the circumstances show judicial relief can redress an actual or imminent injury through declaratory judgment?

HOLDING AND DECISION: (Gajarsa, J.) No. A party does not have to have a reasonable apprehension of imminent suit before a federal court has jurisdiction over a declaratory judgment action so long as all the circumstances show judicial relief can redress an actual or imminent injury through declaratory judgment. The Supreme Court's recent opinion in *MedImmune*, 549 U.S. 118 (2007), disagreed with this court's two-prong *Pfizer* test, 395 F.2d 1324 (Fed. Cir. 2005). The requirement for federal jurisdiction is an actual case or controversy, so the court will no longer apply the *Pfizer* test but the standard of an actual case or controversy as set forth in *MedImmune*. That standard is whether "all the circumstances" show an actual or imminent injury can be redressed by judicial relief justifying a declaratory judgment. Here, the district court was bound by the *Pfizer* precedent, but *MedImmune* is the appropriate standard. Under "all the circumstances" of this case, Teva (P) has a justiciable Article III controversy. Novartis (D) created the controversy when it filed its infringement suit on the fifth patent, thus placing Teva's (P) ANDA in actual dispute. The two are different cases but arise out of the same controversy. Further, Teva's (P) ANDA automatically creates a justiciable controversy regarding infringement, so if Novartis (D) has an Article III case, then it follows that the other party also has an Article III declaratory judgment action. Third, Novartis (D) has tried to claim the protections due a patentee under Hatch-Waxman while avoiding its responsibility to expedite the determination of the validity of the remaining four patents. Fourth, the pending infringement litigation creates uncertainty as to Teva's (P) ANDA, which creates a justiciable controversy. Finally, Novartis (D) has created the possibility of future litigation on the four patents, which could insulate Novartis's (D) patents until they expire. Looking at all the circumstances, Teva (P) has suffered actual injury that can be traced to Novartis's (D) actions and Teva (P) has made out an Article III case or controversy. The court has jurisdiction over the declaratory judgment action. Reversed.

CONCURRENCE: (Friedman, J.) The Supreme Court in *MedImmune* noted in a dicta footnote that it rejected this court's "reasonable apprehension of imminent suit." This court must therefore apply the *MedImmune* test and immediately stop applying the *Pfizer* test. The court came to the correct conclusion today but in an unnecessarily long fashion. The threat to Teva (P) after submission of its Paragraph IV certification creates a justiciable controversy placing the case within the court's jurisdiction.

▶ ANALYSIS

This was the Federal Circuit's first opinion setting forth the new rule governing subject matter jurisdiction of the federal courts over declaratory judgment actions. The majority went out of its way to analyze the totality of the circumstances and demonstrate the applicability of the Supreme Court's decision in *MedImmune*. The case may not have needed such a complicated analysis, as the concurring opinion

Continued on next page.

notes, but the Federal Circuit was overruling its long-standing past precedent.

■==■

Quicknotes

JUSTICIABILITY An actual controversy that is capable of determination by the court.

■==■

Mylan Pharmaceuticals, Inc. v. U.S. Food and Drug Administration

Generic drug manufacturer (P) v. Government agency (D)

454 F.3d 270 (4th Cir. 2006).

NATURE OF CASE: Appeal from dismissal of case.

FACT SUMMARY: Mylan (P) began marketing its generic drug on the same day the NDA holder's licensee began marketing its licensed generic. Mylan (P) argued the FDA (D) should prohibit the sale of an authorized generic within the 180-day exclusivity period granted to the first ANDA applicant approved.

🏛 RULE OF LAW
The FDA is not empowered to prohibit the sale of an authorized generic during the 180-day exclusivity period granted to the first ANDA applicant to file.

FACTS: Mylan Pharmaceuticals, Inc. (P) sought to manufacture a generic version of a drug for which Procter & Gamble was the NDA holder. It filed a paragraph IV ANDA, which the FDA (D) approved. The same day Mylan (P) began sales of its generic, a licensee of Proctor & Gamble began selling its authorized generic of the same drug pursuant to its license. Mylan (P) lost millions of dollars from this competition. Mylan (P) and another generic manufacturer engaged in several suits with the FDA (D) but did not prevail. Mylan (P) resumed its suit against the FDA (D), arguing the FDA should prohibit the sale of the licensed generic during the 180-day exclusivity period granted to the first ANDA applicant to file and get approved. The FDA (D) moved to dismiss for failure to state a claim and the district court granted that motion. Mylan (P) appealed.

ISSUE: Is the FDA empowered to prohibit the sale of an authorized generic during the 180-day exclusivity period granted to the first ANDA applicant to file?

HOLDING AND DECISION: (Michael, J.) No. The FDA is not empowered to prohibit the sale of an authorized generic during the 180-day exclusivity period granted to the first ANDA applicant to file. Mylan (P) argues the denial of its petition was arbitrary and capricious. This court must apply the *Chevron*, 467 I.S. 837 (1984), analysis to determine if the FDA (D) is appropriately interpreting its governing statute, 21 U.S.C. § 355(j)(5)(B)(iv). First, has Congress spoken to this particular issue? The statute language is plain. The statute addresses later-filing ANDA applicants when referencing the 180-day exclusivity period. The FDA (D) would have to redefine paragraph IV certification to include NDA drugs in the 180-day exclusivity. Mylan (P) argues Congress intended for the 180-day exclusivity period to permit solely one manufacturer to market a generic during the period. Mylan (P), however, has no support in text, legislative history, or pre-enactment legislative statements. In fact, the Hatch-Waxman Act attempts to protect the pioneer manufacture's property rights rather than solely concerned with generic marketing rights. Mylan (P) next argues the FDA's (D) position is inconsistent with the agency's position in a prior case. That case was about the proper scope of the commercial marketing trigger, which is not the issue here. The FDA (D) there determined a paragraph IV ANDA applicant's marketing of the authorized generic was the commercial marketing trigger for the 180-day exclusivity period. Mylan's (P) arguments do not show that the FDA (D) was acting in an arbitrary or capricious manner. Affirmed.

▶ ANALYSIS

An "exclusivity" period seems to imply that only one manufacturer should be permitted to manufacture during this period. Nothing indicates, however, this was Congress's intent other than the use of the word "exclusivity." Further, nothing indicates Congress intended for the generic manufacturer to obtain protection to the exclusion of all others.

■══■

Quicknotes

ARBITRARY AND CAPRICIOUS STANDARD Standard imposed in reviewing the decision of an agency or court when the decision may have been made in disregard of the facts or law.

FOOD AND DRUG ADMINISTRATION (FDA) A federal agency responsible for establishing safety and quality standards for foods, drugs, and cosmetics.

■══■

Glossary

Common Latin Words and Phrases Encountered in the Law

A FORTIORI: Because one fact exists or has been proven, therefore a second fact that is related to the first fact must also exist.

A PRIORI: From the cause to the effect. A term of logic used to denote that when one generally accepted truth is shown to be a cause, another particular effect must necessarily follow.

AB INITIO: From the beginning; a condition which has existed throughout, as in a marriage which was void ab initio.

ACTUS REUS: The wrongful act; in criminal law, such action sufficient to trigger criminal liability.

AD VALOREM: According to value; an ad valorem tax is imposed upon an item located within the taxing jurisdiction calculated by the value of such item.

AMICUS CURIAE: Friend of the court. Its most common usage takes the form of an amicus curiae brief, filed by a person who is not a party to an action but is nonetheless allowed to offer an argument supporting his legal interests.

ARGUENDO: In arguing. A statement, possibly hypothetical, made for the purpose of argument, is one made arguendo.

BILL QUIA TIMET: A bill to quiet title (establish ownership) to real property.

BONA FIDE: True, honest, or genuine. May refer to a person's legal position based on good faith or lacking notice of fraud (such as a bona fide purchaser for value) or to the authenticity of a particular document (such as a bona fide last will and testament).

CAUSA MORTIS: With approaching death in mind. A gift causa mortis is a gift given by a party who feels certain that death is imminent.

CAVEAT EMPTOR: Let the buyer beware. This maxim is reflected in the rule of law that a buyer purchases at his own risk because it is his responsibility to examine, judge, test, and otherwise inspect what he is buying.

CERTIORARI: A writ of review. Petitions for review of a case by the United States Supreme Court are most often done by means of a writ of certiorari.

CONTRA: On the other hand. Opposite. Contrary to.

CORAM NOBIS: Before us; writs of error directed to the court that originally rendered the judgment.

CORAM VOBIS: Before you; writs of error directed by an appellate court to a lower court to correct a factual error.

CORPUS DELICTI: The body of the crime; the requisite elements of a crime amounting to objective proof that a crime has been committed.

CUM TESTAMENTO ANNEXO, ADMINISTRATOR (ADMINISTRATOR C.T.A.): With will annexed; an administrator c.t.a. settles an estate pursuant to a will in which he is not appointed.

DE BONIS NON, ADMINISTRATOR (ADMINISTRATOR D.B.N.): Of goods not administered; an administrator d.b.n. settles a partially settled estate.

DE FACTO: In fact; in reality; actually. Existing in fact but not officially approved or engendered.

DE JURE: By right; lawful. Describes a condition that is legitimate "as a matter of law," in contrast to the term "de facto," which connotes something existing in fact but not legally sanctioned or authorized. For example, de facto segregation refers to segregation brought about by housing patterns, etc., whereas de jure segregation refers to segregation created by law.

DE MINIMIS: Of minimal importance; insignificant; a trifle; not worth bothering about.

DE NOVO: Anew; a second time; afresh. A trial de novo is a new trial held at the appellate level as if the case originated there and the trial at a lower level had not taken place.

DICTA: Generally used as an abbreviated form of obiter dicta, a term describing those portions of a judicial opinion incidental or not necessary to resolution of the specific question before the court. Such nonessential statements and remarks are not considered to be binding precedent.

DUCES TECUM: Refers to a particular type of writ or subpoena requesting a party or organization to produce certain documents in their possession.

EN BANC: Full bench. Where a court sits with all justices present rather than the usual quorum.

EX PARTE: For one side or one party only. An ex parte proceeding is one undertaken for the benefit of only one party, without notice to, or an appearance by, an adverse party.

EX POST FACTO: After the fact. An ex post facto law is a law that retroactively changes the consequences of a prior act.

EX REL.: Abbreviated form of the term ex relatione, meaning upon relation or information. When the state brings an action in which it has no interest against an individual at the instigation of one who has a private interest in the matter.

FORUM NON CONVENIENS: Inconvenient forum. Although a court may have jurisdiction over the case, the action should be tried in a more conveniently located court, one to which parties and witnesses may more easily travel, for example.

GUARDIAN AD LITEM: A guardian of an infant as to litigation, appointed to represent the infant and pursue his/her rights.

HABEAS CORPUS: You have the body. The modern writ of habeas corpus is a writ directing that a person (body) being detained (such as a prisoner) be brought before the court so that the legality of his detention can be judicially ascertained.

IN CAMERA: In private, in chambers. When a hearing is held before a judge in his chambers or when all spectators are excluded from the courtroom.

IN FORMA PAUPERIS: In the manner of a pauper. A party who proceeds in forma pauperis because of his poverty is one who is allowed to bring suit without liability for costs.

INFRA: Below, under. A word referring the reader to a later part of a book. (The opposite of supra.)

IN LOCO PARENTIS: In the place of a parent.

IN PARI DELICTO: Equally wrong; a court of equity will not grant requested relief to an applicant who is in pari delicto, or as much at fault in the transactions giving rise to the controversy as is the opponent of the applicant.

IN PARI MATERIA: On like subject matter or upon the same matter. Statutes relating to the same person or things are said to be in pari materia. It is a general rule of statutory construction that such statutes should be construed together, i.e., looked at as if they together constituted one law.

IN PERSONAM: Against the person. Jurisdiction over the person of an individual.

IN RE: In the matter of. Used to designate a proceeding involving an estate or other property.

IN REM: A term that signifies an action against the res, or thing. An action in rem is basically one that is taken directly against property, as distinguished from an action in personam, i.e., against the person.

INTER ALIA: Among other things. Used to show that the whole of a statement, pleading, list, statute, etc., has not been set forth in its entirety.

INTER PARTES: Between the parties. May refer to contracts, conveyances or other transactions having legal significance.

INTER VIVOS: Between the living. An inter vivos gift is a gift made by a living grantor, as distinguished from bequests contained in a will, which pass upon the death of the testator.

IPSO FACTO: By the mere fact itself.

JUS: Law or the entire body of law.

LEX LOCI: The law of the place; the notion that the rights of parties to a legal proceeding are governed by the law of the place where those rights arose.

MALUM IN SE: Evil or wrong in and of itself; inherently wrong. This term describes an act that is wrong by its very nature, as opposed to one which would not be wrong but for the fact that there is a specific legal prohibition against it (malum prohibitum).

MALUM PROHIBITUM: Wrong because prohibited, but not inherently evil. Used to describe something that is wrong because it is expressly forbidden by law but that is not in and of itself evil, e.g., speeding.

MANDAMUS: We command. A writ directing an official to take a certain action.

MENS REA: A guilty mind; a criminal intent. A term used to signify the mental state that accompanies a crime or other prohibited act. Some crimes require only a general mens rea (general intent to do the prohibited act), but others, like assault with intent to murder, require the existence of a specific mens rea.

MODUS OPERANDI: Method of operating; generally refers to the manner or style of a criminal in committing crimes, admissible in appropriate cases as evidence of the identity of a defendant.

NEXUS: A connection to.

NISI PRIUS: A court of first impression. A nisi prius court is one where issues of fact are tried before a judge or jury.

N.O.V. (NON OBSTANTE VEREDICTO): Notwithstanding the verdict. A judgment n.o.v. is a judgment given in favor of one party despite the fact that a verdict was returned in favor of the other party, the justification being that the verdict either had no reasonable support in fact or was contrary to law.

NUNC PRO TUNC: Now for then. This phrase refers to actions that may be taken and will then have full retroactive effect.

PENDENTE LITE: Pending the suit; pending litigation underway.

PER CAPITA: By head; beneficiaries of an estate, if they take in equal shares, take per capita.

PER CURIAM: By the court; signifies an opinion ostensibly written "by the whole court" and with no identified author.

PER SE: By itself, in itself; inherently.

PER STIRPES: By representation. Used primarily in the law of wills to describe the method of distribution where a person, generally because of death, is unable to take that which is left to him by the will of another, and therefore his heirs divide such property between them rather than take under the will individually.

PRIMA FACIE: On its face, at first sight. A prima facie case is one that is sufficient on its face, meaning that the evidence supporting it is adequate to establish the case until contradicted or overcome by other evidence.

PRO TANTO: For so much; as far as it goes. Often used in eminent domain cases when a property owner receives partial payment for his land without prejudice to his right to bring suit for the full amount he claims his land to be worth.

QUANTUM MERUIT: As much as he deserves. Refers to recovery based on the doctrine of unjust enrichment in those cases in which a party has rendered valuable services or furnished materials that were accepted and enjoyed by another under circumstances that would reasonably notify the recipient that the rendering party expected to be paid. In essence, the law implies a contract to pay the reasonable value of the services or materials furnished.

QUASI: Almost like; as if; nearly. This term is essentially used to signify that one subject or thing is almost analogous to another but that material differences between them do exist. For example, a quasi-criminal proceeding is one that is not strictly criminal but shares enough of the same characteristics to require some of the same safeguards (e.g., procedural due process must be followed in a parole hearing).

QUID PRO QUO: Something for something. In contract law, the consideration, something of value, passed between the parties to render the contract binding.

RES GESTAE: Things done; in evidence law, this principle justifies the admission of a statement that would otherwise be hearsay when it is made so closely to the event in question as to be said to be a part of it, or with such spontaneity as not to have the possibility of falsehood.

RES IPSA LOQUITUR: The thing speaks for itself. This doctrine gives rise to a rebuttable presumption of negligence when the instrumentality causing the injury was within the exclusive control of the defendant, and the injury was one that does not normally occur unless a person has been negligent.

RES JUDICATA: A matter adjudged. Doctrine which provides that once a court of competent jurisdiction has rendered a final judgment or decree on the merits, that judgment or decree is conclusive upon the parties to the case and prevents them from engaging in any other litigation on the points and issues determined therein.

RESPONDEAT SUPERIOR: Let the master reply. This doctrine holds the master liable for the wrongful acts of his servant (or the principal for his agent) in those cases in which the servant (or agent) was acting within the scope of his authority at the time of the injury.

STARE DECISIS: To stand by or adhere to that which has been decided. The common law doctrine of stare decisis attempts to give security and certainty to the law by following the policy that once a principle of law as applicable to a certain set of facts has been set forth in a decision, it forms a precedent which will subsequently be followed, even though a different decision might be made were it the first time the question had arisen. Of course, stare decisis is not an inviolable principle and is departed from in instances where there is good cause (e.g., considerations of public policy led the Supreme Court to disregard prior decisions sanctioning segregation).

SUPRA: Above. A word referring a reader to an earlier part of a book.

ULTRA VIRES: Beyond the power. This phrase is most commonly used to refer to actions taken by a corporation that are beyond the power or legal authority of the corporation.

Addendum of French Derivatives

IN PAIS: Not pursuant to legal proceedings.

CHATTEL: Tangible personal property.

CY PRES: Doctrine permitting courts to apply trust funds to purposes not expressed in the trust but necessary to carry out the settlor's intent.

PER AUTRE VIE: For another's life; during another's life. In property law, an estate may be granted that will terminate upon the death of someone other than the grantee.

PROFIT A PRENDRE: A license to remove minerals or other produce from land.

VOIR DIRE: Process of questioning jurors as to their predispositions about the case or parties to a proceeding in order to identify those jurors displaying bias or prejudice.

Casenote Legal Briefs

Administrative Law .... Breyer, Stewart, Sunstein & Vermeule
Administrative Law .... Cass, Diver & Beermann
Administrative Law .... Funk, Shapiro & Weaver
Administrative Law .... Mashaw, Merrill & Shane
Administrative Law .... Strauss, Rakoff, & Farina
(Gellhorn & Byse)
Agency & Partnership .... Hynes & Loewenstein
Antitrust .... Pitofsky, Goldschmid & Wood
Antitrust .... Sullivan & Hovenkamp
Bankruptcy .... Warren & Bussel
Business Organizations .... Allen, Kraakman & Subramanian
Business Organizations .... Bauman, Weiss & Palmiter
Business Organizations .... Hamilton & Macey
Business Organizations .... Klein, Ramseyer & Bainbridge
Business Organizations .... O'Kelley & Thompson
Business Organizations .... Soderquist, Smiddy & Cunningham
Civil Procedure .... Field, Kaplan & Clermont
Civil Procedure .... Freer & Perdue
Civil Procedure .... Friedenthal, Miller, Sexton & Hershkoff
Civil Procedure .... Hazard, Tait, Fletcher & Bundy
Civil Procedure .... Marcus, Redish, Sherman & Pfander
Civil Procedure .... Subrin, Minow, Brodin & Main
Civil Procedure .... Yeazell
Commercial Law .... LoPucki, Warren, Keating & Mann
Commercial Law .... Warren & Walt
Commercial Law .... Whaley
Community Property .... Bird
Community Property .... Blumberg
Conflicts .... Brilmayer & Goldsmith
Conflicts .... Currie, Kay, Kramer & Roosevelt
Constitutional Law .... Brest, Levinson, Balkin & Amar
Constitutional Law .... Chemerinsky
Constitutional Law .... Choper, Fallon, Kamisar & Shiffrin (Lockhart)
Constitutional Law .... Cohen, Varat & Amar
Constitutional Law .... Farber, Eskridge & Frickey
Constitutional Law .... Rotunda
Constitutional Law .... Sullivan & Gunther
Constitutional Law .... Stone, Seidman, Sunstein, Tushnet & Karlan
Contracts .... Barnett
Contracts .... Burton
Contracts .... Calamari, Perillo & Bender
Contracts .... Crandall & Whaley
Contracts .... Dawson, Harvey, Henderson & Baird
Contracts .... Farnsworth, Young, Sanger, Cohen & Brooks
Contracts .... Fuller & Eisenberg
Contracts .... Knapp, Crystal & Prince
Contracts .... Murphy, Speidel & Ayres
Copyright .... Cohen, Loren, Okediji & O'Rourke
Copyright .... Goldstein & Reese
Criminal Law .... Bonnie, Coughlin, Jeffries & Low
Criminal Law .... Boyce, Dripps & Perkins
Criminal Law .... Dressler
Criminal Law .... Johnson & Cloud
Criminal Law .... Kadish, Schulhofer & Steiker
Criminal Law .... Kaplan, Weisberg & Binder
Criminal Procedure .... Allen, Hoffmann, Livingston & Stuntz
Criminal Procedure .... Dressler & Thomas
Criminal Procedure .... Haddad, Marsh, Zagel, Meyer, Starkman & Bauer
Criminal Procedure .... Kamisar, LaFave, Israel, King & Kerr
Criminal Procedure .... Saltzburg & Capra
Debtors and Creditors .... Warren & Westbrook
Employment Discrimination .... Friedman
Employment Discrimination .... Zimmer, Sullivan & White
Employment Law .... Rothstein & Liebman
Environmental Law .... Menell & Stewart

Environmental Law .... Percival, Schroder, Miller & Leape
Environmental Law .... Plater, Abrams, Goldfarb, Graham, Heinzerling & Wirth
Evidence .... Broun, Mosteller & Giannelli
Evidence .... Fisher
Evidence .... Mueller & Kirkpatrick
Evidence .... Sklansky
Evidence .... Waltz & Park
Family Law .... Areen & Regan
Family Law .... Ellman, Kurtz & Scott
Family Law .... Harris, Teitelbaum & Carbone
Family Law .... Wadlington & O'Brien
Family Law .... Weisberg & Appleton
Federal Courts .... Fallon, Meltzer & Shapiro (Hart & Wechsler)
Federal Courts .... Low & Jeffries
Health Law .... Furrow, Greaney, Johnson, Jost & Schwartz
Immigration Law .... Aleinikoff, Martin & Motomura
Immigration Law .... Legomsky
Insurance Law .... Abraham
Intellectual Property .... Merges, Menell & Lemley
International Business Transactions .... Folsom, Gordon, Spanogle & Fitzgerald
International Law .... Blakesley, Firmage, Scott & Williams
International Law .... Carter, Trimble & Weiner
International Law .... Damrosch, Henkin, Pugh, Schachter & Smit
International Law .... Dunoff, Ratner & Wippman
Labor Law .... Cox, Bok, Gorman & Finkin
Land Use .... Callies, Freilich & Roberts
Legislation .... Eskridge, Frickey & Garrett
Oil & Gas .... Lowe, Anderson, Smith & Pierce
Patent Law .... Adelman, Radner & Thomas
Products Liability .... Owen, Montgomery & Davis
Professional Responsibility .... Gillers
Professional Responsibility .... Hazard, Koniak, Cramton & Cohen
Property .... Casner, Leach, French, Korngold & VanderVelde
Property .... Cribbet, Johnson, Findley & Smith
Property .... Donahue, Kauper & Martin
Property .... Dukeminier, Krier, Alexander & Schill
Property .... Haar & Liebman
Property .... Kurtz & Hovenkamp
Property .... Nelson, Stoebuck & Whitman
Property .... Rabin, Kwall & Kwall
Property .... Singer
Real Estate .... Korngold & Goldstein
Real Estate Transactions .... Nelson & Whitman
Remedies .... Laycock
Remedies .... Shoben, Tabb & Janutis
Securities Regulation .... Coffee, Seligman & Sale
Securities Regulation .... Cox, Hillman & Langevoort
Sports Law .... Weiler & Roberts
Taxation (Corporate) .... Lind, Schwartz, Lathrope & Rosenberg
Taxation (Individual) .... Burke & Friel
Taxation (Individual) .... Freeland, Lathrope, Lind & Stephens
Taxation (Individual) .... Klein, Bankman, Shaviro, & Stark
Torts .... Dobbs & Hayden
Torts .... Epstein
Torts .... Franklin & Rabin
Torts .... Henderson, Pearson, Kysar & Siliciano
Torts .... Schwartz, Kelly & Partlett (Prosser)
Wills, Trusts & Estates .... Dukeminier, Johanson, Lindgren & Sitkoff
Wills, Trusts & Estates .... Dobris, Sterk & Leslie
Wills, Trusts & Estates .... Scoles, Halbach, Roberts & Begleiter